Kye-Si Kwon
Steven Ready

**Practical Guide to
Machine Vision Software**

Related Titles

Hornberg, A. (ed.)

Handbook of Machine Vision

2006
Print ISBN: 978-3-527-40584-8; also available
in electronic formats

Cyganek, B., Siebert, J.

An Introduction to 3D Computer Vision Techniques and Algorithms

2008
Print ISBN: 978-0-470-01704-3; also available
in electronic formats

Steger, C., Ulrich, M., Wiedemann, C.

Machine Vision Algorithms and Applications

2008
Print ISBN: 978-3-527-40734-7

Gevers, T., Gijsenij, A., van de Weijer, J., Geusebroek, J.

Color in Computer Vision

Fundamentals and Applications

2012
Print ISBN: 978-0-470-89084-4; also available
in electronic formats

Korvink, J. G., Smith, P. J., Shin, D.-Y. (eds.)

Inkjet-based Micromanufacturing

Series: Advanced Micro and Nanosystems (Volume 9)

2012
ISBN: 978-3-527-31904-6; also available in
electronic formats

Cristobal, G., Perrinet, L., Keil, M. (eds.)

Biologically-inspired Computer Vision

Fundamentals and Applications

2016
Print ISBN: 978-3-527-41264-8; also available
in electronic formats

Kye-Si Kwon and Steven Ready

Practical Guide to Machine Vision Software

An Introduction with LabVIEW

WILEY-VCH

Verlag GmbH & Co. KGaA

Authors

Prof. Kye-Si Kwon
Soon Chun Hyang University
Department of Mechanical Engineering
646 Eupnae-ri
Shinchang-myeon
Chungnam
336-745 Asai-si
South Korea

Steven Ready
Palo Alto Research Center
Electronic Materials and Devices Lab.
3333 Coyote Hill Road
94304 Palo Alto, CA
United States of America

Library of Congress Card No.: applied for

British Library Cataloguing-in-Publication Data
A catalogue record for this book is available from the British Library.

Bibliographic information published by the Deutsche Nationalbibliothek
The Deutsche Nationalbibliothek lists this publication in the Deutsche Nationalbibliografie; detailed bibliographic data are available on the Internet at http://dnb.d-nb.de.

© 2015 Wiley-VCH Verlag GmbH & Co. KGaA, Boschstr. 12, 69469 Weinheim, Germany

Print ISBN: 978-3-527-33756-9
ePDF ISBN: 978-3-527-68412-0
ePub ISBN: 978-3-527-68411-3
Mobi ISBN: 978-3-527-68410-6
oBook ISBN: 978-3-527-68277-5

Cover Design   Formgeber, Mannheim, Germany
Typesetting   Thomson Digital, Noida, India
Printing and Binding   Markono Print Media Pte Ltd, Singapore

Printed on acid-free paper

Contents

*All images containing (LabVIEW, IMAQ and LabVIEW Vision applications in chapter 18) are provided by or originate from the hardware and software of National Instruments Corporation and its affiliates. National Instruments reserves all rights including trademarks in such images.

About the Authors

Kye –Si Kwon
Web site: http://inkjet.sch.ac.kr/
E-mail: kskwon@sch.ac.kr

Kye-Si Kwon is an Associate Professor in the Department of Mechanical Engineering at Soonchunhyang University, Korea. He received his PhD in 1999 from KAIST, Korea. He was a member of research staffs in companies such as Samsung and LG electronics, in charge of hardware and software development based on LabVIEW until he joined Soonchunhyang University in 2006. As a university professor, he has been teaching many LabVIEW-related subjects and carries out his research projects using LabVIEW. His recent works include inkjet-related measurement methods and system developments using LabVIEW. In 2012, he worked for 1 year at PARC (Palo Alto Research Center) in Palo Alto, CA as a visiting researcher. He is also the founder of the start-up company PS. Co. Ltd (www.psolution.kr) and its current CEO. He actively uses LabVIEW Machine Vision for his new business.

Steve Ready
www.parc.com/Steve.Ready

Steve Ready is a Member of the Research Staff at Palo Alto Research Center in Palo Alto, CA. He obtained his degree in Physics from the University of California at Santa Cruz. Since joining PARC, Steve has designed real-time inkjet droplet visualization and analysis tools; designed and developed several high-accuracy inkjet printers for printed organic electronics, document printing, and printing of 3D objects; studied the role of hydrogen and dopants in amorphous, poly-crystalline, and crystalline; and contributed to the development of large-area amorphous and polycrystalline silicon array systems for optical and X-ray imaging, displays, organic semiconductor materials, and devices.

Steve has also made significant contributions to developing laser crystallization of silicon thin films, a fragile book scanner, control software for MOCVD reactors, and a scanning tunneling microscope.

Preface

We believe the basics of engineering and research is measurement. Also, all improvement starts from the measurement. We believe that LabVIEW is one of the best software tools to implement most kinds of measurement. There have been many basic books written for those wanting to learn LabVIEW measurement, which enables one to learn LabVIEW with ease. However, there are not many books on LabVIEW vision for the beginner. The purpose of this textbook is to guide the student in using LabVIEW's Vision Development Module rather than developing deep understanding of the underlying vision algorithms. For this reason, we do not discuss the details behind specific vision algorithms. We do try to explain the concepts involved in programming with the NI Vision Development Module.

In this book the NI Vision Development Module is used to analyze objects in an image. The Vision Development Module includes hundreds of functions to process acquired images. However, for most beginners it may be difficult to understand and use the vision functions. The Vision Assistant, which is a component installed with NI Vision Development Module, is very easy to use and can create LabVIEW or C code in the process of guiding you through image processing steps. Vision Assistant provides access to almost all the vision functionality available in LabVIEW.

The approach of this book is to use the LabVIEW Vision Assistant to create the initial code that can perform vision measurement and provide the beginner a rapid understanding of LabVIEW vision programming. We feel that this is very easy approach for most of users. However, the software created directly from Vision Assistant does not generally provide the final programmed solution to a software project. So, we also guide the readers in how to use and modify the initially generated code from Vision Assistant.

This book assumes that readers have basic experience in LabVIEW programming. If you are a LabVIEW beginner, we suggest you to read a basic book on LabVIEW before starting vision programming. If your intended purpose is to only learn Vision Assistant and apply to your application immediately, we recommend you to use Vision Express. The method of using Vision Express for your application is addressed in each chapter.

In this book, Vision Development Module version 2013 is used for explanation, but the user of other versions can reference the book as there is usually only small difference between current versions.

We have tried to cover many subjects, from edge detection to optical character recognition (OCR), such that readers from various backgrounds can reference the book. Each chapter has examples to practice the vision programming. For real-time acquisition and image analysis, the use of a USB camera is mainly discussed because it is easily available for most of readers. However, LabVIEW provides many ways of acquiring images to apply to image analysis and machine vision.

Kye-Si Kwon
Soonchunhyang University
Republic of Korea

Steven Ready
Palo Alto Research Center
Palo Alto, CA, USA

1
Basics of Machine Vision

1.1
Digital Images

1.1.1
Grayscale Image

The basic digital image is composed of a two-dimensional array of numbers. Each number in the array represents a value of the smallest visual element, a pixel. The indexed location of the pixel value in the array corresponds to the X and Y locations of the pixel within the image, as measured from the top-left corner. The values of a pixel in an X and a Y location in the digital grayscale image, $f(x,y)$, represent the brightness of the pixel in a range from black to white, as seen in Figure 1.1. Let us assume that total number of pixels are 300 (0–299) and 250 (0–249) in the X and Y locations, respectively. Each image can be represented by the array of size 300×250 that has a value for each pixel.

Each image pixel value is related to the brightness of the image at that specific location. For a given camera device, the maximum value recorded for the image pixels is generally related to a characteristic of the camera referred to as the bit depth. For example, if bit depth is **k**, then there will be as much as 2^k levels of brightness that can be defined. For example, if the bit depth is 8 bits, then a pixel can have 256 values (2^8) in the range between 0 and 255.

A grayscale image pixel most often only has brightness information that can be represented in 8 bit values and as such the image is often referred to as an 8 bit image. If the pixel value is 0, then it is the most dark (black) image pixel, whereas a value of 255 means the brightest image (white) pixel. For a better understanding, Figure 1.1 shows a magnified portion of an image where the location range of X pixels is 85–91 and Y range is 125–130 within a total of 300×250 pixels in the image. In the case of pixel location of 85 along the X direction and 125 along the Y direction, the image pixel value is $f(85, 125) = 197$, which is closer to 255 than 0 and therefore is rendered closer to bright end of the image scale (white). On the other hand, the value of image pixel where $X = 91$ and $Y = 125$ is 14, which is close to 0 and thus relatively dark (black).

Practical Guide to Machine Vision Software: An Introduction with LabVIEW, First Edition.
Kye-Si Kwon and Steven Ready.
© 2015 Wiley-VCH Verlag GmbH & Co. KGaA. Published 2015 by Wiley-VCH Verlag GmbH & Co. KGaA.

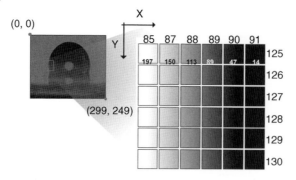

Figure 1.1 Grayscale image.

Due to its simple representation as single pixel values, grayscale images are often used in machine vision applications as a starting point to measure the length or size of an object and to find a similar image pattern via pattern matching. The gray images can be acquired from digital monochrome or color cameras. When the color image is acquired, the color image can easily be converted to a grayscale image by using the color plane extraction function that is provided by NI Vision Development Module.

1.1.2
Binary Image

The most commonly used image format for finding the existence of the object, location, and size information is binary image. The binary image pixel has two digit values, where object has the value of 1 and background has the value of 0 in most cases. Since there are only two values used, it is often called a 1 bit image (bit depth of 1, or 2^1). To make a binary image, the grayscale image is commonly used as a starting point. In general, we use a threshold value to convert a grayscale image to a binary image. In the case that the object of interest in an image is bright against a dark background (the imaged object's pixel value is larger than a chosen threshold value), it is classified as the object (a pixel image value of 1) and if the image value is less than the threshold value, it can be classified as the background (the pixel image value of 0). However, it should be noted that there will be cases where the dark parts of an image may represent the object with the bright part comprising the background.

Once the grayscale image is converted to a binary image, various image processing functions can be used. For example, we can use the particle analysis function from which the size, area, and the center of the object can be easily obtained. Prior to particle analysis, the morphology functions are often used to modify aspects of the image for better or more reliable results. For example, we may want to remove unnecessary parts from the binary image or repair parts of an object that obviously misrepresents the object in the grayscale to binary conversion. By using the morphology functions in the LabVIEW Vision Development module, we can increase the accuracy of image analysis based on the binary image. Details of this process will be discussed later.

1.1.3
Color Image

Digital color images from digital cameras are usually described by three color values: R (red), G (green), and B (blue). The three color values that represent an image pixel describe the color and brightness of the pixel. In other words, the brightness and color of the pixels in an image obtained from a digital color camera are generally defined by the combination of the R, G, and B values. All possible colors can be represented by these three primary colors. The digital color image is often referred to as a 24 or 32 bit image. Figure 1.2 shows the basic concept of a 32 bit color image. Among four possible 8 bit values in a 32 bit word, we use 8 bits for each of the R, G, and B components. The other 8 bit component is not used. This is due to the computer's natural representation of an integer as a 32 bit number.

Figure 1.3 shows an example of a color image. The total size of the image is 800×600. The X direction has 800 (0–799) pixels and Y direction has 600

| Unused | Red | Green | Blue |

Figure 1.2   32 bit color image.

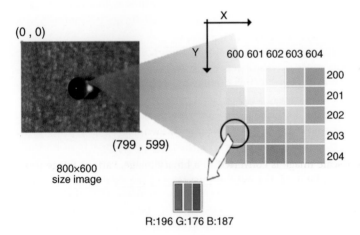

R:196 G:176 B:187

Figure 1.3   Color image ($f(x, y) = 0 \leq R \leq 255, 0 \leq G \leq 255, 0 \leq B \leq 255$).

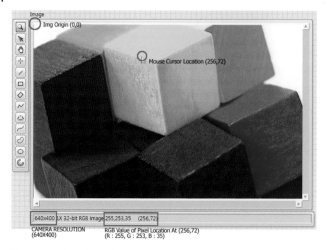

Image

Img Origin (0,0)

Mouse Cursor Location (256,72)

640x400 1X 32-bit RGB image 255,253,35   (256,72)

CAMERA RESOLUTION   RGB Value of Pixel Location At (256,72)
(640X400)   (R : 255, G : 253, B : 35)

Figure 1.4 Acquired color image.

(0–599) pixels. Each pixel has three component values representing R, G, and B. For example, the image value at X = 600, Y = 203, f(600, 203), is R = 196, G = 176, B = 187.

For a better explanation, a USB camera was used to acquire the images via a LabVIEW VI, as shown in Figure 1.4. As seen in the lower part of Figure 1.4, the total size of the image (the number of pixels) is 640 × 480. The pixel location is defined by the X and Y locations, where upper left is (0,0) and lower right is (639,479). Each of the RGB values in a pixel has an 8 bit value, which corresponds to an integer range of 0–255. When we move the mouse cursor over the acquired image, the pixel's RGB values pointed to by the mouse cursor are shown at the bottom of the window. In the example as seen in Figure 1.4, the RGB values at the mouse X/Y image position (257,72) are (255,253,35).

Each pixel color and brightness is the combination of RGB values. For example, R (red) has the range of values between 0 and 255. If the value is close to 0, the R image becomes dark red, which can be seen as black. On the other hand, if the image value of R becomes 255, then the R component becomes the brightest, which is seen as bright red. The green and blue pixel component values have same property. If the R = 255, G = 0, and B = 0, then the pixel appears to be bright red. If all three RGB values are 255, then the pixel appears to be white (bright pixel), whereas if the RGB values are 0, then the pixel becomes dark (black).

One alternative method for color image representation, HSL (hue, saturation, and luminance), can be used instead of RGB (Table 1.1). The three HSL values are also generally represented by 8 bit values for each component. By using proper values of HSL, any color and brightness can be displayed in a pixel.

Table 1.1 The meaning of HSL.

Hue	Saturation	Luminance
Hue defines the color of a pixel such as red, yellow, green, and blue or combination of two of them. It is related to wavelength of a light.	Saturation refers to the amount of white added to the hue and represents the relative purity of a color. If the saturation increases, color becomes pure. If colors are mixed, the saturation decreases. For example, red has higher saturation compared with pink.	Luminance is closely related with the brightness of image. Extracting the luminance values of an HSL color image results in a good conversion of a color image to a grayscale representation.

1.2
Components of Imaging System

Figure 1.5 shows the basic components of imaging systems. Imaging acquisition hardware requires a camera, lens, and lighting source. To get an image from the camera to the computer, we need to select the most appropriate camera communication interface (bus), which connects the camera to the computer. Some cameras require specific types of standardized communication busses integrated into computer interface cards called frame grabbers. Examples of a few standardized frame grabber communication busses are Analog, Camera Link, and Gigabit Ethernet (GigE). Other cameras connect to the computer over more common communication interfaces such as USB, Ethernet, or Fire Wire that are provided as standard configurations in most computers.

Software is also needed to display and extract information from images. In this book, image processing techniques will be described for the purpose of

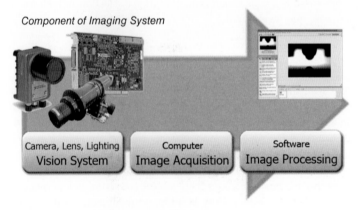

Component of Imaging System

Camera, Lens, Lighting
Vision System

Computer
Image Acquisition

Software
Image Processing

Figure 1.5 Basic component of imaging system.

processing and analyzing the acquired images. While there are a number of software programs that can be used to develop image measurement applications, we will be focusing on methods using the LabVIEW Vision Development module from National Instruments.

1.2.1
Camera

To acquire images, the camera selected must match the requirements suitable to the specifics of imaging task. For this purpose, a brief overview of cameras will be discussed in this section. For better camera selection, we recommend that you should consult with your camera vendor.

Color and Monochrome Camera

If the imaging task can benefit from the additional information provided by the color image of an object or set of objects, a color camera is required. However, one needs to take into account the increased data set size (possibly 4x) and complexity required for processing color images. Therefore, a decision needs to be made as to whether a color camera is required based on the application. As an example, it may be better to enhance the appearance of an object of a specific color by using a monochrome camera in combination with a color filter that may increase the contrast of the object in a grayscale image.

Frame Rate

Frame rate means the number of images (or "frames") acquired per second. The unit is frame per second (fps). The frame rate of most cameras for vision measurement purpose is about 30 fps. This is an historical value based on the development of the television in the United States where the frame rate was determined by half the alternating power current frequency of 60 Hz. On the other hand, when there are needs for high-speed real-time monitoring, the proper selection of high frame rate camera hardware may be required.

Area Scan Camera and Line Scan Camera

Digital cameras can be classified as area scan cameras or line scan cameras according to the scan method. Line scan cameras use one-dimensional sensor arrays that acquire a one-dimensional image in a single frame. Area scan cameras have an image sensor that can acquire a two-dimensional image in a single frame. In most general vision applications, area scan cameras are used. However, in case of inspecting moving object or where the camera is moving, the line scan camera may be best to use for fast inspection. The principle of line scan camera is quite similar to the document scanner. If the object is moving in a perpendicular direction relative to the sensor array in a line scan camera, it can acquire one- or two-dimensional images, as seen in the line camera in Table 1.2.

Table 1.2 Comparison between area scan and line scan camera.

Area scan camera	Line scan camera
AREA SCAN	LINE SCAN
OBJECT	OBJECT
	PROCESS
SENSOR, CAMERA SCANNER	SENSOR, CAMERA SCANNER
Two-dimensional array sensors	One-dimensional array sensors
Commonly used	Image acquisition by moving camera or object

Frame Trigger

The trigger signals from (or to) the camera or frame grabber can be used to synchronize image acquisition with respect to external measurement device, lighting application, or motion of a stage.

Image Resolution

The image resolution is important because it is related to the accuracy of the vision measurement. Resolution is related to the lens image magnification and camera resolution (pixel size and number of pixels). The zoom lens can be used to increase the image resolution. However, increasing the zoom factor of a lens often results in a narrowing of the field of view (FOV), which is defined as the physical dimensions that the image represents. It is often recommended to use a high-resolution camera with more pixels in the image sensors. However, the choice of a high-resolution camera often increases the costs of an imaging system and impacts the computational requirement due to the increased image data set size. So, the proper camera needs to be selected according to imaging task requirements. As a general rule of thumb, two or more pixels are required to detect any defects and more than 10 pixels are required to measure the size of an object. However, it should be noted that the resolution requirement differs according to the specific requirements of the application.

Historically, inexpensive area scan cameras with 30 fps have 640×480 pixel sensor arrays. However, there are cameras available with different numbers of pixel sensor arrays. Table 1.3 shows the example of some commercially available cameras.

In general, the number of camera pixel sensors and the field of view of the camera/lens system are critical factors for determining the image resolution. It should be noted that FOV should be large enough to measure the object of interest. If you know the FOV, you can use the following equation to determine the image resolution:

$$\text{Resolution} = \left(\frac{\text{FOV}}{\text{number of camera pixels in one direction}} \right) \times 2$$

Table 1.3 Example of camera sensors in a camera.

Area scan camera	Line scan camera
640×480	512×1
752×582	1024×1
1024×768	2048×1
1024×1024	4068×1
1280×960	6144×1
1360×1024	8192×1
1620×1220	$12\,228 \times 1$
1920×1080	
2048×2048	
4872×3248	

If the FOV of horizontal direction is 64 mm and the number of sensors in the X direction is 640, the image resolution can be calculated:

$$\text{Image resolution} = \left(\frac{64}{640}\right) \times 2 = 0.2\,\text{mm}$$

Camera Sensor Size

Figure 1.6 shows the relationship between camera sensor size and FOV. The sensor size differs according to the number of pixels and the size of a pixel. As seen in Figure 1.6, the sensor's pixel size is important because it is directly related to the selection of the lens.

Area of Interest

Area of interest (AOI) is used when the fast image acquisition is required by acquiring a part of an image from the camera sensors (Figure 1.7). A similar concept is region of Interest (ROI). ROI differs from AOI in that the former uses the software algorithm to process the part of acquired images, whereas the latter is more hardware-based concept for image acquisition. The concept and application of ROI will be discussed later.

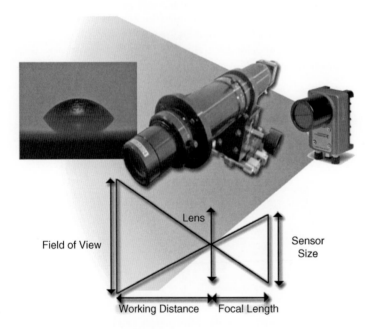

Figure 1.6 Camera lens selection.

area of interst

Figure 1.7   Area of interest.

1.2.2
Camera Bus: The Method to Connect PC and Camera

To acquire an image from a camera, several vision acquisition interface methods have been developed, including analog, camera link, USB, IEEE 1394, and GigE. To determine the proper type of camera bus, we need to compare the camera bus' capabilities according to the specific application of interest. Once we decide the right camera bus, the National Instruments (NI) Web site (http://www.ni.com/camera) can be referred to select an appropriate camera.

You may call NI technical center to get information on the proper image acquisition board from NI products according to your application.

Analog Camera

To acquire images from the analog signal produced by an analog camera, BNC or RCA cables are commonly used, as seen in Figure 1.8.

There is no power source provided for the camera in the analog camera bus. Therefore, analog cameras generally require an external power source (such as

Figure 1.8   Analog camera connected to an analog frame grabber card with a BNC cable. Video standards for color and monochrome analog camera are summarized in Table 1.4.

Table 1.4 Standard analog video.

	Standard	Number of image sensors	Frame rate (fps)	Comments
Color	NTSC (National Television Systems Committee)	640 × 480	29.97	North America, Japan
	PAL (Phase Alternative Line)	768 × 576	25	Europe
Monochrome	RS170 (Electronic Industries Association)	640 × 480	30	North America
	CCIR (Consultative Committee for International Radio)	768 × 576	25	Europe

12V DC). Analog cameras also require an analog frame grabber to convert the composite video analog signal to digital image.

Camera Link

One standard for a high-speed video bus is known as Camera Link, which was determined by the Automated Imaging Association (AIA). The standard defines the cable between the camera and a frame grabber, the connectors, and the signals and their functions (Figure 1.9).

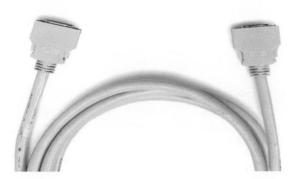

Figure 1.9 Camera link cable.

Cameras designed to the Camera Link standard work with all the Camera Link-specific frame grabbers. Camera Link is a specially designed high-speed digital bus. Some base-priced Camera Link cameras can acquire 1 megapixel image at 50 fps. Medium- and high-performance cameras acquire 510 and 680 MB/s, respectively. Some higher performance cameras can acquire 1280 × 1024 images at 500 fps.

The Camera Link camera bus is designed for middle- or high-end applications and the price of these imaging systems reflects this capability. In addition, Camera Link cameras require a frame grabber that is capable of high-speed processing. The price of a Camera Link frame grabber is more than that of analog frame grabbers. However, as the digital camera systems become of more standard and the analog systems less standard, it would be harder to find electronics to support analog systems.

National Instruments requires Camera Link cameras to have special camera description files, which have information on image acquisition and the communication method that can be used by the NI software to acquire the camera image. Camera description files can be found from http://www.ni.com/cameras.

USB Camera

The initial USB 1.1 standard did not have enough speed or bandwidth to support the data requirements of most imaging applications. However, the USB 2.0 standard has increased bandwidth capable of video streaming and comparable speeds to IEEE 1394a. USB 3.0 has even greater capability.

The advantage of USB cameras is that they are relatively inexpensive and do not require a frame grabber. As a result, USB cameras are convenient for research purposes and even in industry when there are cost issues and special functions may not be required (e.g., triggering, etc.).

IEEE 1394

Historically, the initial image acquisition speed of FireWire, or IEEE 1394a (Figure 1.10), was much faster than USB 1.1. So, due to the high bandwidth requirements of cameras, it has been a standard in many vision acquisition systems. Since the 1394 camera does not require the frame grabber and power can be provided from the cable, the vision system can be simplified.

The drawback to 1394 imaging systems is the relatively higher price compared with USB camera systems. In addition, due to the development of USB 2.0 and

Figure 1.10 IEEE 1394.

USB 3.0, the communication speed of USB cameras is now becoming comparable with that of the 1394 cameras.

Nonetheless, there are several merits in 1394 camera compared with USB. The
IEEE1394 camera can work independently and can communicate with other
devices without a computer. In comparison, USB cameras need a master con-
troller and are required to operate under the master control, which is usually
supplied in the form of a computer. Also, it is known that the 1394 camera systems are generally considered more reliable in an industrial environment compared with USB camera.

Gigabit Ethernet

GigE cameras (Figure 1.11) use gigabit Ethernet (LAN cable) for real-time data
and image transfer to computer. There is no need for an additional frame grabber with the GigE camera. As a result, high-speed and low-cost image acquisition is possible by using GigE camera. The GigE camera can use very long
camera cables up to 100 m. However, external power is still required.

1.2.3
Lens

The selection of an appropriate lens is crucially important for any application
being considered. The choice of lens has significant effects on the FOV, working

Figure 1.11 GigE camera.

Table 1.5 Various lightings.

Ring light	Back light	Strobe light	Diffused lighting
Ring-shaped LED arrays or fiber optic ring lights can be used to focus the light on the object located in the left of the ring for clear images	By using the back light, the object shape and size can be investigated. Relatively small amount of light is required. It is a useful method for inspecting an object's outer shape, but there can be objectionable effects such as light diffraction around the object	This method can be used to obtain images of object frozen in motion The light needs to be synchronized with respect to the image capture timing and position of the object of interest in motion	The light passes through a diffused plate such that it can result in uniform lighting on the area of interest

Figure 1.12 The importance of lighting.

distance, and optical image resolution at the camera's sensor. To select a proper lens, the focal length of the lens is often used. Focal length is defined by distance between lens and the image plane at the sensor in the camera. Figure 1.6 shows the relationship among focal length, FOV, sensor size, and working distance. Here, the working distance means the distance between lens and object to measure. If you know the FOV, sensor size, and working distance, you can calculate focal length of lens by the following equation:

$$\text{Focal length} = \frac{\text{sensor size} \times \text{working distance}}{\text{FOV}}$$

1.2.4
Lighting

The main purpose of lighting is to differentiate the background from the object to be measured by providing contrast. The contrast means the light intensity difference between the background and the object to measure. To extract image information for vision analysis, the imaged object should have enough light intensity difference to distinguish it from its imaged surroundings. To optimize the contrast in the acquired images, proper lighting is essential prior to image acquisition. Figure 1.12 shows an example of the importance of corrected lighting. If the lighting is inadequate, we cannot get the required information from the acquired image.

As a power source for lighting, DC or high-frequency lighting is commonly used. In specific applications, a strobe light synchronized with motion of objects of interest can be used very effectively. There are many lighting tricks that can be applied in specific applications. Table 1.5 shows the few examples.

2
Image Acquisition with LabVIEW

This chapter describes how to acquire and display images using a USB camera. A USB camera is used in this book because these cameras can be inexpensive, easy to use, and easily acquired.

The methods for image acquisition using a USB camera are different according to which LabVIEW version is used, although the 2013 version of LabVIEW as well as versions later than LabVIEW 2009 is compatible with the methods described in this book. Readers having earlier software versions may still be able to refer to this book since most image processing functions are the same or very similar irrespective of software version.

When using a USB camera, ensure that the camera is compatible with Microsoft's multimedia API (DirectShow or Media Foundation). Also, the software driver for the USB camera, National Instruments LabVIEW software, and LabVIEW Vision Acquisition Module will need to be installed. The installation instructions for the camera drivers may be found at the http://www.ni.com/drivers/. LabVIEW NI Vision Acquisition software module allows you to acquire, process, display, and save images. LabVIEW and the Vision Development module can be purchased through the National Instruments Web site at www.ni.com. A trial version of the software can also be acquired from http://www.ni.com/downloads/evaluation.htm.

2.1
Acquiring Images with MAX

With the image acquisition software installed, run the **Measurement & Automation Explorer** (MAX) application (which is installed with the LabVIEW software) to configure and test your imaging system. Throughout your vision programming tasks, **MAX** is always a good utility to test and ensure your imaging system is working satisfactorily prior to programming.

Practical Guide to Machine Vision Software: An Introduction with LabVIEW, First Edition.
Kye-Si Kwon and Steven Ready.
© 2015 Wiley-VCH Verlag GmbH & Co. KGaA. Published 2015 by Wiley-VCH Verlag GmbH & Co. KGaA.

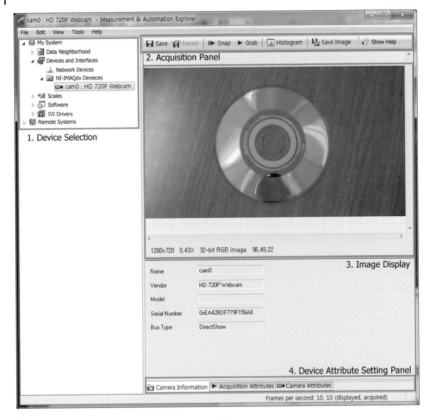

Figure 2.1 Imaging system configuration via **MAX**.

In order to configure your imaging system, it will be useful to complete the following steps:

1) Launch **Measurement & Automation Explorer** by double-clicking the **MAX** icon on the desktop (or navigating to **Start»All Programs»NI Max**).

2) Within **MAX**, find your USB camera from **Devices and Interfaces»NI-IMAQdx device**. As an example, *cam0: HD 720P Webcam* is displayed in Figure 2.1.

3) You may need to modify the image acquisition parameters located in tabs at the bottom of the user interface if images are not acquired properly. Different parameters are available for the various types of cameras according to their capability. To test and acquire images from the camera, click on the **Grab** or **Snap** buttons in the tool bar menu as seen in Figure 2.1. By selecting the **Grab** button you can acquire images continuously. The **Snap** button will acquire and display a single image.

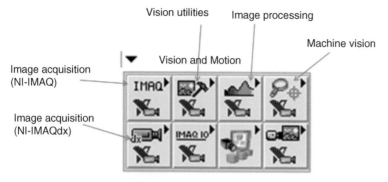

Figure 2.2 Vision function palettes.

2.2
Acquiring Images Using LabVIEW

Vision function palettes within the LabVIEW programming environment are organized in subpalettes such as **Vision Utilities**, **Image Processing**, **Machine Vision**, **NI-IMAQ**, and **NI-IMAQdx**, as seen in Figure 2.2.

- **Vision Utilities** include image file handling, image management, and pixel editing functions to manipulate and display images.
- **Image Processing** includes low-level VIs used to analyze, filter, and process images.
- **Machine Vision** consists of high-level functions that simplify common machine vision tasks.
- **NI-IMAQ** and **NI-IMAQdx** provide functions involved with image acquisitions.

2.2.1
IMAQdx Functions

In LabVIEW 2009 or later version, **NI-IMAQdx** functions are used to acquire images from digital cameras, as in the case of USB cameras. Image acquisition functions such as **Configure Grab** and **Grab** functions can be found in the **IMAQdx** function palette, as seen in Figure 2.3. If **NI-IMAQdx** functions are not found within the Vision function palette, check to see if Vision Acquisition Software is properly installed.

In this section, several functions needed for image acquisition using a USB camera are explained in detail. Image acquisition functions for cameras connected through different interfaces will be similar.

IMAQdx Open Camera
The **IMAQdx Open Camera** function allows you to open, or acquire, a camera reference (connection or Session) to a designated camera (Figure 2.4).

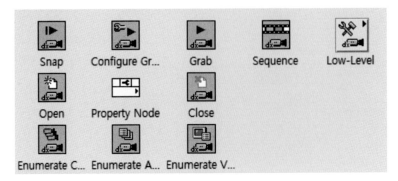

Figures 2.3 IMAQdx functions (**Vision and Motion»IMAQdx**).

IMAQdx Open Camera.vi

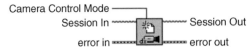

Figure 2.4 IMAQdx Open Camera.

IMAQdx Configure Grab

When the **Configure Grab** function is called, the grab method of image acquisition is configured and initiated. Acquired images are continuously captured and stored to internal buffers. This function is often used for high-speed, continuous image acquisition and video capture. If **IMAQdx Open Camera** is not used prior to **IMAQdx Configure Grab**, the default camera designator, *cam0*, is automatically selected for image acquisition (Figure 2.5).

IMAQdx Grab

The function (**IMAQdx Grab**) can be used only after **IMAQdx Configure Grab** has been executed (Figure 2.6). The latest acquired image frame in the camera driver memory buffer is copied to a LabVIEW image memory buffer via the **Image Out** connected wire.

NI_Vision_Acquisition_Software.lvlib:IMAQdx Configure Grab.vi

Figure 2.5 IMAQdx Configure Grab.

NI_Vision_Acquisition_Software.lvlib:IMAQdx Grab.vi

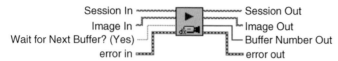

Figure 2.6   IMAQdx Grab.

NI_Vision_Acquisition_Software.lvlib:IMAQdx Close Camera.vi

Figure 2.7   IMAQdx Close Camera.

IMAQdx Close Camera

IMAQdx Close Camera stops image acquisition and closes the camera session that has previously been opened to acquire images (Figure 2.7).

2.2.2
Image Management Functions

Image management VIs are used to create (allocate image memory), dispose, and copy images. They can also get and set image information and characteristics. For example, as seen in Figure 2.8, IMAQ create and dispose functions can be found in function palette: **Vision and Motion»Vision Utilities»Image Management**.

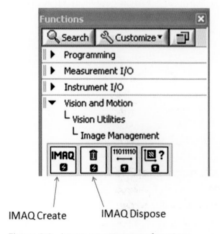

Figure 2.8   Image management functions.

IMAQ Create

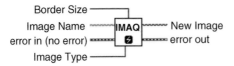

Figure 2.9   IMAQ Create.

IMAQ Create

To show the captured images on image display, the memory for images needs to be allocated. For this purpose, the **IMAQ Create** function is used to create memory space in LabVIEW for image acquisition, manipulation, and display (Figure 2.9).

When you create a memory location for an image, one of the following image types can be selected as an **Image Type**: Grayscale (U8), Grayscale (I16), Grayscale (SGL), Complex (CSG), RGB (U32), HSL (U32), RGB (U64), and Grayscale (U16). These image types are described in Table 2.1.

IMAQ Dispose

The memory allocated for an image can be disposed of and thus be freed for other uses with the use of **IMAQ Dispose** (Figure 2.10). The function is usually used when the image acquisition program is terminated and/or the image is no longer needed in your application.

Table 2.1   Image type.

Image type	Bits per pixel	Comment
Grayscale (U8)	8 bits per pixel	Unsigned, standard monochrome
Grayscale (I16)	16 bits per pixel	Signed
Grayscale (SGL)	32 bits per pixel	Floating point
Complex (CSG)	2×32 bits per pixel	Floating point
RGB (U32)	32 bits per pixel	Red, green, blue, alpha
HSL (U32)	32 bits per pixel	Hue saturation, luminance, alpha
RGB (U64)	64 bits per pixel	Red, green, blue, alpha
Grayscale (U16)	16 bits per pixel	Unsigned, standard monochrome

Imaq Dispose

Figure 2.10   IMAQ Dispose.

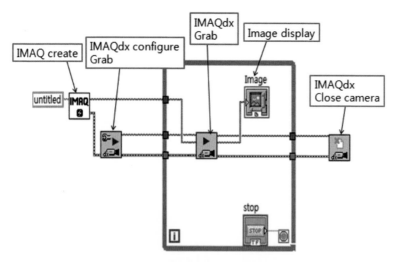

Figure 2.11 Typical block diagram for image acquisition using LabVIEW.

2.2.3
Block Diagram for Image Acquisition

A typical image acquisition routine is comprised of several Vis, including **IMAQ Create, IMAQdx Configure Grab**, and **IMAQdx Grab** function, as seen in Figure 2.11.

Note that **IMAQdx Open Camera** was not used in this example. In such case, **IMAQdx Configure Grab** function will start a camera session automatically using the default "cam0" camera.

In order to show acquired images, an image display (**Image**), front panel indicator (**Control Palette»Vision»Image Display**), is placed on the front panel. With the associated control panel icon **Image** on the block diagram connected with the image wire from the **IMAQdx Grab** function, the acquired images can be displayed in the front panel.

2.2.4
Image Acquisition from Example

It is often useful to study examples provided in LabVIEW that are referenced for image acquisition and processing. If the image acquisition software is installed, example VIs for image acquisition using a USB camera can be found from the following folder (or similar path according to the version of LabVIEW installed):

C:\Program Files\National Instruments\LabVIEW 2013\Examples\Vision Acquisition\NI-IMAQdx\High Level\Grab.vi

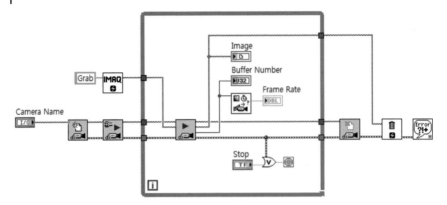

Figure 2.12 Example VI of image acquisition using **Grab** function (block diagram).

The block diagram for this example of image acquisition is shown in Figure 2.12 and the front panel is shown in Figure 2.13.

Note that the camera name as set in **MAX** needs to be selected from the front panel. In this example, the camera name **cam1** was selected before running the program, as seen in Figure 2.13. The VI displays a frame rate via the **Frame Rate** indicator, which shows how many image frames per second (fps) are being acquired.

The visible image on the image display can be enlarged or reduced by using the zoom tool (magnifying glass icon) located in the ROI tools of the image display. If the ROI tools are not present next to the image display, the ROI tools can be made visible with the following procedure.

1) Move the mouse pointer over the image display and click the right mouse button to display the pop-up menu.

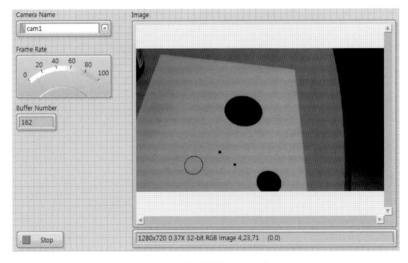

Figure 2.13 Image acquisition using LabVIEW (front panel).

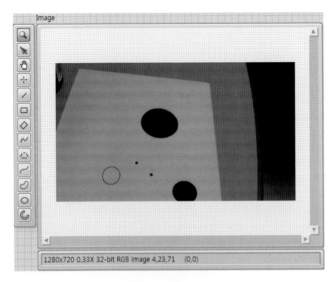

Figure 2.14 Image zoom in/zoom out.

2) From this menu, the following item should be selected: **Visible Items»ROI Tools»Visible**. Now that the ROI tools on the left-side of the image display are available, select the **Zoom Tool** icon ( ).

3) Then by left-clicking the mouse on the image at a part of the image you want to magnify, the image portion will be enlarged (zoom in). To reduce the image (zoom out), hold down the shift key and left-click on the image. You may need to click several times to zoom out to see the overall image on the image display (Figure 2.14).

A quicker way to view the whole image is to right-click the mouse on image to show the pop-up menu and select the **Zoom to Fit** menu item. The image display is automatically changed so that the entire image fits in to the image display window.

It should be noted that image zoom does not change resolution of the acquired image in memory. It only changes how the image is displayed.

In the next chapter, image processing methods will be discussed in detail in order to extract information on objects from acquired images. Before proceeding with learning more about vision programming, we recommend that readers review vision techniques by running the example VIs provided with LabVIEW. The examples of many vision functions and applications can be found in the following folder.

C:\Program Files\National Instruments\LabVIEW 2013\Examples\Vision

2.2.5
Vision Acquisition Express

As an alternative, Vision Acquisition Express provides a simple and easy method to set up vision acquisition. If readers feel that it is difficult or time consuming to build a routine from scratch using the individual LabVIEW image acquisition functions, Vision Acquisition Express is provided as a quick way to start.

The Vision Acquisition Express function may be used by itself or you can use it as a way to automate the creation of a LabVIEW VI (LabVIEW code). The automatic code generation feature of Vision Acquisition Express provides an easy approach that has advantages. However, the resulting code may not be optimized for the intended purpose and may require further modification.

There are actually two different Vision Express functions in the Vision Express palette: Vision Acquisition Express and Vision Assistant Express. Vision Acquisition Express can either acquire images from a camera using the **NI-IMAQ** or **NI-IMAQdx** functions or read in an image file or video (AVI) file. The Vision Assistant Express function can automate the creation of image processing tasks within the LabVIEW environment. In this section, the Vision Acquisition Express VI will be used to acquire image from a USB camera. Complete the following steps to configure an acquisition on a remote target.

1) Launch LabVIEW and create a new blank VI (**File»New VI** from the menu bar).
2) Right-click the block diagram of the new VI to display the **Functions Palette**. Select **Vision and Motion»Vision Express»Vision Acquisition Express VI** and drag it onto the block diagram, as seen in Figure 2.15.

The NI Vision Acquisition Express wizard is launched when the icon is placed on the block diagram. As seen in Figure 2.16, the wizard window displays five icons across the top of the window, which represent the steps that guide us through the process of setting up image acquisition. The five steps are **Select**

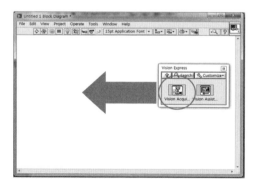

Figure 2.15 Selection of Vision Acquisition Express from the function palette.

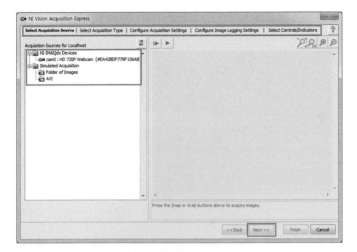

Figure 2.16 Select acquisition source.

Acquisition Source, **Select Acquisition Type**, **Configure Acquisition Setting**, **Configure Image Logging Settings**, and **Select Controls/Indicators**. With each step, option selections are displayed in the areas below.

STEP 1: Select Acquisition Source
All the available devices recognized by **NI MAX** will appear in the list of camera devices in the **Acquisition Sources** control in the **Vision Acquisition Express wizard window**.

The first step is to select an Image Acquisition Source. You are given the option to select image files, video files (AVI), or an imaging device. In this example, a camera imaging device is selected from the available **NI-IMAQdx** devices as the source for image acquisition. To proceed to the next step (**Select Acquisition Type**), click **Next**.

STEP 2: Select Acquisition Type
In this step, we select the acquisition type by which the image acquisition takes place from the camera device (Figure 2.17). You are presented with four acquisition types to choose from:

- **Single Acquisition with Processing**: Acquires a single image.
- **Continuous Acquisition with Inline Processing**: Continuously acquires and performs image processing on each image in sequence until an event stops the acquisition.
- **Finite Acquisition with Inline Processing**: Acquires a specified number of images and returns each image as it is acquired. Image processing occurs while images are acquired.

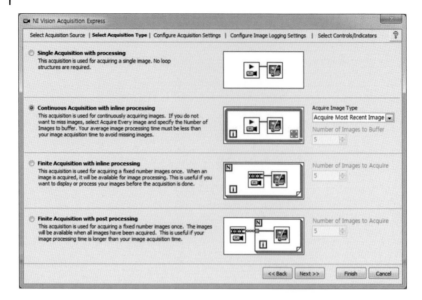

Figure 2.17   Select acquisition type.

- **Finite Acquisition with Postprocessing**: This mode is the same as **Finite Acquisition with Inline Processing**, except the images are acquired and image processing is performed only after the specified number of images are already acquired.

Continuous Acquisition with inline processing is selected in this example.

STEP 3: Configure Acquisition Settings
By clicking on the **Test** button in the right-hand subwindow, images are continuously acquired from the camera and displayed (Figure 2.18). The **Video Mode** and **Camera Attributes** in the left-hand subwindow can be modified to adjust the acquisition parameters to improve the quality of the images as they are acquired and displayed.

STEP 4: Configure Image Logging Settings
The capture image logging setting is used only in the case where the programmer desires to save a stream of images to a designated folder (Figure 2.19). For the purposes of this example, the image logging option is not used. Therefore, the **Enable Image Logging** box is not selected and we proceed to **Next≫**.

STEP 5: Select Controls/Indicators
Select Control/Indicators offers you the option to select controls and indicators that will be available to a calling program. As seen in Figure 2.20, **Stop (F)** that

Figure 2.18 Configure acquisition settings.

will cease acquisition is selected automatically as required controls. **Stopped** and **Image Out** on the right-hand side are selected as required indicators. In addition, the **Camera Attributes** set of controls that establish camera settings are optional controls and **Image Number** and **Frame Rate** are optional indicators.

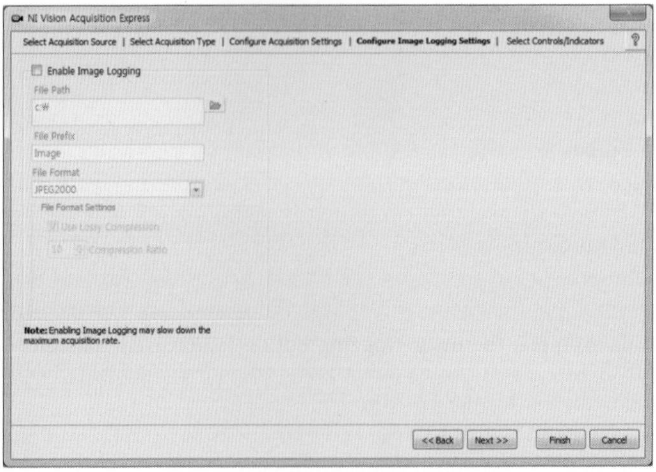

Figure 2.19 Configure image logging setting.

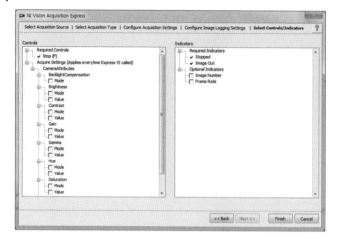

Figure 2.20   Select controls and indicators.

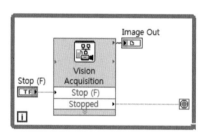
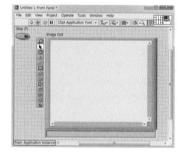

Figure 2.21   VI for image acquisition.

Upon selecting **Finish**, you will see the block diagram for capturing images with the USB camera as a result of using the Express VI, as seen in Figure 2.21. If you run the VI, images are acquired continuously and displayed on the front panel in the **Image Out** display indicator.

Upon using the mouse to right-click on the Vision Acquisition Express icon on the block diagram, a pop-up menu will appear. You can select **Open Front Panel**, as seen in Figure 2.22. By doing this you will be converting this express VI to standard SubVI where you can examine the automatically generated program structure and make it available for editing if needed.

You can then save the resulting SubVI under a chosen file name. The resulting block diagram of the newly saved SubVI is shown in Figure 2.23.

Using the Vision Express VI described above provides a simple and easy method for most of readers to generate an image acquisition routine. However,

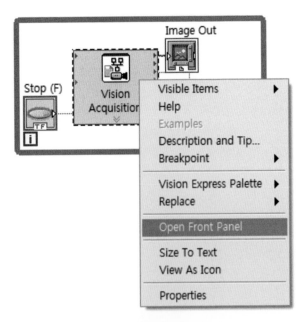

Figure 2.22   Conversion of Express VI to standard SubVI.

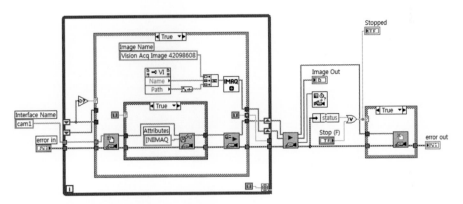

Figure 2.23   Converted SubVI.

if we open the converted VI, the image acquisition functions and block diagram look complicated and it may be difficult to change it for your specific purpose. Since both approaches have benefits and weaknesses, both Vision Acquisition Express and the standard VI creation methods are discussed in this book.

3
Particle Analysis

Particle analysis is one of the most commonly used machine vision techniques. A *particle* refers to connected regions (or groupings) of pixels to be measured. Particle analysis is effectively used when you want to find out the size, location, orientation, and/or number of objects in an image.

Particle analysis refers to a set of image analysis functions that operate on binary images, that is, those images that have only two values of a pixel: 1 and 0. The reason for using the binary image is that it is an easy and fast way to analyze objects by differentiating the objects (or particles) from the image background. Before particle analysis can be performed, a proper binary image needs to be created from the acquired grayscale or color image. The transformation to a binary image needs to be done in a manner such that the objects of interest in the image have pixels values of 1 and background is comprised of pixels of values 0.

Most acquired images from cameras are either color or grayscale images. Therefore, an image conversion process is needed. When a color camera is used, the acquired color image must first be converted to a grayscale image. The grayscale image is then converted to a binary image. Conversion methods will be discussed in detail later. Once the color or grayscale image is converted to binary, you may then need to apply various morphology functions prior to particle analysis. Morphology functions have the ability to effectively remove unwanted objects as well as modify the objects of interest for more accurate measurement.

An example of particle analysis provided in LabVIEW can be referred to from the following folder:

> *C:\Program Files\National Instruments\LabVIEW 2013\Examples\Vision\Particle Filter.vi*

Figure 3.1 shows the results of particle analysis from the example VI. By running the VI and clicking on the tabs, the basic process of particle analysis including binary image conversion and morphology functions can be explored and understood.

Practical Guide to Machine Vision Software: An Introduction with LabVIEW, First Edition.
Kye-Si Kwon and Steven Ready.
© 2015 Wiley-VCH Verlag GmbH & Co. KGaA. Published 2015 by Wiley-VCH Verlag GmbH & Co. KGaA.

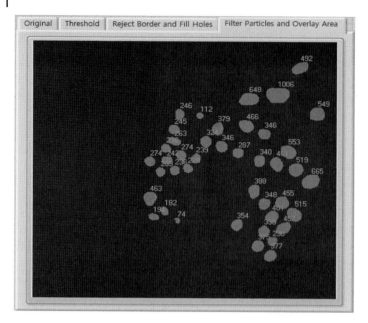

Figure 3.1 Example VI for particle analysis provided by LabVIEW.

3.1
Particle Analysis Using Vision Assistant

In this section, the use of Vision Assistant is discussed in detail. Vision Assistant is a tool for prototyping, testing, and perhaps providing an accelerated start to creating image processing applications. However, it often does not result in providing a complete solution to the application required. Initial code can be generated, but in most cases the code will require modification to meet the needs of the final application. Readers will be guided through practical examples to complete their image processing applications and will then be presented with example problems.

Example: Particle Analysis

To learn how to use Vision Assistant, a simple example of particle analysis is presented. As seen in Figure 3.2, the three circles to be analyzed are printed on a paper: circle 1 and circle 3 are filled, while circle 2 is not filled. In addition, there are two small dots that should not be part of the measurement. Binary-based particle analysis will be completed using Vision Assistant. In this example, the center and size of each circle in the image is to be measured. We then build a LabVIEW VI that can analyze circles from video images acquired in real time.

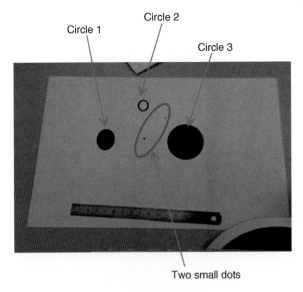

Circle 1

Circle 2

Circle 3

Two small dots

Figure 3.2 Example for particle analysis.

3.1.1
Image Acquisition Using Vision Assistant

To start Vision Assistant, select **Start»All Programs»National Instru-ment»Vision»Vision Assistant 2013**. When you start Vision Assistant, you will see a pop-up welcome screen, as seen in Figure 3.3. You can either select **Open**

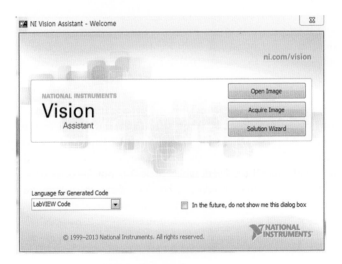

Figure 3.3 Vision Assistant-Welcome Screen.

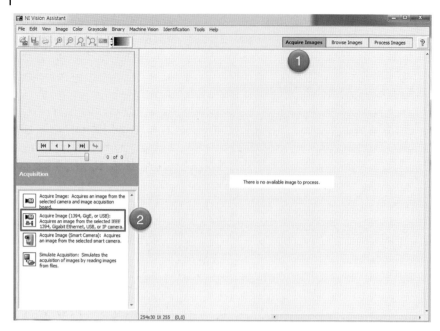

Figure 3.4 Vision Assistant.

Image to load an image from a file or **Acquire Image** to acquire an image from a camera. In this example, **Acquire Image** is selected from the welcome screen. You will then be presented with the NI Vision Assistant window, as seen in Figure 3.4.

Complete the following steps to use Vision Assistant for image acquisition.

1) From the upper right corner of Vision Assistant, select **Acquire Images**, as seen in Figure 3.4 ①. If you select **Acquire Image** from the welcome screen, **Acquire Images** is already selected in the Vision Assistant window. **Acquisition** options are displayed in the lower left-hand portion of the application window.

2) Select **Acquire Image (1394, GigE, or USB)** to acquire images using USB camera, as seen in Figure 3.4 ②. The **Acquisition** subwindow will then be replaced with the **Acquire Image (1394, GigE, or USB) Setup** options subwindow (Figure 3.5).

3) Select the **Acquire Continuous Image** ([▶]) indicated in Figure 3.5 ① to start image acquisition. Vision Assistant offers three types of image acquisition: snap([▶]), grab([▶]), and sequence([▦]). Here, grab acquisition is used to acquire continuous images. However, you may wish to select **Snap Acquisition (single image)** or **Sequence Acquisition** instead.

Reference window   Acquired Image

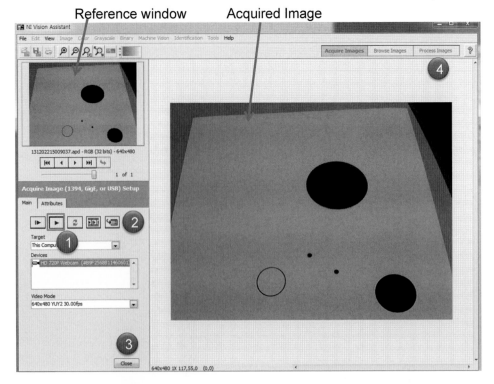

Figure 3.5 Image acquisition.

4) Selecting **Store Acquired Image in Browser** ( ) indicated in Figure 3.5
   ② stores the acquired image as a reference image and displays it in the
   image browser window in the left-hand portion of the window.
5) Clicking the **Close** button in Figure 3.5 ③ closes the image acquisition
   operation and proceeds on to the next step.
6) Select **Process Images** in Figure 3.5 ④ to begin to define image processing tasks. You will see the **Processing Functions: Image**, reference window and processing subwindow, as seen in Figure 3.6. Note that browser
   reference window is provided to display the original image, whereas the
   larger processing window will show results as the image is processed.

3.1.2
Image Processing Functions

The image processing functions in Vision Assistant are classified according to
the type of images and processing functions, as seen in Table 3.1. Each of the
processing function will be discussed later in the appropriate chapters.

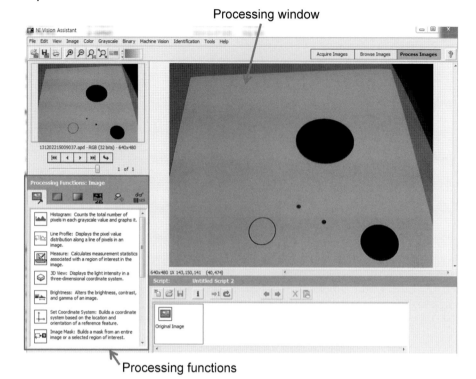

Figure 3.6 Image processing using Vision Assistant.

3.1.3
Setting a ROI (Region of Interest)

In viewing the window in Figure 3.6, there may be objects included in the image that are of no interest. These unwanted objects need to be excluded from any image processing or image analysis. The existence of unwanted objects makes the image analysis complicated. One of the ways to simplify the image processing is to use ROI. By using ROI, a portion of image can be specifically isolated for image processing. To define a ROI in the acquired image, we can use the **Image Mask** function in Figure 3.7, which can be found in **Vision Assistant»Processing Function: Image** (Figure 3.6).

By selecting **Image Mask** and then using the option menu of **Image Mask Setup** located in the lower left portion of Figure 3.8, complete the following steps to finish ROI setups:

1) Select **Create from ROI**.
2) From the **Mask Pixels** select **Outside of the ROI** to exclude image features outside of ROI for image processing.

Table 3.1 Image processing functions in Vision Assistant.

Icon	Processing function	Features
	Image	Image functions are used to manipulate images of all types. It includes image histogram, coordinate system, ROI setting (Image Mask), and overlay functions.
	Color	Color functions are used for dealing with RGB and HSL representations of color images. For example, the color functions include color plane extraction, color (pattern) matching, and color location functions.
	Grayscale	To use these functions, the image should already be a grayscale image. In case of color image, the image should be converted to a grayscale image prior to use of these functions. The grayscale functions include filters, threshold, operators, and so on.
	Binary	From the binary image, the object size and location can be effectively calculated by using particle analysis. For better results, various morphology functions are used prior to particle analysis. To use the functions, the image should be converted into a binary image, which easily differentiates objects from background. Binary functions include morphology, particle analysis, shape matching, and so on.
	Machine vision	Machine vision functions include pattern matching, shape detection, shape matching, and caliper, which are high-level operations used in machine vision applications.
	Identification	Identification functions include bar code reading and OCR.

3) Select the rectangle tool at the top of the processing window and draw out a rectangle ROI by right click dragging the mouse in processing window of Vision Assistant, as seen in Figure 3.8.

4) Select **Extract Masked Region** from the lower left side of the menu.

   Note: As a result of selecting **Extract Masked Region**, the size of resulting image will be reduced to the ROI region. Otherwise, the image size will

 Image Mask: Builds a mask from an entire image or a selected region of interest.

Figure 3.7 Image Mask.

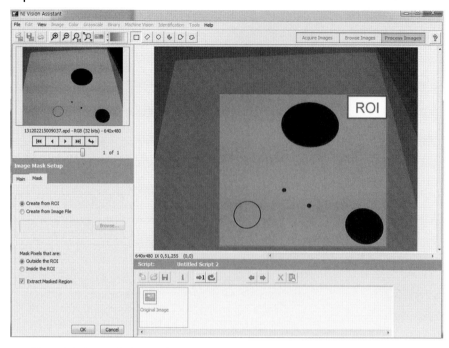

Figure 3.8 Image Mask setup (ROI setup).

remain the same as original image, but the image value outside of ROI becomes black (or zero).

5) As a final step, click the **OK** button to complete the ROI setup.

Figure 3.9 shows the reduced image area of 405×358 due to the selection of **Extract Mask Region**. Note that the size of original image was 640×480. At this point you can see **Image Mask 1** has been added to the **Script** located at the bottom of Figure 3.9. A series of image algorithm steps in Vision Assistant is called a script.

3.1.4
Binary Image Conversion

To perform particle analysis, the acquired image needs to be converted to a binary image. In the case where a color camera is used, two steps are required to convert the color image to a binary image. The process steps are shown in Figure 3.10. First, the color image needs to be converted to a grayscale image. Second, the grayscale image is converted to a binary image by means of a threshold operation. Note that if you need to threshold a color image instead of gray image, you must specify thresholds for each of the color planes; either the red, green, blue planes or the hue, saturation, luminance planes depending on the color image format.

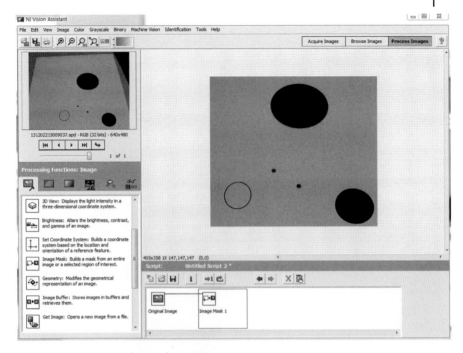

Figure 3.9 Image size reduction due to ROI.

Step 1: From Color to Grayscale Image

1) Select **Color Plane Extraction** function tab from **Processing Functions: Image » Color**.
2) Select **HSL-luminance** plane from color plane extraction setup.
3) Click **OK** button to finish image conversion from color to gray image.

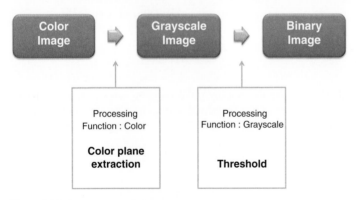

Figure 3.10 Image conversion process.

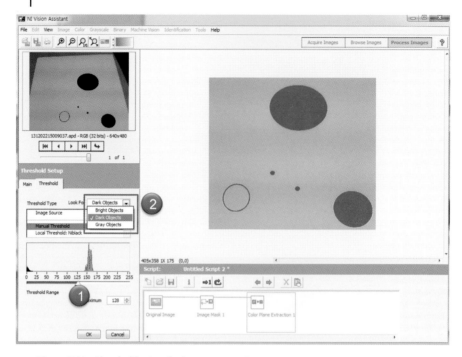

Figure 3.11 Threshold setup for image conversion.

Step 2: From Grayscale to Binary Image

1) Select **Threshold** function from **Processing Functions:Image » Grayscale**.
2) Select a proper threshold value from threshold setup, as seen in Figure 3.11.
3) Select **OK**.

Proper selection of a threshold value is important to obtain an accurate representation of the object's boundaries for image analysis. If the threshold value is not chosen correctly, the converted binary image will not accurately represent the object characteristics. The selection of the threshold value is a critical step prior to particle analysis. The threshold values for 8 bit gray images range from 0 to 255.

As seen in Figure 3.11, the threshold range slider bar (①) can be used to easily adjust the threshold value. By moving the slider bar, you can observe changes to the converted binary image as the threshold value changes. The binary image pixels with a value of 1 are indicated as red color in the processing window. Note that in this example, the image objects were dark relative to the background. As seen in Figure 3.11 ②, the option for **Dark Objects** is selected when the objects of interest are darker than background.

From Figure 3.11, we can confirm that the image pixel values for the object become 1 and the background pixels are 0 by using the threshold value of 128.

Note that a correctly chosen threshold value can differ according to various conditions such as lighting, object and background color, and so on. So, the threshold value may need to be adjusted according to the specific image conditions.

3.1.5
Morphology

Once the acquired image is converted to binary, morphology functions can be used to modify objects in the image. The primary reasons to use morphology functions are to remove unwanted particles, isolate connected particles, or improve the binary representation of the particles. In the previous section, the method using a ROI was discussed to exclude the unwanted part from image processing by reducing the image processing area. However, in some cases, unwanted objects might not be completely excluded by using the ROI only. Morphology functions can be useful to eliminate such unwanted objects. In this example, two small unwanted objects appear in the acquired image, as seen in Figure 3.11. The morphology functions will be used to remove these two small particles. Morphology functions can also be used to modify objects. In this example, the unfilled circle in the image is filled by using morphology functions.

For this purpose, complete the following steps:

1) Select **Processing Functions: Image»Binary** tab.
2) Select **Adv. Morphology** (🔲) and then **Fill Hole** (to fill the circle) from the available list. Then, Select **OK**.
3) Select **Adv. Morphology** again and then **Remove Small Object**. (to remove the small dots) If the small objects are not removed after clicking the **OK** button, increase the number of iterations and try again.
4) Select **OK** button.

As seen in Figure 3.12, by using morphology functions, the unfilled circle is filled and small objects were removed.

Morphology: Another Method to Remove Small Objects

Unwanted small objects can be removed by using **Erode** and **Dilate** functions. The Erode function reduces all the objects size by eroding the contour of the object. The Dilate function increases the size of the objects by expanding the particle contours. In this way, the Erode and Dilate functions can be used to eliminate tiny objects or fill small holes in particles.

Erode function can effectively eliminate small objects. If the iteration number of erode function is increased, the size of all objects can be further reduced. It is a good method to remove small objects, but it affects the size of other objects. So, the Dilate function is usually used after using the Erode function. Note that the number of iteration used in Dilate function needs to be the same as that of

Erode function. Otherwise, the measured size of the objects of interest might not reliably represent the original objects. The following steps are needed for removing small objects:

1) Select **Processing Functions: Binary**.
2) Select **Basic Morphology** (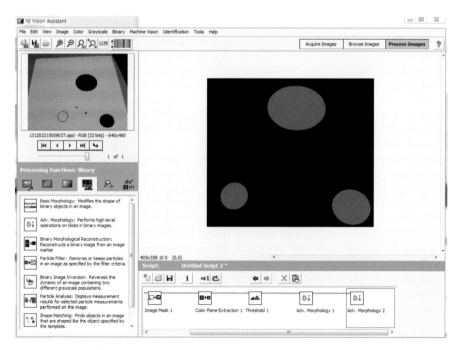).
3) Select **Erode** and increase Iteration number to eliminate unwanted small objects.
4) Select **OK** and then select **Basic Morphology** again.
5) Select **Dilate** and ensure that iteration number is the same as that of the Erode function. Even though the dilate function increases the size, the removed small objects do not appear.

3.1.6
Particle Analysis

If you have a converted binary image and the binary image has been modified by using morphology functions, the objects identified with pixel values of 1, as represented in red, can be analyzed by the **Particle Analysis** function. For this purpose, complete the following steps.

Figure 3.12 Morphology.

Particle Analysis: Displays measurement results for selected particle measurements performed on the image.

Figure 3.13 Particle Analysis function.

1) Select the **Particle Analysis** function from **Processing Function: Binary** tab in Vision Assistant (Figure 3.13).
2) Click **Select Measurements** from **Particle Analysis Setup** shown in Figure 3.14.
3) Select the measurement items from **Select Measurements**, as seen in Figure 3.15. In this example, **Center of Mass X, Center of Mass Y**, and the bounding rectangle information are selected as measurement items. With items selected, we will obtain information on the size and location of three circles, as seen in Figure 3.16. Note that the size of each circle can be easily calculated from the bounding rectangle information.

Final results can be seen in the lower part of Figure 3.16:

Circle 1: center location is (345.89, 121.09).
Circle 2: center location is (61.49, 432.03).
Circle 3: center location is (489.73, 510.51).

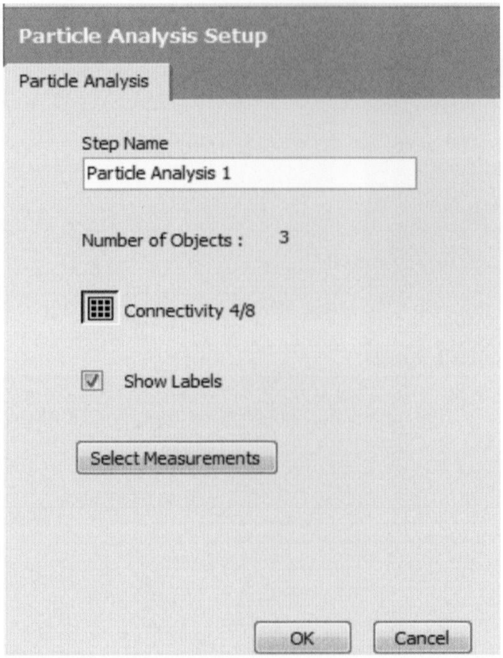

Particle Analysis Setup

Particle Analysis

Step Name

Particle Analysis 1

Number of Objects :   3

Connectivity 4/8

☑ Show Labels

Select Measurements

OK   Cancel

Figure 3.14 Particle analysis setup.

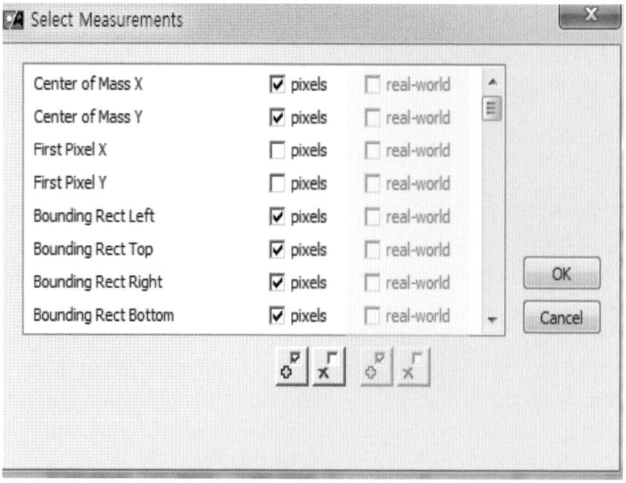

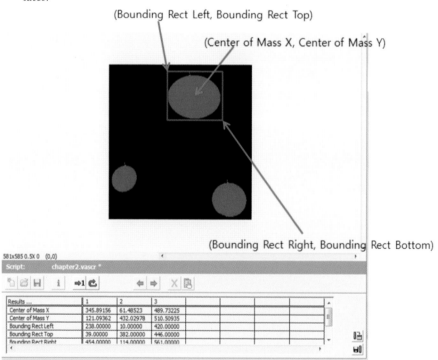

Figure 3.15 Measurement selection.

Here, the center location and bounding rectangle information are in units of pixels. The units of pixels may need to be converted to real-world units of measure (i.e., millimeters). The method for unit conversion will be discussed later.

Figure 3.16 Particle analysis results.

3.2
LabVIEW Code Creation Using Vision Assistant

LabVIEW code can be generated from Vision Assistant by selecting **Create Lab-VIEW VI** from the **Tools** (drop down menu at the top of the window), as seen in Figure 3.17.

The **LabVIEW VI Creation Wizard** will appear and guide you through four steps (Figure 3.18).

As a first step, you may need to select the version of NI Vision to use if you have more than one version on your system. In the second step, a file name and path for the new view VI is selected. By clicking on **Next** to proceed to step 3, the image source is selected, as seen in Figure 3.19. If you want to use a USB camera for real-time image processing from the camera, **IMAQdx Image Acquisition** should be selected, as seen in Figure 3.19.

Figure 3.17 LabVIEW code generation.

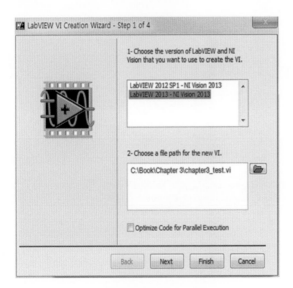

Figure 3.18 VI Creation Wizard (step 1 of 4).

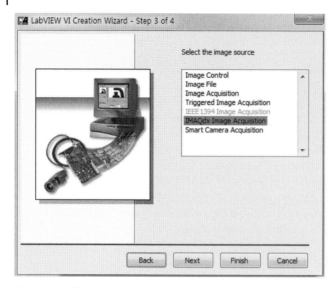

Figure 3.19 VI Creation Wizard (step 3 of 4).

Click on **Next** to proceed to the final step where controls and indicators are selected. As an example, the **ROI Descriptor** and **Out/In** from **Image Mask 1** is selected for controls in order to have them available to VIs that may call this one. As indicators, **Number of Particle** and **Particle Measurements** were selected, as seen in Figure 3.20.

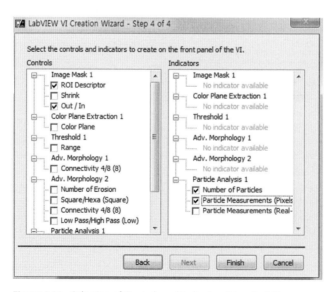

Figure 3.20 Selection of Controls and Indicators (step 4 of 4).

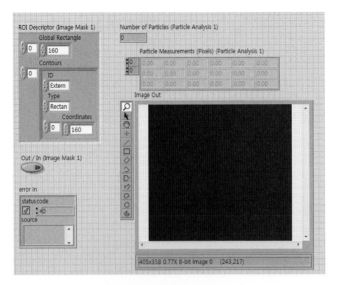

Figure 3.21 Created LabVIEW software.

Then, select **Finish** from the step 4 to create the LabVIEW VI. Sometimes, it can take about a minute to create the VI code.

Figure 3.21 shows the created LabVIEW VI's front panel. However, the created code may not be complete and you may want to modify the code with the follow suggestions:

1) In the created code, we chose to select **IMAQdx Image Acquisition** to acquire images from camera. However, it is based on single image acquisition. You may want continuous image acquisition. Alternatively, you may want to change the VI to use a saved image files for image processing. In such cases, you will need to modify the created VI for your own purpose.

2) The image displayed in Figure 3.21 is not the original image. The size as well as the image type has been changed because the ROI selection and threshold were used for binary particle analysis. However, you may want to show and keep the original image even after the image processing and analysis. In addition, you may wish to indicate the found objects with identifiers overlaid on the original image as a verification of the image analysis results.

3) In the created code, the location of the ROI was defined as constant value since the ROI position information that was entered in Vision Assistant becomes a constant during the code creation. However, the ROI could be defined interactively since the object's location may change when images are acquired continuously. In this case, you may want to modify the ROI location and size either interactively by mouse selection on image display or automatically by program software.

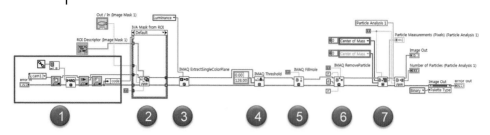

Figure 3.22 Block diagram of created VI from Vision Assistant.

3.2.1
Block Diagram of Created LabVIEW Code

In this section, the created VI will be analyzed. The created VI code has the same functionality as the script created in Vision Assistant. Therefore, it is easy to understand the resulting block diagram (Figure 3.22). If you can understand the VI code, you can easily modify it for your own application. We will present certain aspects of the Vision Assistant created code that may be considered for modification to make the final program more useful.

Modification of Image Read or Image Acquisition Code

If you select **Image Source from File** from the Vision Assistant wizard setup, you will see a function to read in an image file, as seen in Figure 3.23. For your application, you may want to modify this part so that the camera can continuously acquire images for real-time image analysis.

If you select **IMAQdx Image Acquisition** from the Vision Assistant wizard setup, the image is acquired once with the snap function, as seen in Figure 3.22 ①. However, for your application, the continuous image acquisition for real-time analysis might be required.

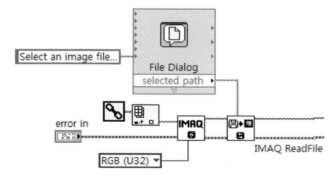

Figure 3.23 Image file read (need modification).

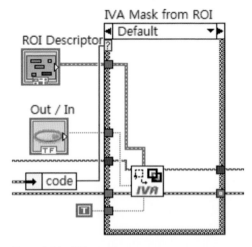

Figure 3.24 ROI setup.

Region of Interest (Figure 3.22 ②)

Figure 3.24 shows the ROI setup part that was created from Vision Assistant. Here, the VI icon that has the **IVA** label indicates that a SubVI was generated from Vision Assistant. The ROI region is passed to the **IVA Mask** from the **ROI Descriptor**. As seen in Figure 3.24, an **ROI Descriptor** control was generated, but it contains set values that were initially entered using the Vision Assistant. However, the objects in the image may move to different regions in future images or you may need to inspect different regions. In this case, you would want to be able to change the area specified by the ROI interactively with the mouse on the image display.

Image Conversion from Color to Grayscale Image (Figure 3.22 ③)

IMAQ Extract Single Color Plane function is used to extract luminance plane from color planes (Figure 3.25). In this way, a 32 bit color image is easily converted to 8-bit grayscale image.

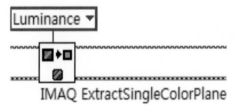

Figure 3.25 Extracting the luminance plane of a color image for conversion to a grayscale image.

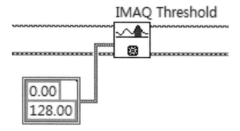

Figure 3.26 Threshold setting.

Binary Image Conversion (Figure 3.22 ④)

A thresholding operation on the image, as seen in Figure 3.26, is required to change the grayscale image to a binary image. Here, the pixels identifying dark objects are converted to image values of 1, whereas the brighter background pixels are converted to image values of 0. In this example, threshold value for image conversion was set to 128, which is about half in the image value range of an 8 bit gray image (0–255). Consider that the threshold value might need to be altered due to a change in lighting conditions.

Fill Hole (Morphology) (Figure 3.22 ⑤)

The **Fill Hole** function in Figure 3.27 is one of the morphology functions for binary images that can modify objects. By using the Fill Hole function, an unfilled object with a closed boundary can be filled and thus be made more readily available for identification and measurement functions.

Morphology: Removing Small Objects (Figure 3.22 ⑥)

Figure 3.28 shows the **IMAQ RemoveParticle** function to remove the small objects in a binary image. The input setting values come from those originally set from Vision Assistant. As seen in Figure 3.28, the iteration numbers are set to 4. Note that the iteration number may need to be increased if the particle size of unwanted object is larger.

Particle Analysis (Figure 3.22 ⑦)

Figure 3.29 shows the VIs for particle measurements. You may consider modifying this to display the result of measurements overlaid on image display for verification of the results.

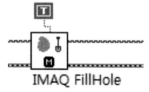

IMAQ FillHole

Figure 3.27 Fill hole function.

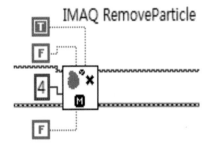

Figure 3.28 Remove small particles.

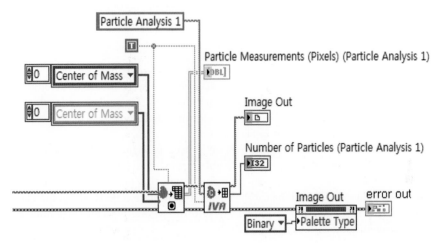

Figure 3.29 Particle analysis measurements.

Palette Type Modification

The palette type used for the image display on the front panel needs to match with the type of images to be shown. The image display's palette type may need to be modified by means of setting the image display property node as seen in Figure 3.30. Here, Vision Assistant has changed the palette type automatically during the code creation since the image is converted to binary image with **Threshold** function.

Figure 3.30 Image-type modification.

3.2.2
Image Type Modification

In the case where the palette type of image display does not match the image type, the image will not appear properly on the image display. In this section, image type modification method is briefly discussed.

The palette type of the image display can be changed by using either of the following steps.

Palette Type Change from Image Display
Mouse is moved onto the image display in front panel, as seen in Figure 3.31, and the right mouse button is held down. A menu will appear, as seen in Figure 3.32. From the menu, the palette type for the image display can be changed by selection of a proper image type.

Palette Type Modification Using Property Node
As seen in Figure 3.33, the palette type can be changed via property node of the image display indicator within the block diagram. Move the mouse to the indicator icon for the image display in the block diagram. Then, click and hold the right button of mouse. The property node for palette type can be created by using the several steps shown in Figure 3.33.

With the mouse on the property node as seen in Figure 3.33 ⑥, the palette value can be generated by clicking right button of the mouse and selecting **Create>Constant** from the pop-up menu. From this palette-type value constant, the correct palette type can be chosen from the selections within the constant. Now you can connect the constant to the palette-type property node of the image display, as seen in Figure 3.34.

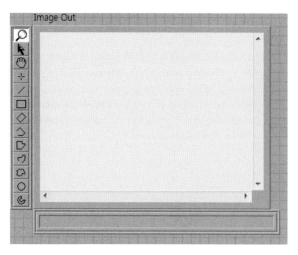

Figure 3.31   Image display.

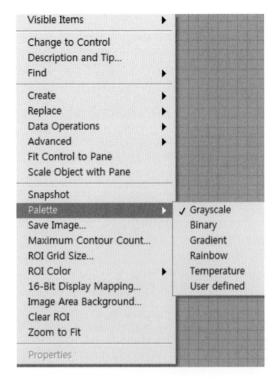

Figure 3.32 Palette-type selection from image display.

3.3
LabVIEW Code Modification

In this section, VI modification techniques will be used with the Vision Assistant-created VI to enhance the real-time image acquisition and analysis. For this purpose, the basic structure of the vision program shown in Figure 3.35 will be used where the framework is based on the grab method of image acquisition and subsequent image processing.

For easy integration of the image processing code in the framework, creating a SubVI for the image analysis is recommended to simplify the main VI structure and thereby make it easier to read and understand.

3.3.1
SubVI for Particle Analysis

To simplify the code, the program routine created from Vision Assistant is converted to SubVI. Here, the input and output of SubVI for particle analysis is defined, as seen in Figure 3.36.

Table 3.2 summarizes the input and output of the SubVI in Figure 3.36.

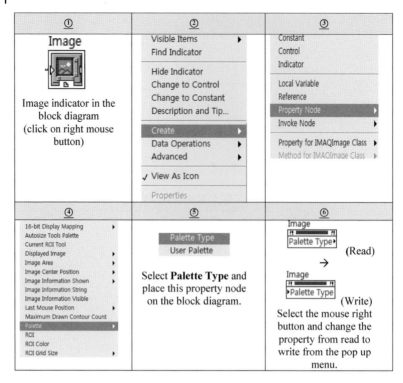

Figure 3.33 Palette-type selection method using property node.

Figure 3.34 Image palette-type modification.

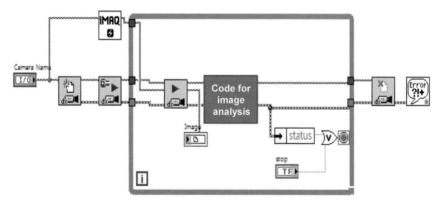

Figure 3.35 Basic code structure for real-time image processing.

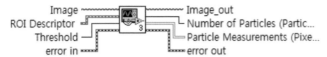

SUB_binary.vi

Image ～～～～～～ Image_out
ROI Descriptor ⊐ ⌐ Number of Particles (Partic...
Threshold ─ ├ Particle Measurements (Pixe...
error in ⋯⋯⋯ ⌊⋯⋯ error out

Figure 3.36 SubVI for particle analysis.

Table 3.2 Inputs and outputs of SubVI.

Inputs	Outputs
Image in (acquired original image)	Image_out (converted Binary image)
Threshold (threshold value for Binary image)	Particle Measurements (Pixels) (Particle analysis results)
ROI Descriptor (ROI information)	Number of particles (the number of Particles)
Error in	Error out

To build the SubVI shown in Figure 3.36, the created VI from Vision Assistant (Figure 3.22) was saved as SUB_binary.vi. It will now be modified to be used as a SubVI for image analysis. The method for making SubVI will be discussed in detail.

Inputs of the SubVI

The acquired image in the main program shown in Figure 3.35 is now to be used as input for the image analysis SubVI (Figure 3.37). A part of the code shown in Figure 3.22 ① that performs the single image acquisition needs to be replaced by an image control input to the SubVI. The image control can be created by using mouse to drag the image control onto the front panel, as seen in Figure 3.38.

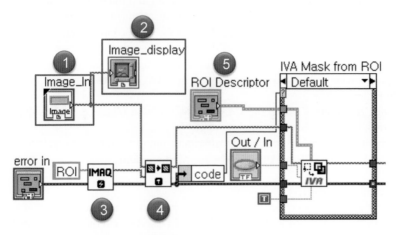

Figure 3.37 Inputs of particle analysis.

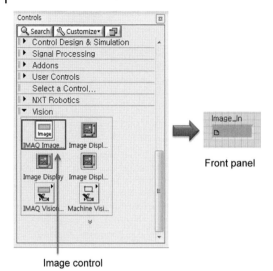

Image control

Figure 3.38   Image control (Figure 3.37 ①).

The resulting image control in Figure 3.37 ① is used as an input of SubVI to receive the acquired image from the main VI.

To show the image from the main VI, an image display indicator is placed on the front panel of the SubVI. The image display indicator name is changed to **Image_display** (Figure 3.37 ②). It is then connected (wired) to the image control, **Image_In** (Figure 3.37 ①) in block diagram. In this way, you will be able to see the acquired image in the SubVI when its front panel is displayed.

Image Copy

From our previous discussion above, as a consequence of particle analysis, the image size is reduced as a result of the ROI operation and the image is converted to a binary image. Therefore, the image will be changed from the original acquired image. To preserve the original image for later comparison, a copy of the original image needs to be kept so that the changes to the image for image processing are applied only to the copied image. To copy the image, the memory for copied image needs to be created by using **IMAQ Create** (Figure 3.39) as seen in Figure 3.37 ③.

To copy the original image, the **IMAQ Copy** function (Figure 3.40) was used in Figure 3.37 ④.

The functions for image copy and create can be found from function palette in **Vision and Motion»Vision Utilities»Image Management.**

ROI Description (Figure 3.37 ⑤)

By using the ROI information, we can obtain a new image for processing that is reduced in size as defined by the ROI. The **ROI Descriptor** (control) generated from Vision Assistant has the ROI information defined by the mouse selection in

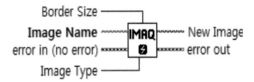

Creates a temporary memory location for an image.

Figure 3.39 IMAQ Create.

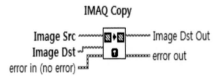

Figure 3.40 IMAQ Copy.

the Vision Assistant processing window, as shown in Figure 3.8. In some cases, you may want to create a control (or indicator) for a **ROI Descriptor** directly from control palette so that it can be used as an input (control) of the SubVI. For this purpose, the **ROI Descriptor** (control) can be found from the control palette: **Vision»IMAQ Vision Controls**, as seen in Figure 3.41, and can be placed on the front panel.

You will be able to use the **ROI Descriptor** to receive the ROI information from the main VI.

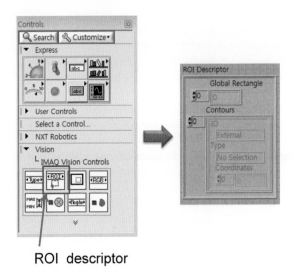

Figure 3.41 ROI Descriptor creation.

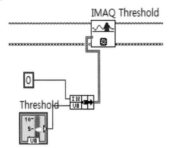

Figure 3.42 IMAQ Threshold.

Threshold Value Change
To obtain a binary image from the grayscale image, an appropriate threshold value is needed. The optimal threshold value differs according to the contrast of the objects in the image, which in turn is affected by the camera position relative to the scene under investigation and the lighting conditions. The threshold value may need to be adjusted according to changes in these conditions. Note that the **Auto-Threshold** function available in LabVIEW may be useful if changing the threshold value automatically works well in your imaging setup.

In this example, the program is modified such that a threshold value is used as input of the SubVI, as seen in Figure 3.42. In this way, the threshold value input to the threshold function in the SubVI can be made available to the main program. The program user can then adjust the threshold value according to changes of the image brightness.

Particle Analysis
After image conversion to binary by means of the threshold function, the particle analysis function can be used to analyze the objects in the image. The last part of the created VI (Figure 3.22 ⑦) is modified as seen in Figure 3.43 so that main VI can receive the particle analysis results from the SubVI.

Figure 3.43 ① shows the measurement items required for the particle analysis. The measurement choices can be edited, as shown in Figure 3.44, by moving the mouse to ① and right clicking the mouse to select **Edit Items**.

In this example, the center locations of the circles and bounding rectangle information of the particles were selected from the Vision Assistant as the measurements, as seen in Figure 3.44. We can also add or delete items from this list. The number of objects (in Figure 3.43 ②) and measurement results from the particle analysis (Figure 3.43 ③) are used as outputs of the SubVI so that they can be made available to the main VI. The measurement results are in the form of 2D array, as seen in Figure 3.45. The columns represent the measurements selected. In this case they are the particles X and Y center locations and bounding rectangle coordinates. The number of columns is the same as that of measurement items selected, whereas the number of rows corresponds to the number of particles found in the image. Note that the results have subpixel

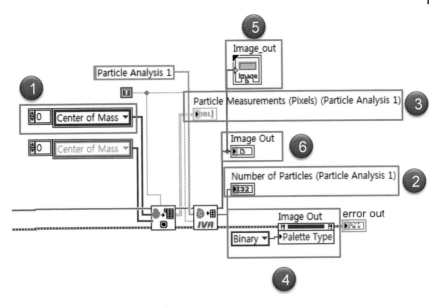

Figure 3.43 Defining outputs of particle analysis.

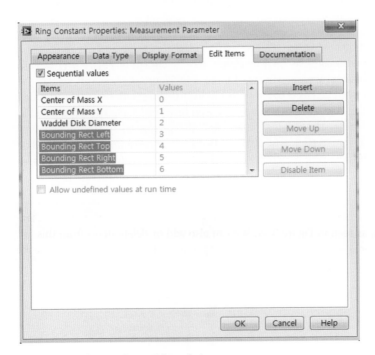

Figure 3.44 Edit Items for particle analysis.

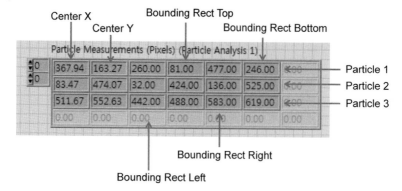

Figure 3.45 Particle analysis results (Particle Measurements in Figure 3.43 ③).

precision since software algorithm uses an interpolation function over all the pixel locations to get the measurement information.

Figure 3.43 ④ changes type of the image display. Image control of Figure 3.43 ⑤ is used as output of the SubVI to pass the processed image (binary image with reduced size) to the main program. One way to do this is to place an image control on the front panel from **Vision»IMAQ Image.ctl** and use the mouse right button on the control to select and change it to an indicator. The image display of ⑥ is used to show the resulting binary image that has been processed in the SubVI for the purpose of debugging the SubVI. As a final step, the terminals are connected to define inputs and outputs of SubVI, as seen in Figure 3.46 ① and ②.

The SubVI defined so far (Figure 3.46) is used for image analysis of continuously measured images, as seen in Figure 3.47 ②. **Image** in Figure 3.47 ③ is to display the original image, whereas **Image 2** in Figure 3.47 ④ will display the binary image with reduced size due to the ROI (Figure 3.47 ①). When running the VI, you can compare both images, as seen in Figure 3.48. The front panel in Figure 3.48 shows the original image and the processed image modified by binary image conversion and ROI, respectively. Programmatically, the ROI region is to be defined interactively by having the user specify the ROI area using

Figure 3.46 Inputs and outputs of the SubVI.

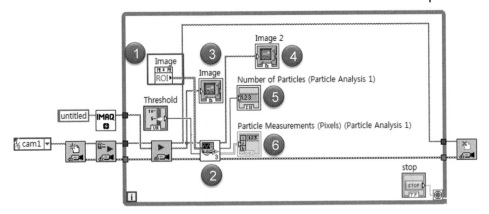

Figure 3.47 Block diagram for image analysis.

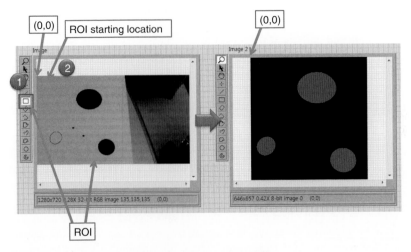

Figure 3.48 Identifying the positions of objects using a ROI.

mouse on image display in front panel during program operation. For this purpose, the ROI tool is selected from the vertical tool bar (Figure 3.48 ①). Since the
ROI information is an imbedded property of the **Image**, a property node is created from the **Image** to retrieve this information. To create this property node,
the mouse cursor is moved over the image indicator on the block diagram
(Figure 3.47 ③: **Image**) and the mouse right button is held down to display a
pop-up menu. From the menu, select **Create»Property Node»ROI** to create
property node that supplies the ROI information from the image (Figure 3.47 ①)
and wire this to the ROI input of the SubVI.

Upon running the VI in Figure 3.47, you will see the binary image
(Figure 3.47 ④: **Image 2**) with the reduced size defined by the ROI, as seen in
Figure 3.48b. For example, the size of the original image was 1280 × 720, but the

reduced size of the processed image was 646×657 due to the ROI. From the binary image analysis, the results can be obtained in terms of particle number and particle measurements indicators (Figure 3.47 ⑤ and ⑥).

Particle Analysis Result Overlay

One good way to display and verify the image processing results is to show them on the main program's image display via overlay. This nondestructive overlay enables you to overlay text, line, and geometric shapes without affecting the image itself. The creation of another SubVI for overlaying results is discussed in this section.

The particle location information from the particle analysis results is used for the overlay. However, since the location of the particles was obtained from the reduced size binary image, we need to use the ROI location information to readjust the location information so that it relates to the original image. Therefore, the location of the ROI in the original image needs to be added to the particle analysis location results to overlay the results on original image in the correct location.

The inputs and outputs of the SubVI for overlaying results can be defined, as seen in Figure 3.49. The ROI information and particle measurement results are required to calculate the overlay location on original image. Be aware that the image input (**Image**) in Figure 3.49 will be the original image.

Figure 3.50 shows an example of the block diagram of a SubVI to overlay the particle analysis results on the original image.

Figure 3.50 ① uses the ROI Descriptor information to get the offset location of the ROI. An ROI descriptor that needs to be placed on the front panel can be found in the control palette: **Vision and Motion»IMAQ Vision Controls» ROI Descriptor.** This ROI descriptor is used as the input of the SubVI so that the ROI information from the main program can be passed to the SubVI.

To retrieve the ROI offset location, the first and second coordinate array values can be obtained from the first array element of the **Contours** cluster unbundled from the **ROI Descriptor**. Then, the unbundled **Coordinates** are extracted, as in Figure 3.50 ①. The array values (X_s, Y_s) correspond to the X and Y origin locations of the ROI relative to the original image. This information will

Figure 3.49 SubVI for overlay.

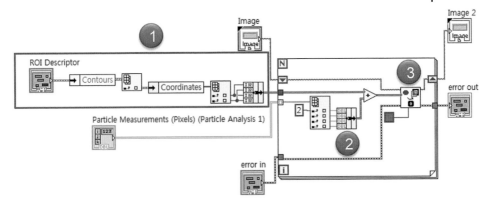

Figure 3.50 Block diagram of SubVI for overlaying.

be added to the particle analysis results to locate the objects in the original image. Since there may be more than one found object in the image to identify with overlay, the **Particle Measurements** (array) is used in a FOR loop. We can use the auto-indexing feature of the FOR loop to convert the 2D measurement results array to a 1D array of particle location results corresponding to each particle (each row of information from the 2D array results, shown in Figure 3.45, will be used to draw an overlay in each loop).

We will use the **IMAQ Overlay Oval** function (**Vision and Motion»Vision Utilities»Overlay**), as shown in Figure 3.51 and as seen in Figure 3.50 ③, to overlay circles (or ovals) on the boundary of the objects in the image.

To use this overlay function, the bounding rectangle of an oval, defined by left-upper (x_1, y_1) and right-lower (x_2, y_2) coordinates, is used to define an input cluster to the overlay function. The bounding rectangle information for each object from the particle analysis $(X_{\text{Left}}, Y_{\text{Top}}, X_{\text{Right}}, Y_{\text{Bottom}})$ is used to build the cluster information, as seen in Figure 3.50 ②. By using the ROI offset location and particle analysis results, we can calculate the bounding rectangle location information for the overlay function as

$$x_1 = X_{\text{Left}} + X_s; \quad y_1 = Y_{\text{Top}} + Y_s;$$
$$x_2 = X_{\text{Right}} + X_s; \quad y_2 = Y_{\text{Bottom}} + Y_s.$$

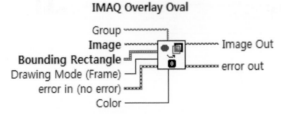

Figure 3.51 IMAQ Overlay Oval function.

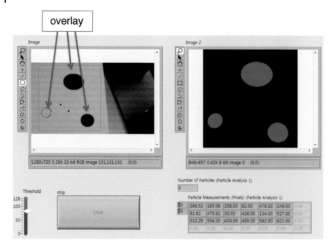

Figure 3.52 Main program for particle analysis.

Real-Time Image Processing Program

Figure 3.52 shows the resulting front panel of the main VI, which analyzes the acquired image to find the location of particles and overlays the results graphically. The binary image is also shown on the front panel (**Image 2**) and gives useful information feedback to the user on whether the threshold value is correct and the morphology functions are working properly.

Figure 3.53 shows the block diagram of the main program. In this case, two SubVIs are used: a SubVI for particle analysis (①) and a SubVI for overlaying (②). The methods for building the two SubVIs have already been discussed. The **Image** property node that contains the information on the current ROI is used as input for the two SubVIs.

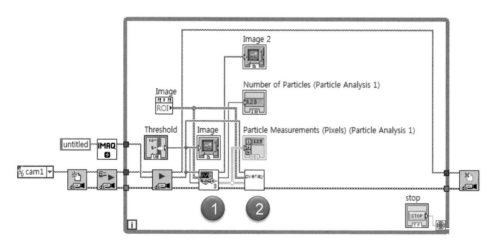

Figure 3.53 Block diagram for particle analysis.

Image display (**Image 2** in Figure 3.52) shows the binary image, which is converted in the SubVI (①). Here, the image palette type should be set to be binary. For this purpose, image display on the front panel was clicked by the right mouse button and **Palette»Binary** was selected from the menu. If the image display palette type does not match with image type, the image cannot be shown properly on image display as discussed earlier.

Note that the **IMAQ Dispose** function can be used to free memory for images after image analysis. This function can be found from Vision and **Motion» Vision Utilities»Image Management»IMAQ Dispose**.

3.4
Particle Analysis Using Vision Express

Vision Acquisition Express was discussed in Chapter 2. In this section, the use of Vision Express VIs will be discussed to help readers quickly develop common processing applications. In this section, an example shown in Figure 3.2 will be used to explain the particle analysis using Vision Express VI.

3.4.1
Vision Acquisition Express

To acquire image, Vision Acquisition Express can be used by dragging the **Vision Acquisition Express** function on the block diagram (Figure 3.54). Then, selecting the camera and continuous acquisition with inline processing will result in a block diagram that acquires continuous images, as seen in Figure 3.55. The details describing image acquisition using Vision Express can be found in Chapter 2.

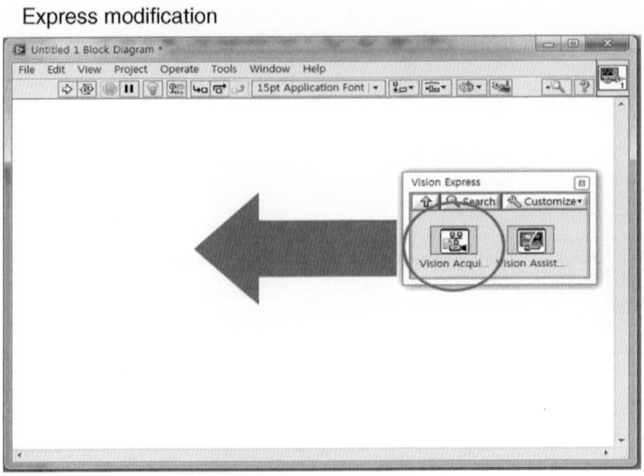

Figure 3.54 Vision Acquisition Express.

3.4.2
Vision Assistant Express

As a first step for setting up **Vision Assistant Express**, an image file may be required. For this purpose, when we run the VI from Figure 3.55, the acquired image in the front panel (Figure 3.56) can be used. The image can be saved to a file by right clicking on the front panel image display and selecting the **Save Image**, as seen in Figure 3.56. This method will be referred to in the following chapters for obtaining images as needed.

As a next step, a **Vision Assistant Express VI** is placed on the block diagram. This operation will result in the NI Vision Assistant window appearing as seen in Figure 3.57. There is slight difference in the menu compared with Vision Assistant in Figure 3.4. As seen in Figure 3.57 ①, this row of buttons are used in the final steps of Vision Assistant to define inputs and outputs and return to the block diagram.

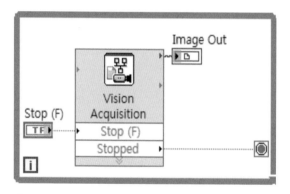

Figure 3.55 Continuous image acquisition.

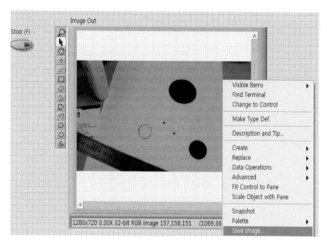

Figure 3.56 Saving image file from image display.

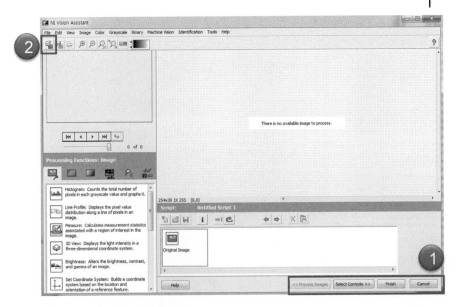

Figure 3.57   Vision Assistant Express.

To start image analysis, the saved image to be analyzed can be opened by selecting Open Image ( ) from the menu bar in Figure 3.57 ②.

Once you have loaded the image into Vision Assistant as seen in Figure 3.58, the same process can be followed as discussed earlier (Figures 3.8–3.16). When image analysis from Vision Assistant is complete, click on **Select Controls≫** in the bottom menu, as seen in Figure 3.58 ①. You will then see the controls and indicators (Figure 3.59) available for the resulting Vision Express VI, which will be used in your applications. This is very useful because the selected controls and indicators can be automatically added to the resulting code.

In this example, **Image Mask 1»ROI Descriptor** and **Threshold 1»Range** are selected for controls. For indicators, the **Particle Analysis 1» Number of Particles** and **Particle Measurements (Pixels)** are selected. To return to LabVIEW, click **Finish**, as seen in Figure 3.57 ①. Then, the Vision Assistant Express VI can be used in the same way as a SubVI in the block diagram. This can significantly reduce the effort to make an image analysis SubVI manually as described in previous sections.

To acquire continuous image and inline processing, the block diagram can be completed by wiring the inputs and outputs of the Vision Assistant Express VI, as seen in Figure 3.60. The acquired image is wired to **image src** (image source) of the Vision Assistant Express VI. To keep the original image after binary image analysis, additional image memory needs to be created, as seen in Figure 3.60 ①, and connected to **image dst** (image destination) input of the Vision Assistant Express VI. To access the ROI information defined by the user on image display (**Image Out**), the ROI property node of **Image Out** (Figure 3.60 ③) is created and connected to input of the **ROI Descriptor** in the Vision Assistant Express VI.

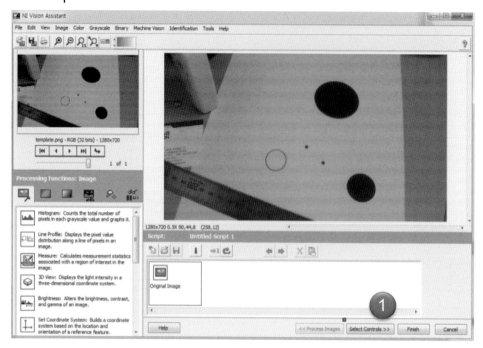

Figure 3.58 Image analysis using Vision Assistant.

If you define a ROI area from image display, the binary image bounded by this ROI area (Figure 3.61 ②) and the particle analysis results can be obtained (Figure 3.61 ④). You can dynamically adjust the threshold value (Figure 3.61 ①) from front panel to obtain proper binary image (Figure 3.61 ③) for particle

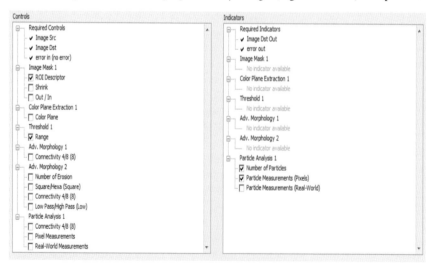

Figure 3.59 Selection of Indicators and Controls for Vision Express VI.

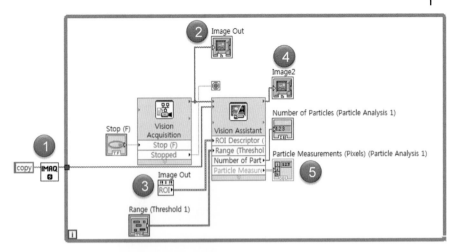

Figure 3.60 VI for particle analysis using Vision Express VI.

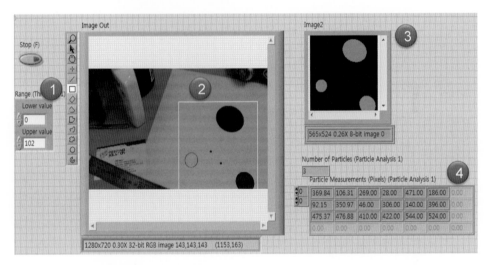

Figure 3.61 Front panel of particle analysis.

analysis while the program is executing. As discussed earlier, the image display palette of **image2** should be set to binary image type to show the image properly.

3.5
Conversion of Pixels to Real-World Units

The identified length and size of an object from vision analysis are in units of pixels. In many applications one would want the results of the measurements to be converted into real-world units. To do this, the dimensions of an image pixel,

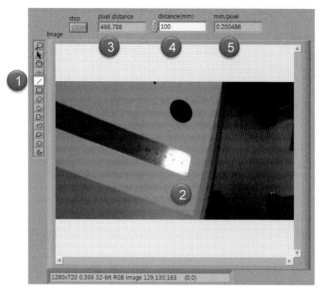

Figure 3.62 Image pixel to distance conversion using line ROI.

in the form of a ratio, needs to be calculated in advance to determine real-world dimension measurements from image processing. As an example of obtaining the conversion ratio, a simple manual method using line ROI will be used. Note that you may use other methods to obtain the conversion ratio, such as the image calibration method provided in LabVIEW Vision. That image calibration method will be discussed in Chapter 14.

Figure 3.62 shows an example of a stand-alone program to calculate the distance-to-pixel ratio. As seen in Figure 3.62, the ROI Line tool ( ) is selected from image display tools in ①. We can then draw a line ROI by clicking and dragging the mouse as seen in ②, which will appear as a line on the image display.

From the ROI line, the line length can be obtained in units of pixels retrieving the start and end of the line coordinates. For this purpose, the **IMAQ Convert ROI to Line** function in Figure 3.63 is used.

IMAQ Convert ROI to Line

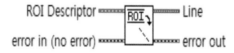

ROI Descriptor ━━━━━ Line

error in (no error) ━━━━━ error out

Converts an ROI Descriptor to a line.

Detailed help

Figure 3.63 IMAQ Convert ROI to Line function.

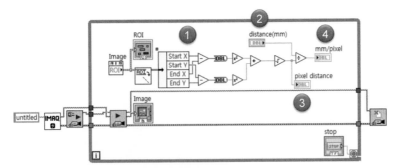

Figure 3.64 Pixel to distance ratio calculation. ① and ③: calculation of length of ROI line in pixels. ②: Control of VI to get the user-entered real distance, for example, 100 mm. ④: Indicator of VI to show the calculated distance-to-pixel ratio.

By using the **Convert ROI to Line** function, the start and end locations of the ROI line can be obtained. As in this example, you can draw a ROI line along the 100 mm length of a ruler. By this you will know the real distance of the ROI. You can calculate the distance in pixels along the line by using the convert **ROI to Line** function. Knowing the real distance and the distance in number of pixels, you can calculate conversion ratio, that is distance to pixel ratio.

Figure 3.64 shows a block diagram to calculate distance in mm/pixel. The real distance in mm (②) and ROI length in pixels (①) are used to calculate mm/pixel (④).

As seen in front panel (Figure 3.62), the real length of the ROI line (100 mm) is entered as the distance (④). Then, the real distance per 1 pixel can be calculated. Here the value is 0.20 mm/pixel (⑤). This conversion ratio may change according to lens selection and the working distance between the camera and the object. It is therefore recommended that the distance to pixel ratio be calibrated prior to image processing to get the distance in the real-world units.

Based on the results of this example, image processing results in real-world units can be obtained by multiplying the conversion ratio (mm/pixel) by the image locations, which are in units of pixels as a result of the image analysis.

$$\text{Distance (or position) in mm} = \text{(image analysis results in pixels)} \times (0.2 \text{ mm/pixel})$$

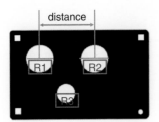

Figure 3.65 Size and the distance between two circles.

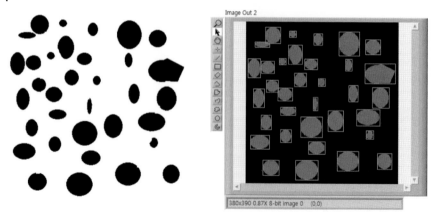

Figure 3.66 Particle analyses and overlay exercise.

Exercise 3.1

Find the image (**Holes.tif**) from folder *C:\Program Files\National Instruments \Vision\Example\Image*. By using particle analysis, calculate the size of each circle and the distance between the two large circles (Figure 3.65).

Exercise 3.2

Find the image (**Particle 2.png**) from the folder (*C:\Program Files\National Instruments\Vision\Example\Image*). By using the particle analysis, find the number of particles and show the result by overlaying the rectangle around each of particle (Figure 3.66).

Exercise 3.3

Add overlay function in VI shown in Figure 3.60 to show the results on original image of Exercise 3.2.

4

Edge Detection

Edge detection is used to find locations in the digital image where the image brightness changes abruptly along a line of pixels. These abrupt changes usually define the edge of an object in an image. By using the edge detection, boundaries of an object can be identified. Once the boundary of an object is located, the size as well as other features of the object can be determined.

Note that the type of ROI used for edge detection is defined as a line in the image display, whereas in Chapter 3 a two-dimensional area is used as a ROI for particle analysis. To use the edge detection algorithm, color image should be converted to either a grayscale or a binary image in advance.

The basic example for Edge detection can be found from the following folder:

> C:\Program Files\National Instruments\LabVIEW 2013\Examples\Vision\Caliper\
> Edge Detection.vi

The concept of edge detection can be understood from the example provided with LabVIEW. As shown in Figure 4.1, by defining a ROI line across the object, the pixel values along the line's path provide a profile of the object that is represented in the **Line Profile** graph seen at the top right of Figure 4.1. The profile values display an abrupt change at the edge of the object. As seen in Figure 4.1, the small dots at the object's edges indicate that the program has found the edge locations along the ROI line. The dots appear on the image by means of an overlay function.

4.1
Edge Detection via Vision Assistant

In this section, a method using Vision Assistant for edge detection will be discussed.

1) As a first step, an image needs to be acquired either from a camera or read in from a file for the image analysis.

Practical Guide to Machine Vision Software: An Introduction with LabVIEW, First Edition.
Kye-Si Kwon and Steven Ready.
© 2015 Wiley-VCH Verlag GmbH & Co. KGaA. Published 2015 by Wiley-VCH Verlag GmbH & Co. KGaA.

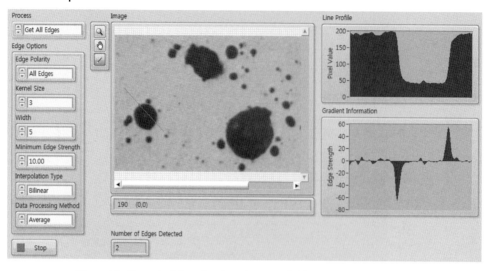

Figure 4.1 Example VI for edge detection provided by LabVIEW.

2) Once the image is acquired, select **Process Images** (Acquire Images | Browse Images | **Process Images**) as described in Chapter 3 to start image processing.

3) In the case of color images, select **HSL-Luminance** plane from color plane extraction (**Processing Functions: Color»Color Plane Extraction**) to obtain gray image. This process was discussed in detail in Chapter 3.

4) Now, by selecting **Processing Functions: Machine Vision»Edge Detector**, you will see the menu for **Edge Detector Setup**, as shown in Figure 4.2.

As seen in Figure 4.2, a line (①) is drawn using the mouse to define a ROI. In this example, the **Simple Edge Tool** function is selected as the **Edge Detector**. With the line defined, the image values along the line ROI are used to find the object's edge locations. The image values along the ROI line are shown in **Line Profile** subwindow (④). From this profile you can see how the image values of the object and background are differentiated. The inside part of the circle object is dark since it has image values close to 0 and the background is brighter with higher image values of around 150, as seen in Figure 4.3. Note that the relative image value of the background with respect to the object is important since these absolute values might be subject to change due to image brightness from imaging conditions.

In this example, the simple edge tool is used for edge detection. To obtain the best results from edge detection, determining an appropriate value for the threshold is important. For this purpose, the **Threshold Level** can be adjusted as represented in Figure 4.2 ③.

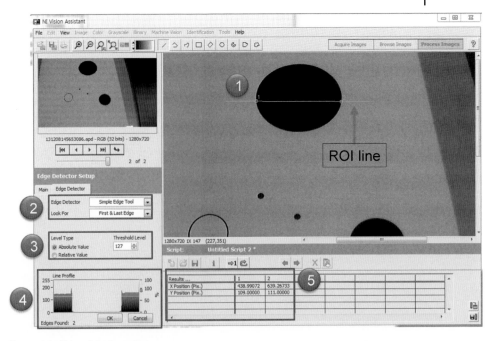

Figure 4.2 Edge detector setup.

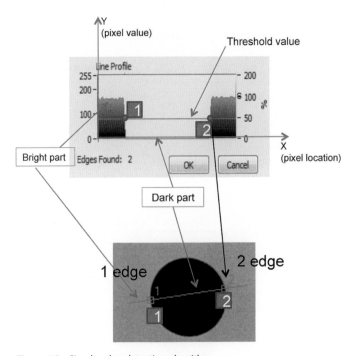

Figure 4.3 Simple edge detection algorithm.

After defining a threshold value, the edge measurement results including the X and Y edge location values are displayed, as seen in Figure 4.2 ⑤. Using the detected edge locations, we can calculate the distance between the edges to gain knowledge about the size of the object.

LabVIEW code can be created upon completion of the Vision Assistant setup. The created code can then be modified to calculate the location as well as the size of the object. The methods for modifying code as a result of using Vision Assistant have been extensively discussed in Chapter 3. To explore another approach in this chapter, an example VI, as shown in Figure 4.1, will be modified. This example VI is included with the LabVIEW Vision software installation.

4.2
LabVIEW Code for Edge Detection

In this section, we will briefly examine the example VI in Figure 4.1 to learn more about edge detection. Figure 4.4 shows the block diagram of the example VI shown in Figure 4.1.

Figure 4.4 ① shows the code to read in an image from a file. The **ROI** property node (⬚) of the image display provides information about the ROI. This information includes the location and size of the **ROI** as drawn with mouse on the image. The image values along the ROI line are obtained by using **ROI Profile** function in Figure 4.4 ②. The **ROI Profile** function (Figure 4.5) can be found from function palette in **Vision» Image Processing»Analysis**.

The **Edge Tool** function in Figure 4.4 ③ and Figure 4.6 is used to find the edge along the ROI line. The **Edge Tool** function can be found in **Vision»Machine Vision»Caliper**. The Edge Tool function returns location and statistical results in **Edge Information** shown in Figure 4.6b.

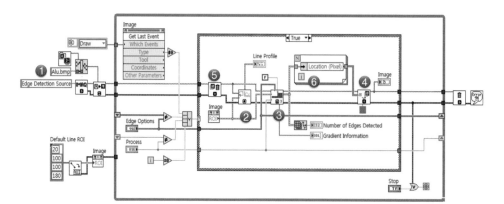

Figure 4.4 Block diagram of example VI in Figure 4.1 (provided by LabVIEW).

NI_Vision_Development_Module.lvlib:IMAQ ROIProfile

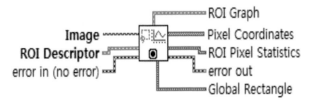

Figure 4.5   ROI Profile.

NI_Vision_Development_Module.lvlib:IMAQ Edge Tool 2

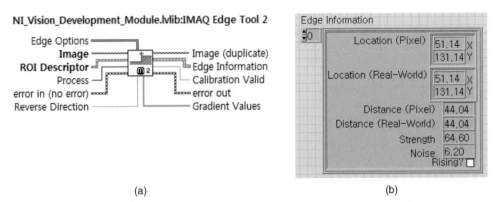

(a)   (b)

Figure 4.6   IMAQ Edge Tool. (a) Edge Tool function. (b) Edge Information (output of Edge Tool).

In Figure 4.4, the **Overlay VI** (④) uses the image processing edge coordinate results and displays these locations as small ovals overlaid on the image. The block diagram of the **Overlay Points with User Specified Size** VI is shown in Figure 4.7b. This VI requires the edge locations **(Points)** obtained by edge detection algorithm as the inputs. The **Location (Pixel)** values in the **Edge Information** cluster in Figure 4.4 ⑥ provide the information required. However, the **IMAQ Overlay Oval** function used to overlay in this example requires the location information to be in the form of an array of clusters containing bounding rectangle corner locations. The bounding rectangles are used to define filled circles at the edge locations of the object. The **Location (Pixel)** values will be used to create the bounding rectangle for the circle overlays.

To define the bounding rectangle information, the value from the **Point Diameter** control is used so that the calling routine can adjust the size of the circles as needed (Figure 4.7 ①). To create the bounding rectangle, the edge **Location (Pixel)** (Xp, Yp) and the **Point Diameter** (D) are used as

$$X1 = Xp - D/2, \quad Y1 = Yp - D/2, \quad X2 = Xp + D/2, \quad Y2 = Yp + D/2 \quad (4.1)$$

The resulting boundary rectangle information (X1, Y1, X2, Y2) is assembled into a cluster using bundle function, as seen in Figure 4.7b ③.

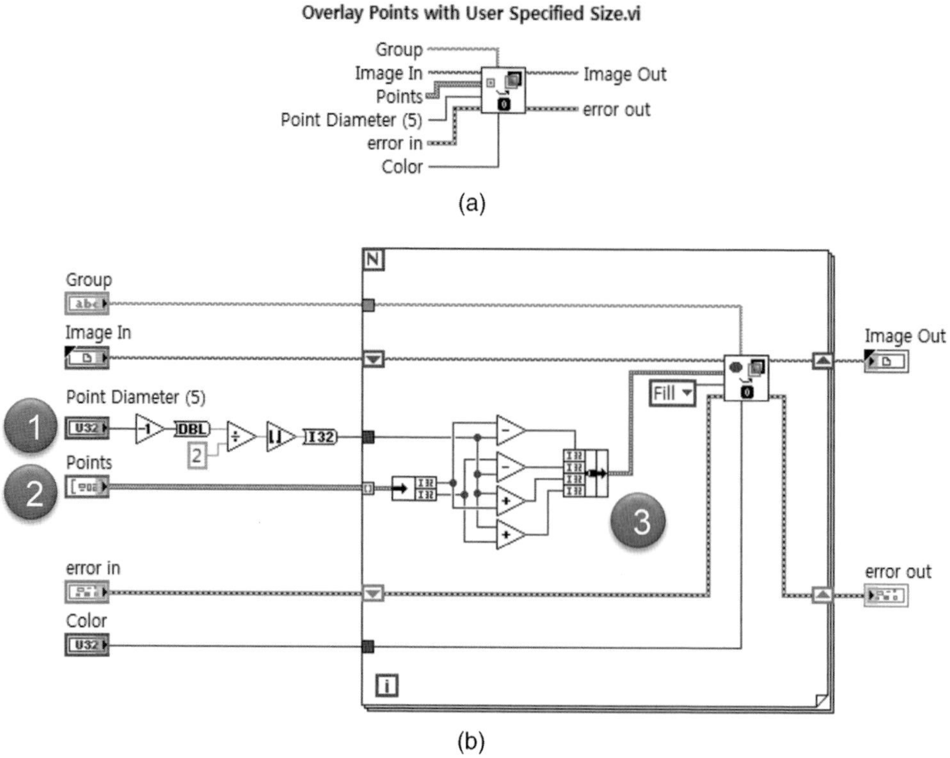

Overlay Points with User Specified Size.vi

Group
Image In
Points
Point Diameter (5)
error in
Color

Image Out
error out

(a)

Group
Image In

Point Diameter (5)
Points

error in

Color

Image Out

error out

(b)

Figure 4.7 Overlay VI in example VI provided by LabVIEW. (a) SubVI for overlay points. (b) Block diagram for overlay VI.

The cluster containing the bounding rectangle information shown in Equation 4.1 was wired to the **Bounding Rectangle** input of the **IMAQ Overlay Oval** function and used to overlay the edge results (Figure 4.8). The **IMAQ Overlay Oval** function can be found from the function palette: **Vision and Motion»Vision Utilities» Overlay**.

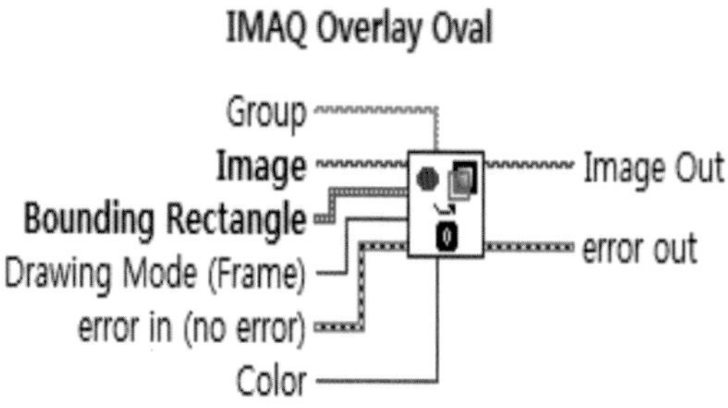

IMAQ Overlay Oval

Group
Image
Bounding Rectangle
Drawing Mode (Frame)
error in (no error)
Color

Image Out
error out

Figure 4.8 Overlay Oval function.

Clears the image overlay

Figure 4.9 Clear Overlay.

As seen in Figure 4.7, the number of iterations needed in the FOR loop to overlay all the edges is the same as the number of edges. Thus, the autoindexing feature of LabVIEW FOR loops is used to cycle through the number of elements in the array of points. Note that any previous overlaid objects can be deleted by using **Clear Overlay** function (Figure 4.9) prior to overlaying the currently detected edges as seen in Figure 4.4 ⑤.

The example VI for edge detection was briefly reviewed. Now, you may want to modify the VI according to your needs.

4.3
VI for Real-Time-Based Edge Detection

Example: Edge Detection
Create a VI that finds edges along a ROI line defined by mouse selection on image display. For example, you may want real-time edge detection, as seen in Figure 4.10. By using the edge detection, boundaries of objects are located as video images are acquired and ROIs are dynamically redefined. The detected edges can be presented and verified by means of overlay.

Figure 4.11 shows the block diagram for edge detection, which has been modified from the example VI shown in Figure 4.4.

As seen in Figure 4.11 ①, the color image is first converted to a grayscale image. This is accomplished by selecting the luminance color plane from the **IMAQ ExtractSingleColorPlane** function (Figure 4.12) that can be found in **Vision and Motion»Vision Utility»Color Utility**. If a grayscale image is acquired from the camera, this step can be skipped.

After the luminance plane is obtained, the palette type of the image display needs to be changed from color to grayscale. The **Image** indicator property node is used to change the palette type. Create the property node by positioning the mouse over the **Image** display indicator (Image) icon in the block diagram and use the right mouse button to select **Create»Property Node»Palette»Palette Type** from the pop-up menu. Then with the mouse on the newly created

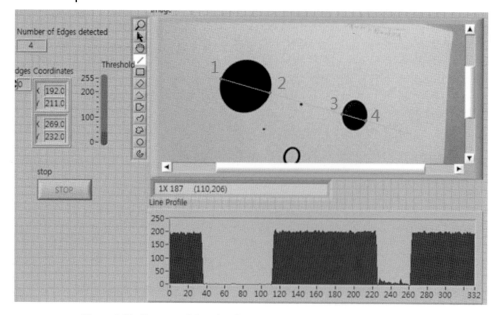

Figure 4.10 Front panel for edge detection.

property node, select **Change to Write** from the menu that appears using the right mouse button. When the property node is changed to write, the property shape appearance is changed as seen in Figure 4.13.

From the wire input position of the property node, use the mouse right button to show a pop-up menu and select **Create»Constant** to create constant value for

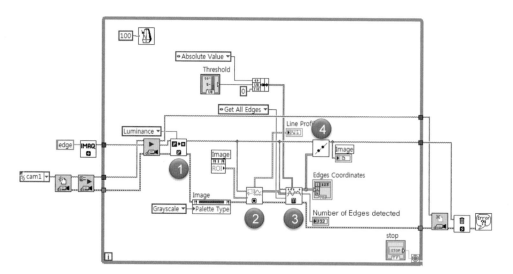

Figure 4.11 Block diagram for Edge detection.

IMAQ ExtractSingleColorPlane

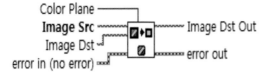

Figure 4.12 IMAQ ExtractSingleColorPlane function.

Figure 4.13 Property node for palette type (changing from read to write).

palette type. Set the constant to **Grayscale** in order to allow the **Image** display to render the image as a grayscale image on the front panel.

Before using the edge detection functions, a line profile graph can be used to represent the image values along the ROI line, as seen in Figure 4.11 ②. The **IMAQ ROI Profile** function can be found from **Vision and Motion»Image Processing»Analysis**.

The **IMAQ Simple Edge** function in Figure 4.14 is used here for the edge detection. The simple edge function requires **Pixel Coordinates** from the ROI line information and **Threshold Parameters** as inputs.

The **IMAQ Simple Edge** function returns the **Edges Coordinates**, as seen in Figure 4.15. The **Edges Coordinates** are in the form of an array of clusters that contain X/Y coordinate values. The array contains the same number of cluster elements as detected edges. In this example, four edges are detected resulting in an array of four clusters. The array front panel indicator in Figure 4.15 shows the first two clusters of the array that hold location information of the first and second edges. To see the information on other edges, change the array index (0).

NI_Vision_Development_Module.lvlib:IMAQ Simple Edge

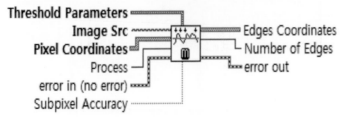

Figure 4.14 IMAQ Simple Edge (Vision»Machine Vision»Caliper).

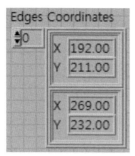

Figure 4.15 Edge coordinates.

Draw Edges Position 2(Clear Overlay).vi

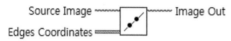

Figure 4.16 Modified Overlay function.

Edge Coordinates from the **IMAQ Simple Edge** function consists of X and Y coordinates only. To indicate the edge detection results on image display, a modified form of the overlay SubVI from Figure 4.7 is used. This modified form is defined in Figures 4.16 and 4.17.

Here, the main differences between the SubVIs in Figures 4.17 and 4.7 are (1) the form in which the **Edge Coordinates** information is supplied and (2) that all previous overlays are cleared.

It should be noted that the detected location and size of the overlaid ovals are in units of pixels. To have the results reported in real-world measurement

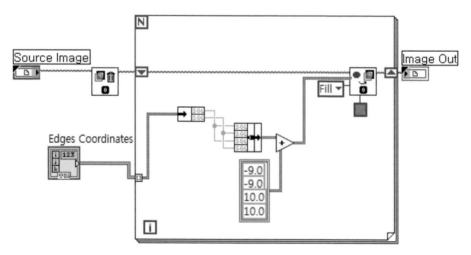

Figure 4.17 Block diagram for modified overlay SubVI.

values, we need to multiply the pixel units with a conversion ratio that has the unit of mm/pixels to convert the measurements to a measured real-world dimensional units (mm).

In this section, an example provided by NI was used as a starting point to create a modified VI for edge detection without using Vision Assistant. It is up to readers whether to use Vision Assistant to create a VI for image analysis or to build it explicitly from scratch. In the next section, perhaps an even easier approach that uses Vision Assistant Express for edge detection will be examined.

4.4
The Use of Vision Assistant Express for Real-Time Edge Detection

In this section, Vision Assistant Express will be used for real-time edge detection. The real-time aspect will involve continuous image acquisition using the image grab method, as seen in Figure 4.18.

Since the Vision Assistant Express initially requires the use of a reference image to build the image processing algorithm, a previously saved image file needs to be supplied.

The Vision Assistant Express can be easily started by dragging Vision Assistant Express VI to the block diagram. Once the Vision Assistant Wizard is running, the previously saved image file will need to be opened. If the image is color, you need to convert the color image to a gray image by **Color Plane Extraction**

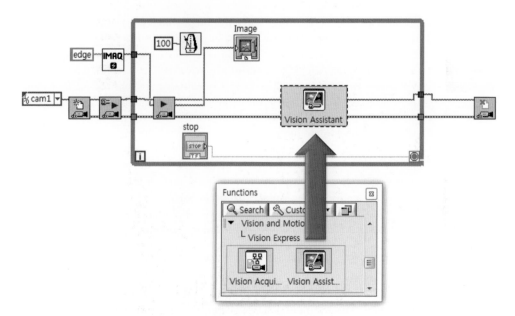

Figure 4.18 Vision Assistant Express.

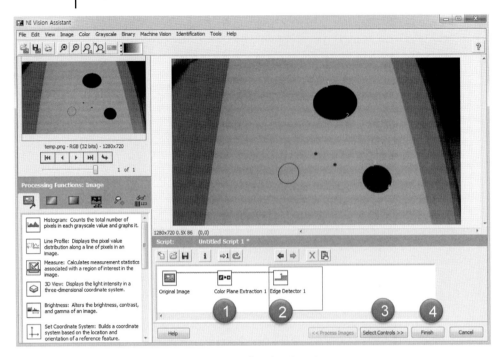

Figure 4.19 Vision Assistant Express for edge detection.

function (Figure 4.19 ①). Then, select the **Edge Detector** (Figure 4.19 ②) from **Processing Functions: Machine Vision**, as discussed in Figure 4.2.

Then, click **Select Controls>>** (Figure 4.19 ③) to select controls and indicators. In this example, the **ROI Descriptor** is selected (Figure 4.20 ①) for controls and **Number of Edges** as well as **Edge Coordinates** are selected for indicators as seen in Figure 4.20 ②. Here, the **Edge Coordinates** indicator is an array of clusters containing the X and Y coordinates of the detected edges.

After selecting **Finish** and returning to LabVIEW, the inputs and outputs of created VI can be wired, as seen in Figure 4.21. To provide a user-defined ROI from the image display as input to the created VI, an **Image** ROI property node (Figure 4.21 ①) is generated by right mouse clicking on **Image** indicator icon in Figure 4.21 ② and selecting **Create»Property Node»ROI**.

Note that the image display in Figure 4.22 is a grayscale image because the original color image was converted in Vision Assistant Express. To keep the color image, another allocation of image memory using the **Image Create** function could be added and connected to **Image dst** (image destination) of Vision Assistant Express.

As an additional step, an image overlay routine could be created to indicate the locations of the detected object's edges.

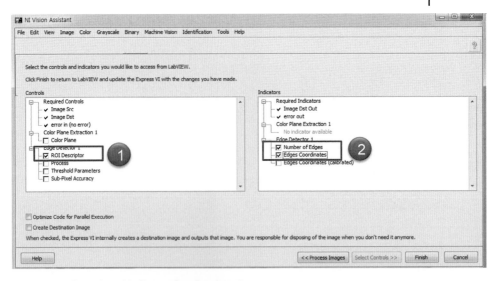

Figure 4.20 Controls and Indicators for edge detection.

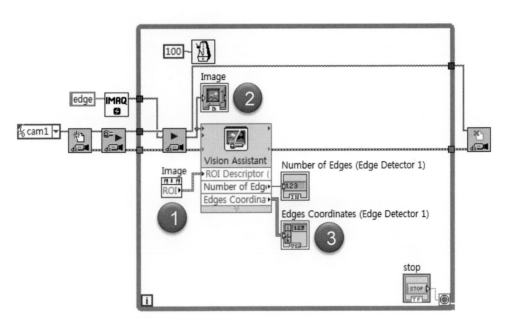

Figure 4.21 VI for edge detection.

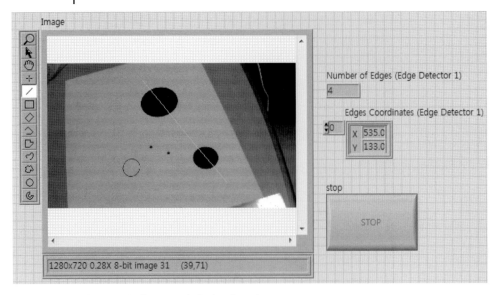

Figure 4.22   Front panel of edge detection.

Exercise 4.1

Using the NI supplied image, **Clamp.png** from *C:\Program Files\National Instruments\Vision\Examples\Images*, create a VI to perform edge detection in order to calculate **Distance 1** and **Distance 2** from the edge coordinate information (Figure 4.23). Use the Vision Acquisition Express VI to read in the image file. Methods for reading and writing image files using LabVIEW standard VIs will be discussed in Chapter 15.

Exercise 4.2

Add an overlay to the image in Figure 4.22 so that edge detection results can be examined easily on the image display.

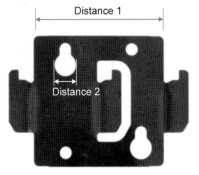

Figure 4.23   Dimension measurement using edge detection.

5
Pattern Matching

Pattern matching is a method for finding regions in a grayscale image that match a reference image pattern. If the initial image source is a color image, the image needs to be converted to grayscale first in order to use pattern matching. The pattern matching VI uses a reference or template image to find like images within a new image regardless of location, rotation, or scaling of the template.

Pattern matching is often used to locate the positions of a fiducial mark, or unique characteristic features, of an object in an image. You can use the positions to compute length, angles, and other measurements. As a result, pattern matching has been widely used in various applications such as alignment, gauging, and inspection. Pattern matching has an advantage over particle analysis or edge detection because the pattern search does not rely on distinct brightness of the imaged object compared with the image background.

Figure 5.1 shows an example VI provided in LabVIEW, which can be found in the following folder:

> *C:\Program Files\National Instruments\LabVIEW 2013\Examples\Vision\Pattern Matching*

As seen in Figure 5.1, pattern matching requires several steps.

Run the example VI above to gain an understanding of LabVIEW pattern matching concept:

1) Click on **Image File Path** to select and read in an image file (Figure 5.1 ①).
2) Select **Create Template** (Figure 5.1 ②) and a pop-up **ROI Constructor** window will appear. Using the **Rectangle ROI** tool, select the part of the image to be used as the reference or template (right mouse button on the image to drag out a rectangle). Then, select **OK** to return to main VI. The selected image portion will appear as the **Template**, as seen in Figure 5.1 ③ and will be used for pattern matching in a target image.
3) Select **Match** (Figure 5.1 ④) to search for the matched pattern in the image. The matching results include locations, number of matches, and

Practical Guide to Machine Vision Software: An Introduction with LabVIEW, First Edition.
Kye-Si Kwon and Steven Ready.
© 2015 Wiley-VCH Verlag GmbH & Co. KGaA. Published 2015 by Wiley-VCH Verlag GmbH & Co. KGaA.

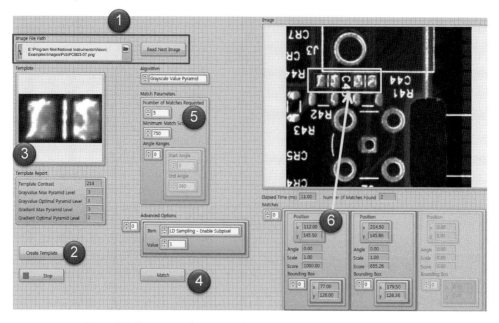

Figure 5.1 Pattern matching example VI.

boundary rectangle information, as seen in Figure 5.1 ⑤. The found patterns will then be shown on **Image** display via overlay, as seen in Figure 5.1 ⑥.

Example: Pattern Matching

In order to practice pattern matching, several types of patterns can be printed on paper, as seen in Figure 5.2. A USB camera can then be used to continuously acquire images of printed patterns. The task for this chapter is to build a VI that can find patterns that match with the reference image shown in Figure 5.2.

5.1
Pattern Matching Using Vision Assistant

To find patterns that match with a reference pattern, Vision Assistant will be used for this section. Perform the following steps:

1) Acquire or read in an image for image processing by using Vision Assistant.
2) Color images will need to be converted to grayscale via the **Color Plane Extraction** function (**Processing Function: Color» Color Plane Extraction**). This process has been discussed in Chapter 3.

Reference template

Figure 5.2   Image for pattern matching example.

3) From Vision Assistant, select the pattern matching function from **Processing Functions: Machine Vision»Pattern Matching**.

4) Select **New Template** from **Pattern Matching Setup**, as seen in Figure 5.3 ①.

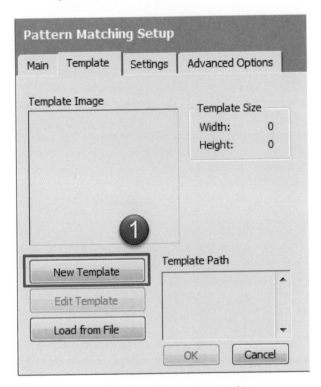

Figure 5.3   Create New Template for pattern matching.

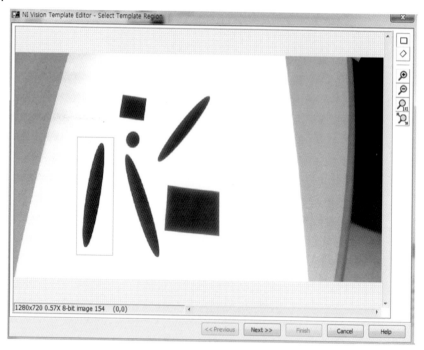

Figure 5.4 Selection of template region from the image.

5) You will be presented with a pop-up window to select a region of the image as the reference pattern for the pattern matching operation using the mouse, as seen in Figure 5.4. After the image template is selected, click on **Next**≫ to proceed.

6) From the **NI Vision Template Editor** as shown in Figure 5.5, you can select the regions in the template image to ignore by using the drawing tool ( ) to draw a region around the object. Here, the ignored area is indicated in Figure 5.5. This area will not be used for pattern matching and more accurate matching results can be obtained by excluding unnecessary parts.

7) Select **Next**≫ to adjust the desired X and Y coordinates within the matched object, as seen in Figure 5.6. This **Match Offset** point will identify the object's point of location when it is found in the searched image. Now, select **Finish** to save the Template image for pattern matching.

8) The resulting template image and template image path can now be seen in the **Template** tab of the **Pattern Matching Setup**, as seen in Figure 5.7.

9) By selecting the **Settings** tab from **Pattern Matching Setup** in Figure 5.7, you can set parameters values, as seen in Figure 5.8 ① and ②. Table 5.1 summarizes the parameter settings for pattern matching.

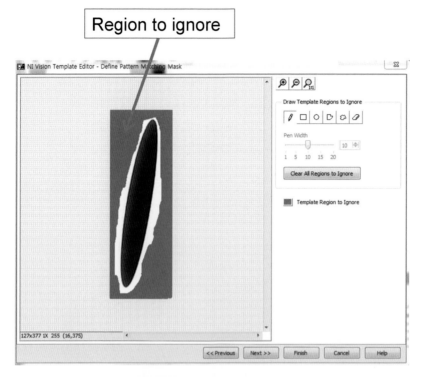

Figure 5.5 Regions to Ignore (Define Pattern Matching Mask).

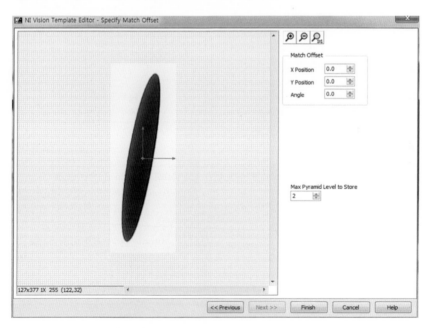

Figure 5.6 Matching offset adjustment.

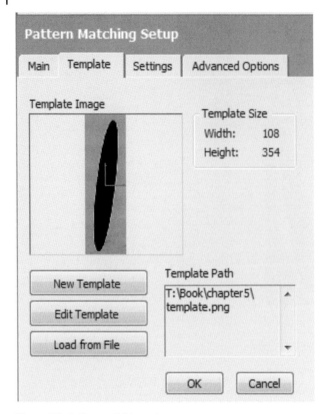

Figure 5.7 Pattern matching setup.

Table 5.1 Parameters for pattern matching.

Number of matches to find (Figure 5.8 ①)	Minimum score (Figure 5.8 ①)	Search for rotated pattern (Figure 5.8 ②)
In this example, the value of 3 is used to find three ovals that match with template pattern.	Only objects with higher matching score than the minimum score are considered valid in the search. The score value ranges from 0 to 1000. If matching score of an object is close to 1000, the matched object is likely to be perfectly matched with the reference template. However, if the value of minimum score is set too high, some of matched patterns with low matching score may not be found.	Rotated pattern can be found by using Search for Rotated Patterns. Note that allowable angle of 180° ranging from −90 to 90 is selected since the oval is symmetrical in shape.

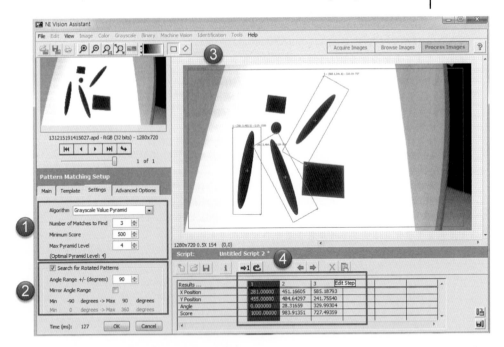

Figure 5.8 Pattern matching setup and the results.

10) Select a ROI rectangle in the image to define the area (Figure 5.8 ③) to perform pattern matching.

11) Observe and confirm the pattern matching results, as seen in Figure 5.8 ④. The results include X and Y coordinate locations, angle of rotation, and score. Three patterns are found in this example. Note that matched pattern 1 has the score value of 1000 since this pattern was used as the reference template image. The scores of other matched patterns are 983.9 and 727.5. From the score values, the level of similarity of matched patterns can be evaluated. If you set the minimum score to 900, the pattern with score value of 727.5 will not be included in the set of found objects. Note that the score can be affected by differences in lighting conditions as well as object similarity. The rotation angle of matched patterns with respect to reference pattern can be obtained, as seen in Figure 5.8 ④. If you had set allowable angle range to 30°, the pattern with a 329.9° rotation (result 3) would not have been reported in the search results.

12) If the parameters are acceptable, select **OK** from the **Pattern Matching Setup** to finish pattern matching using Vision Assistant. You are now ready to create a VI to build your own program for pattern matching.

5.2
LabVIEW Code Creation and Modification

Now we can use Vision Assistant to create a LabVIEW VI (**Tools»Create Lab-VIEW VI**). The created VI needs to be modified according to your needs. Lab-VIEW programming skills are required for this purpose. You may want to skip Sections 5.2 and 5.3 if you prefer an easier approach with the use of Vision Express, which will be presented in Section 5.4.

Within the **LabVIEW VI Creation Wizard**, you may select **Image File** as the image source (step 3 of 4). Note that the VI code that specifies the image source may not be appropriate for the intended application and may need to be modified. To build the SubVI for your applications efficiently, select the indicators and controls for the created VI (step 4 of 4), as seen in Figure 5.9.

The created VI from Vision Assistant will need to be modified in order to be used for real-time analysis. In this section, modification techniques are discussed for real-time pattern matching. However, before any modifications are performed, save the created LabVIEW code under the name **pattern_maching_SUB.vi**. The resulting LabVIEW SubVI has inputs and outputs, as seen in Figure 5.10.

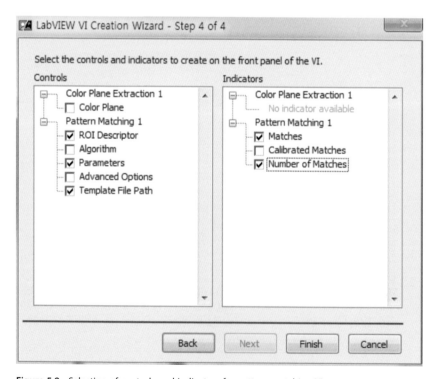

Figure 5.9 Selection of controls and indicators for pattern matching VI.

pattern_matching_SUB.vi

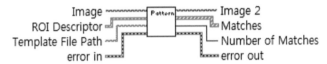

Figure 5.10 SubVI for pattern matching.

Figure 5.11 shows the SubVI that has been slightly modified from the created VI to add controls and indicators, as shown in Figure 5.10. Note that most of the indicators and controls were created automatically by the **VI Creation Wizard** (step 4 of 4). The parts of the VI to be discussed are indicated as circled numbers in Figure 5.11.

① shows an **Image** control that is placed on the front panel (**Vision»IMAQ Image ctl**) so that the image can be used as an input of the SubVI. In this way, the SubVI can receive an acquired image from the main or calling VI.

② shows error controls to handle possible errors for debugging purpose and used as an input of the SubVI.

③ shows the control for a **ROI Descriptor**, which was automatically generated during the VI creation. The ROI is often used to define image processing area. Initially, the **ROI Descriptor** control was given default values, which were defined in Vision Assistant prior to the SubVI code creation. However, the ROI information needs to be changeable either interactively or programmatically according to the location of object. The ROI information will be defined and updated from the main VI.

④ shows the control for the **Template File Path**, which is the file path for the reference template image. The **File Path** control was created in the control selection from VI Creation Wizard. Note that the reference image was defined and saved using the Vision Assistant, as seen in Figure 5.7.

⑤ shows the control for the pattern matching parameters. From the front panel, the number of matches requested, minimum match score, and angle range can be modified. Note that the default values for this control were generated from Vision Assistant. By using this control as an input for the SubVI, the parameters can be modified and passed from the main VI.

⑥ shows the pattern matching part, which searches for the matched pattern.

⑦ shows the indicator, **Matches**, which contains the results from pattern matching. The results include position, angle, scale, and bounding box. **Matches** is an array of clusters and will have the same size as the number of found patterns. The position and bounding box information will be used to overlay the searched patterns on image.

⑧ **Number of Matches** receives the number of matched (or searched) objects.

⑨ shows a **Vision Image.ctl** indicator that is placed on the front panel so that the image can be used as an output of the SubVI.

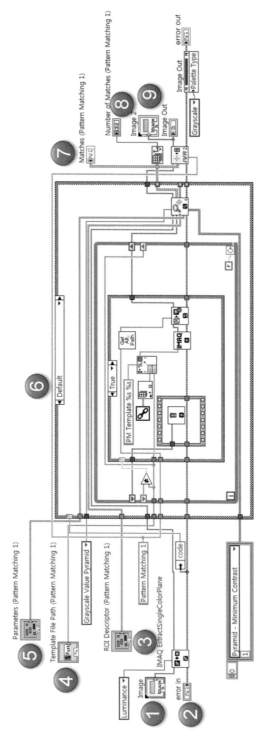

Figure 5.11 Block diagram of pattern matching SubVI.

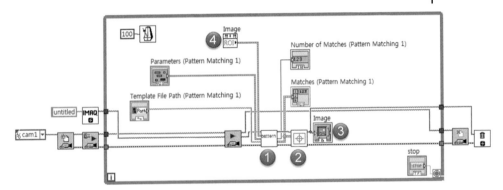

Figure 5.12 Main VI for pattern matching.

5.3
Main VI for Pattern Matching

Figure 5.12 shows the main VI's block diagram for pattern matching. In this main program, there are two SubVIs: one is to find matched patterns as seen in ① and the other is to overlay the matched pattern on image display as seen in ②.

The method to make the SubVI for pattern matching (**pattern_matching_SUB.vi**) was discussed in previous section. In the main program, all the inputs of the SubVI in ① are provided to perform the pattern matching. The inputs of the SubVI include acquired images from a camera, ROI information (property node of **Image ROI**) defined by mouse selection, and the template file path. The property node of the **Image ROI** (Figure 5.12 ④) can be generated by using the right mouse click on the **Image** indicator (Figure 5.12 ③).

To indicate the matched results on the **Image** display, an overlay function is used (Figure 5.13). For this purpose, you may reference the example provided in LabVIEW from *C:\Program Files\National Instruments\LabVIEW 2013\Examples\Vision\Pattern Matching*. The example VI, **Overlay Pattern Matching Results.vi** effectively overlays the results of pattern matching on the image display. Here, we slightly modify this code as seen in Figure 5.14.

Matches, which is one of the inputs to the SubVI is a cluster array, has the same number of elements as matched objects. To overlay the matched results, autoindexing of the **Matches** array in the FOR loop is used to overlay each of the resulting matched objects. There are two sets of location information for each matched object: position and boundary box. Both locations are used for overlaying the matched results.

Draw Pattern Matches Position.vi

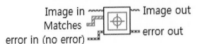

Figure 5.13 Overlay SubVI from NI provided example program.

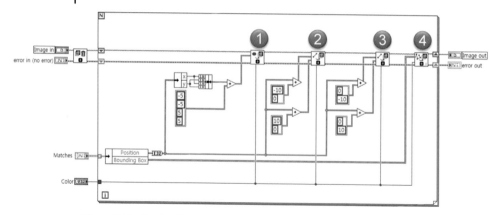

Figure 5.14 Overlay for Matches.

In Figure 5.14 ①, the **Overlay Oval** function (**Vision and Motion»Vision Utilities»Overlay»Overlay Oval**) is used to draw a circle around the position indicator of the matched objects. Additionally, two overlay line functions (Figure 5.14 ② and ③) are used to draw crosses at the indicator positions. The bounding box information, which defines the boundary of each object, can be used to draw a boundary line by using the **Overlay Multiple Lines** function (Figure 5.14 ④).

Figure 5.15 shows the final result of pattern matching when the main VI is run. As seen in Figure 5.15, template image file path as saved in Vision Assistant is selected in ① (refer to Figure 5.5). In the process of running the VI, define the ROI area (Figure 5.15 ③) on image display after selecting the rectangle tool (Figure 5.15 ②) from ROI tool menu. You can adjust the pattern matching

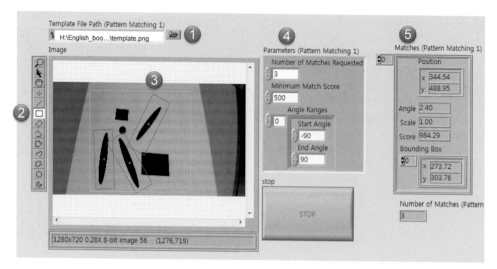

Figure 5.15 Pattern matching results.

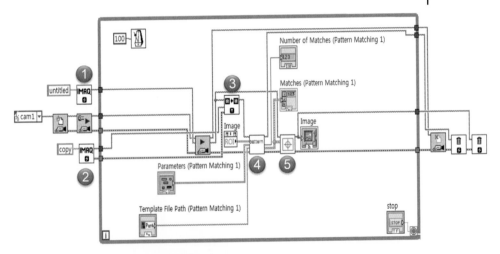

Figure 5.16 Modified VI to keep original image.

parameters (Figure 5.15 ④) in order to provide tuned real-time pattern matching results, as seen in Figure 5.15 ⑤. As a result of pattern matching, the position, angle, size, and score of the objects are determined. Note the angle indicates the amount of rotated angle of matched pattern with respect to reference template image. Matched results (**Matches**) are in the form of an array, of which the size is the same as the number of located matched patterns.

Note that the acquired color image was converted to a grayscale image because the pattern matching function requires a grayscale image. If you want to show original color image, **Image Copy** can be used to keep original image. The **IMAQ Image Create** function in Figure 5.16 ① is used to allocate memory for the original image acquired by camera. The **Overlay** SubVI in Figure 5.16 ⑤ can then be configured to overlay on the original image. To keep the original image, the copied image should be used for image processing. The image processing includes image conversion of the color image to a grayscale image. For this purpose, additional image memory is allocated, as seen in Figure 5.16 ②, and is connected to the **destination (Dst)** of IMAQ Copy (**Vision and Motion»Image Management»IMAQ Copy**) in Figure 5.16 ③ in order to make a copy of the acquired image. The copied image is connected to the pattern matching SubVI (**pattern_matching_SUB.vi**) in Figure 5.16 ④. In this way the original color image can be used to display the result, while the copy is used for conversion to grayscale and image processing.

5.4
Vision Assistant Express

Creating a pattern matching VI by using Vision Express is discussed. Prior to creating pattern matching using Vision Express, a VI for the continuous image

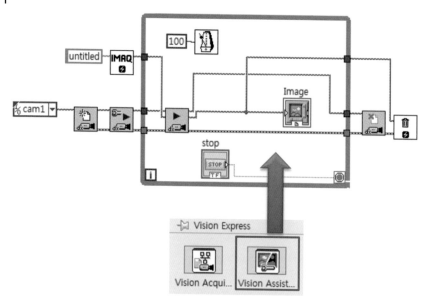

Figure 5.17 Vision Assistant Express.

acquisition using the **Grab** function (**Vision and Motion»NI-IMAQdx»Grab**) can be used, as shown in Figure 5.17, to capture and save an image for analysis using Vision Assistant Express. The image can be saved by right mouse clicking on the front panel image display and selecting **Save image** from the pop-up menu.

Then, the Vision Assistant Express function is dragged down onto block diagram, as seen in Figure 5.17.

As a result of the drag the function onto the block diagram, the Vision Express wizard will appear. As a first step, open the saved image to use for pattern matching using Vision Assistant. Then, the same process (described in from Figures 5.3–5.8) can be used for pattern matching. Since it is the same Vision Assistant process for pattern matching, a detailed discussion will be skipped. As a final step, you can select controls and indicators, as seen in Figure 5.18, by clicking on **Select Controls»**. In this way, the inputs and outputs can be easily accessed by the LabVIEW main VI.

As a final step of Vision Assistant Express, select **Finish** to return to LabVIEW. The created Vision Assistant Express VI for pattern matching will have controls and indicators, as seen in Figure 5.19 ③. The image source and destination controls are automatically selected and generated so that the acquired image (related to create memory in Figure 5.20 ①) is connected to **Image Src** (source) and the additional created memory (Figure 5.19 ②) is connected to **Image Dst** (destination) for copying and processing the image. In this way, the original acquired image is left unchanged, while the **Image Dst Out** can be converted to a grayscale image for pattern matching. Finally, the overlay SubVI

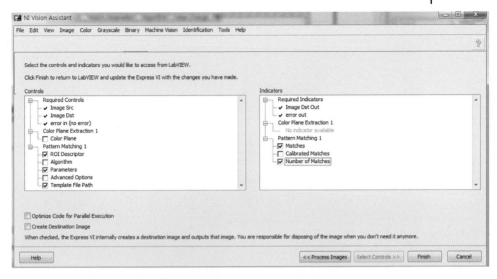

Figure 5.18 Selection of controls and indicators from Vision Assistant Express.

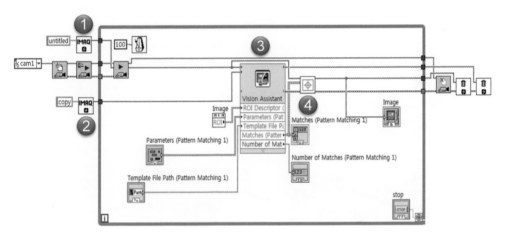

Figure 5.19 Final code for pattern matching using Vision Assistant Express.

described in Figure 5.13 is used for overlaying the matched results on the original image, as seen in Figure 5.19 ④.

By using the Vision Assistant Express, image processing subroutines can be easily created and directly inserted into LabVIEW VIs. In Chapter 6, Vision Assistant Express will be mainly discussed as a means to create VIs for your application.

Exercise 5.1

Nano-imprinted patterns are inspected to find any defects. The image has 100 imprinted patterns. Use the pattern matching to obtain the correct number of

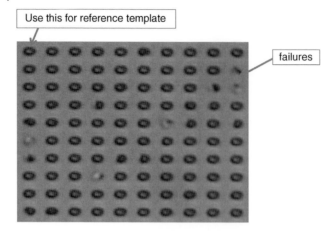

Figure 5.20 Acceptable pattern search based on pattern matching.

valid patterns. As matched results, display the number of acceptable patterns and overlay the pattern with boundary rectangle around acceptable patterns.

Exercise 5.2

Find the image *C:\Program Files\National Instruments\Vision\Example\ Images\Particle 01.png* (**Figure 5.21**). From the image, find the screws by using pattern matching and overlay the boundary box at position of matched screws. Incomplete screw images should be ignored.

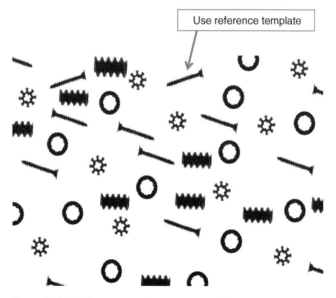

Figure 5.21 Finding screws using pattern matching.

6
Color Pattern Matching

Pattern matching based on grayscale images is a well-established tool for alignment, gauging, and inspection applications. However, grayscale images may have contrast problems due to non-optimum lighting conditions. If the object and background have similar grayscale intensities, grayscale pattern matching may not give accurate results. On the other hand, color pattern matching searches for color patterns and can improve the matching results significantly when the color of an object provides greater object differentiation from the background.

An example for color pattern matching can be found from the following folder:

> *C:\Program Files\National Instruments\LabVIEW 2013\Examples\Vision\Color*
> *Color Pattern Matching.vi*

Figure 6.1 shows a screen-captured image of the example VI. As seen in the figure, color pattern matching is effectively used in finding matched patterns with distinctive colors and shapes in comparison with the background. In the same manner as in Chapter 5, color pattern matching consists of two main steps: (1) learning template information and (2) searching for patterns based on the template.

Upon running the example VI, select a **Template** (Figure 6.1 ①) part for color pattern matching by drawing ROI on the image display. Then, you will see the selected reference image on image display of template (Figure 6.1 ②). Based on the template images and color pattern matching parameters (Figure 6.1 ③), patterns can be searched for and located in terms of location and score, as seen in Figure 6.1 ④.

6.1
Color Pattern Matching Using Vision Assistant Express

In this section, you will learn how to build color pattern matching VI by using Vision Assistant Express.

Practical Guide to Machine Vision Software: An Introduction with LabVIEW, First Edition.
Kye-Si Kwon and Steven Ready.
© 2015 Wiley-VCH Verlag GmbH & Co. KGaA. Published 2015 by Wiley-VCH Verlag GmbH & Co. KGaA.

Figure 6.1 Example VI for color pattern matching.

Example: Color Pattern Matching

Several kinds of colored patterns are printed on a paper, as seen in Figure 6.2. Four out of seven patterns are oval shapes. Here, the color of five of the objects is blue. In this example, you will find blue oval patterns by using color pattern matching. There are only two blue oval objects on the printed paper. Note that the paper may move or be rotated during image acquisition. So, the locations and angular aspects of the matched patterns need to be determined from real-time acquired images. Here we use Vision Assistant Express to make a VI for color pattern matching. The results will be shown as indicators and are graphically overlaid on the image display.

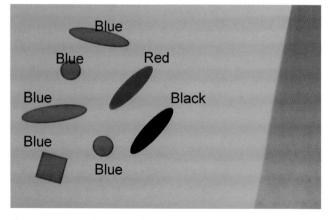

Figure 6.2 Example patterns for color pattern matching.

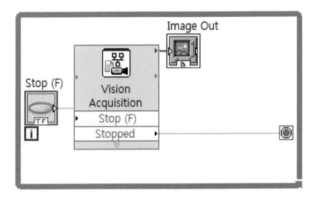

Figure 6.3 Image acquisition using Vision Acquisition Express.

6.1.1
Vision Acquisition Express

As a first step, acquire continuous images by dragging down Vision Acquisition Express from the function palette onto the block diagram. From pop-up window of Vision Acquisition Express wizard, complete the operations to implement continuous acquisition with inline processing, as seen in Figure 6.3. The details of Vision Acquisition Express have been discussed in Chapter 2.

By running the VI in Figure 6.3, continuous images are acquired from the camera, as seen in Figure 6.4. On the front panel, right mouse click on the

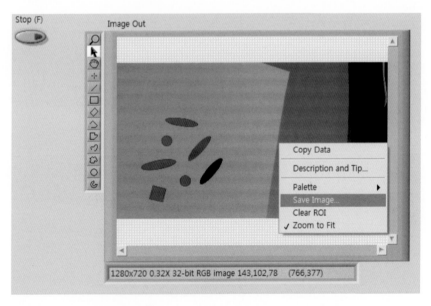

Figure 6.4 Saving image to a file.

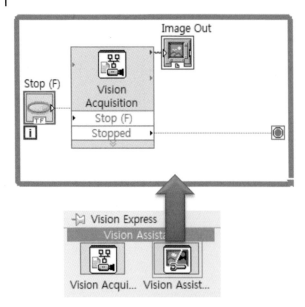

Figure 6.5 Vision Assistant Express for image processing.

image. From the pop-up window, select **Save Image** to save the image to a file for future use with Vision Assistant Express.

6.1.2
Vision Assistant Express

By dragging the Vision Assistant Express icon from the function palette onto the block diagram, you will be presented with the Vision Assistant wizard pop-up window (Figure 6.5). Initially, you will need to load the image from the previously saved image file (Figure 6.6 ①) to begin building the image processing process.

Perform the following steps to complete color pattern matching:

1) Select **Color Pattern Matching** from **Processing Functions: Color** as seen in Figure 6.6 ③.
2) From **Color Pattern Matching Setup**, select the **Template** tab, as seen in Figure 6.7.
3) By selecting **Create Template** from Figure 6.7, you will then see the pop-up window to select the reference (template) image, as seen in Figure 6.8. Here, a blue oval pattern is selected as the template. Note that accurate choice and selection of a reference template is important because the matched patterns are searched based on the template. Also, the rotation angle of matched pattern is calculated with respect to the template. Select

Figure 6.6 Vision Assistant for color pattern matching.

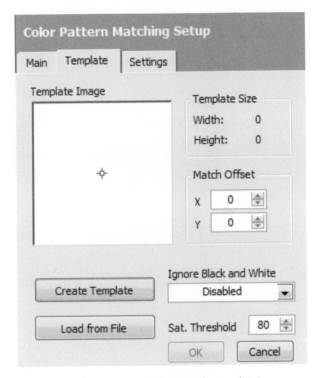

Figure 6.7 Color pattern matching setup for template image.

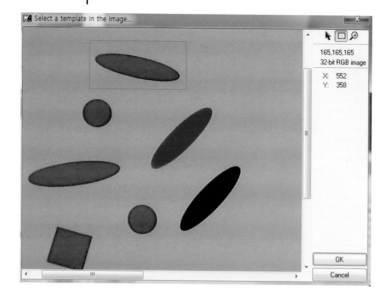

Select OK, then
Save the template.png

Figure 6.8 Selecting template image.

OK in Figure 6.8 when a template is selected. You then need to save the template image before returning to the Vision Assistant wizard.

4) If you create a template successfully, you will find the template image displayed in the **Template** tab in the **Color Pattern Matching Setup**, as seen in Figure 6.9 ①. Note that the **Match Offset** position in ②, the location

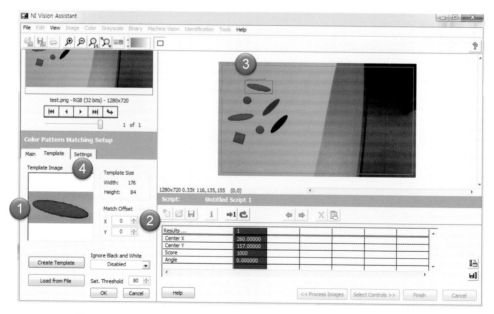

Figure 6.9 Color pattern matching setup.

Table 6.1 Setup values for color pattern matching.

Number of matches to find	Minimum score	Color score weight
In this example, the number of matches is set to 2 because there are two matched patterns to find.	The value for minimum score ranges from 0 to 1000. The higher value means that the more perfectly matched results will be searched.	The value for color score weight ranges from 0 to 1000. The higher value means the more perfectly matched object in terms of color. The software uses the color score weight for the final match ranking. If the value is 500, it indicates that the match score uses an equal combination of the color and shape scores.

coordinate results, will be reported based on the selected offset in the template.

5) Select the **Settings** tab from **Color Pattern Matching Setup**, as seen in Figure 6.9 ④. From the **Settings** Tab, determine setting values, as shown in Figure 6.10 ①. The guideline for setting values is summarized in Table 6.1.

Figure 6.10 ② shows setup parameters for rotated patterns. In this example, we select allowable rotation angle ranging from −90 to 90° because ovals are symmetric (mirror angle) and any angle of rotation within 180° is enough to find all

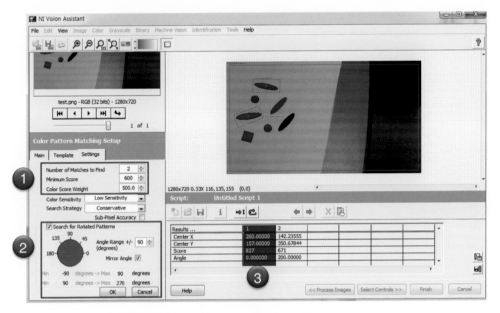

Figure 6.10 Settings for color pattern matching setup and the results.

orientations. Figure 6.10 ③ displays the numerical results of the pattern matching. These include the X and Y locations, score, and rotation angle of the matched objects. Here, the score indicates similarity in both shape and color. The value ranges from 0 to 1000 according to the determined amount of similarity.

When the color pattern matching setup using Vision Assistant is complete, select **Select Controls≫** to create controls and indicators that you can access from LabVIEW. In this example, we select **ROI descriptor**, **File Path**, **Number of Matches Requested**, **Minimum Score**, and **Color Score Weight** for controls. For indicators, **Matches** and **Number of Matches** are selected. **Matches** contains the resulting information of matched objects, including score, location, angle, and so on.

6.1.3
Main VI

After selecting controls and indicators as seen in Figure 6.11, click **Finish** to return to LabVIEW. You will then see the resulting Vision Assistant Express function on the block diagram having inputs and outputs, as seen in Figure 6.12 ②. The inputs and outputs of the Vision Assistant Express are connected, as seen in Figure 6.12. If you want to make changes to the image processing algorithm, double click on Vision Assistant Express icon in Figure 6.12 ② and you will be

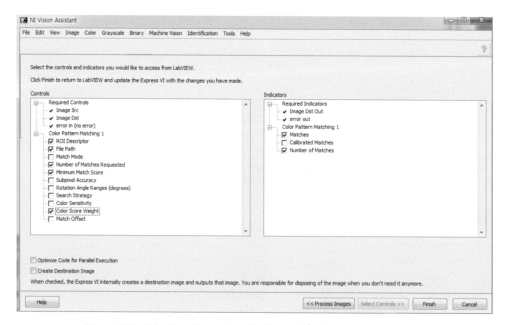

Figure 6.11 Selection of controls and indicators for color pattern matching.

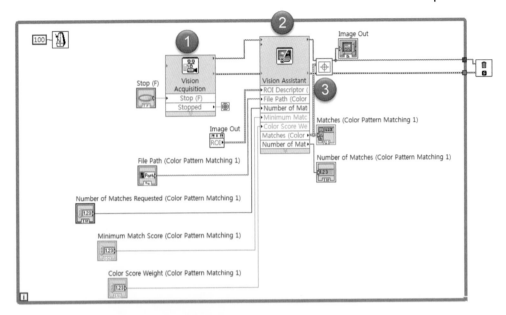

Figure 6.12 Block diagram for pattern matching.

brought back into the Vision Assistant Express wizard application. You can then modify and rebuild the image processing from within Vision Assistant Express. To show the matched results, the **Overlay** SubVI (Figure 5.13) discussed in Chapter 5 can be used, as seen in Figure 6.12 ③.

Figure 6.13 shows the front panel of main VI when the matched patterns are searched. As seen here, the parameter controls for color pattern matching have default values as set from Vision Assistant Express. However, you can modify these from main VI to tune the results. Other parameters that were not selected as controls will be shown as constant values in the block diagram and can only be modified in the block diagram.

The result of **Matches** can be easily accessed by LabVIEW because it was selected as an indicator in Vision Assistant Express. Shown here in the form of an indicator on the front panel, the results are available to use in other application tasks such as alignment, gauge, and so on. Also, the information can be used to overlay location information to confirm the matched results. As seen in front panel, we understand from the overlay that the target objects (blue ovals) are found successfully. The score of each matched pattern can be used to judge the similarity of matched object with template image.

We have the option to convert Vision Assistant Express function to a standard SubVI. The advantage of using converted standard SubVI is that you may open it and modify image processing functions and parameters according to your needs. To convert the Vision Assistant Express to a standard VI, move the mouse to

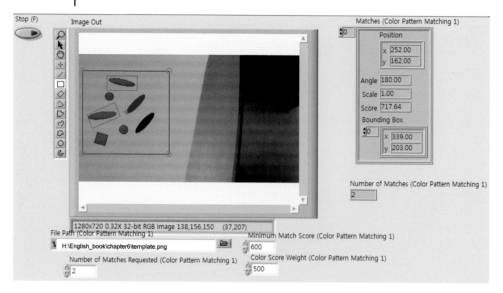

Figure 6.13 Front panel for color pattern matching.

Vision Assistant Express and click the right button. Then, from the resulting pop-up menu, select **Open Front Panel**, as seen in Figure 6.14.

You can then select **Convert** from the pop-up dialog box. As seen in the message, you need to be confident of the imaging processes you have established as

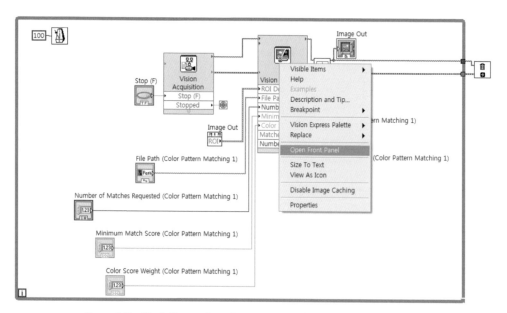

Figure 6.14 Block diagram for color pattern matching.

Figure 6.15 Converting Express VI to a standard VI.

you will not be able to return to use the Vision Assistant Express wizard for any modifications if you select **Convert**, as shown in Figure 6.15.

Once converted, you will need to double click on the converted SubVI and save it as a named VI (e.g., **color_pattern_sub.vi**) (Figure 6.16 Figure 6.16. Vision Assistant Express provides a very easy method to generate a SubVI compared with the direct use of Vision Assistant. However, the converted VI may seem to be complicated and not optimized. We recommend the direct use of Vision Assistant to convert to a LabVIEW VI rather than using a VI created from Vision Assistant Express as a starting VI to modify according to your needs.

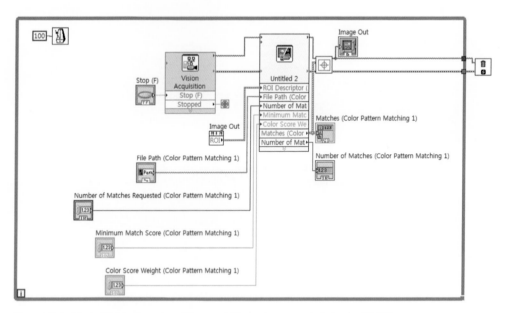

Figure 6.16 Block diagram for color pattern matching using converted standard SubVI.

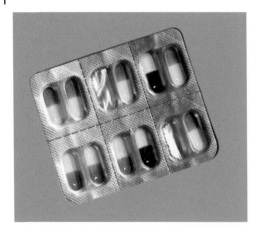

Figure 6.17 Example of finding green pills (Blister 13.jpg).

Exercise 6.1

Find the image **Blister 13.jpg** in the folder *C:\Program Files\National Instruments\Vision\Examples\Images\Blister*. Using the color pattern matching method, find the number of green pills and construct an overlay SubVI to overlay the results on the source image (Figure 6.17).

7
Dimension Measurement

Particle analysis analyzes complete objects rather than a part of an object. So, it is difficult to measure the size of a specific part in an object. On the other hand, the method using edge detection can measure the dimension of parts of objects. In this section, the edge detection method is extended to two dimensions (2D) to measure an object's dimensions. One way to do this is to cover a two-dimensional area with many search lines over which edge detection is performed. The measurement of an object's dimension in this manner can give accurate dimensional information since the outline of an object can be obtained by using a set of line ROIs to define 2D area. The **Clamp** function based on 2D edge detection is often used to detect locations that define the maximum or minimum length of a part of an object. Then, **Caliper** function can be used to determine the distances between edges. An example VI of measuring dimension by using a **Clamp** function can be found from the following folder:

C:\Program Files\National Instruments\LabVIEW 2013\Examples\Vision\Caliper\ Clamp.vi

Figure 7.1 shows the front panel of this dimension measurement example. In this example the maximum horizontal size of a hole in an object can be measured. Note that if you change the location and size of the ROI, you can measure the dimension of different parts of the object.

7.1
Dimension Measurement Using Vision Assistant Express

In this section, you will learn how to use Vision Assistant Express to measure dimensions of objects in an image.

Practical Guide to Machine Vision Software: An Introduction with LabVIEW, First Edition.
Kye-Si Kwon and Steven Ready.
© 2015 Wiley-VCH Verlag GmbH & Co. KGaA. Published 2015 by Wiley-VCH Verlag GmbH & Co. KGaA.

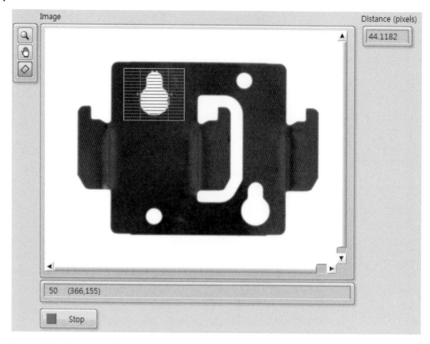

Figure 7.1 Example VI for **Clamp** function (**Clamp.vi**).

Example: Dimension Measurement

By using the **Clamp** function and the **Find Circular Edge** function, find the center location of two circles (circle 1 and circle 2), as shown in Figure 7.2. Then, use the **Caliper** function to obtain the distance between two circles.

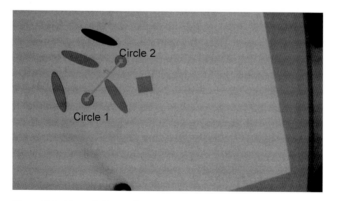

Figure 7.2 Example image for dimension measurement.

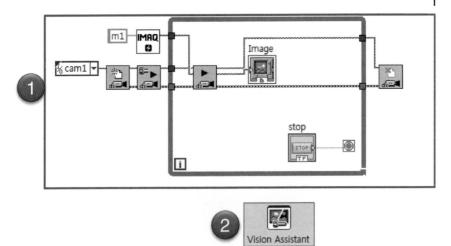

Figure 7.3   Vision Assistant Express for image processing of continuously acquired images.

7.1.1
Find Circular Edge Function

Complete the following steps in Vision Assistant Express to measure the dimension of circle 1 using **Find Circular Edge**.

1) Build a VI for continuous image acquisition, as seen in Figure 7.3 ①. Note that this part will be modified later to be used in an **Event** structure.
2) Save one of the acquired images from the **Image** display on the front panel.
3) From the function palette, drag Vision Assistant Express onto the block diagram, as seen in Figure 7.3 ②. You will then see the Vision Assistant Express wizard window.
4) Select the **Find Circular Edge** function from **Processing Functions: Machine Vision»Find Circular Edge**.
5) Move the mouse near the center of circle 1 and define an annular (circular) ROI around circle 1 with the left mouse button, as seen in Figure 7.4. There are two circles in an annular ROI: the inner circle should be placed inside of the circle 1 and outer circle should be placed outside of the circle 1.
6) As seen in Figure 7.5, it is possible to measure the center location and radius of circle 1 by using the **Find Circular Edge** function.

7.1.2
Clamp Function

The **Clamp** function can be used to measure the radius as well as the location of circle 2. The reason for using **Clamp** function here is to help readers understand

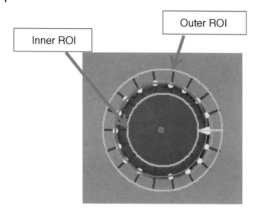

Figure 7.4   ROI for **Circular Edge**.

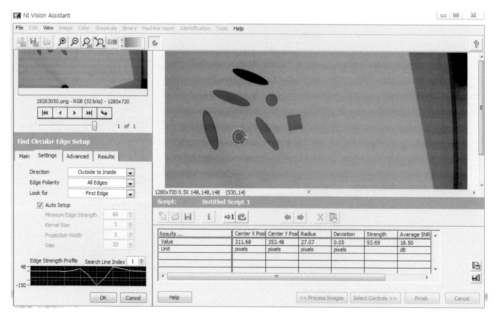

Figure 7.5   **Find Circular Edge** Results.

different dimension measurement approaches. Note that the **Find Circular Edge** function could be more effectively used to measure circle 2 instead of the **Clamp** function. In the case of using the Clamp function, the image should be converted to 8 bit grayscale image (or binary image) since the clamp function is based on edge detection techniques. So, you need to convert color image to grayscale image via color plane extraction function (**Processing Functions:**

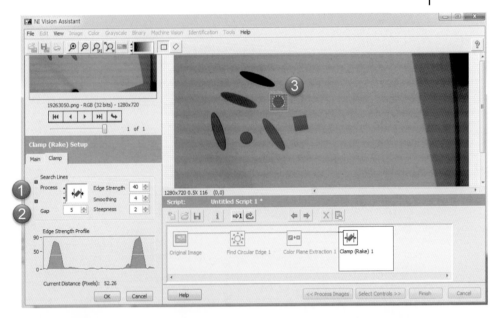

Figure 7.6 **Clamp** Setup.

Color» Color Plane Extraction» HSL-Luminance Plane) prior to using **Clamp** function.

Complete the following steps to measure circle 2 based on **Clamp** function.

1) Select the **Clamp** function from **Processing Functions:Machine Vision» Clamp**. Then, select the **Clamp (Rake) Setup** parameters, as seen in Figure 7.6.

2) Select **Horizontal Max Caliper** from **Process** selection and in this case set the value for gap to 5, as seen in Figure 7.6 ① and ②. You may want to select different parameters according to your needs. Tips for selecting these parameters are discussed in the following.

Search Lines: Process

You can select various clamp processes, as seen in Figure 7.7, depending on what dimension you are measuring. Table 7.1 summarizes the process for dimension measurement.

Search Lines: Gap

The **Gap** among ROI lines for edge detection can be modified. As seen in Table 7.2, smaller gap can reduce the distance among ROI lines for edge detection. Small gaps give better results in terms of accuracy. However, it may not be efficient in terms of computation time because there will be more edge data to

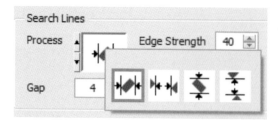

Figure 7.7 Clamp function process.

Table 7.1 Clamp process.

Horizontal max caliper	Horizontal min caliper	Vertical max caliper	Vertical min caliper
The maximum length in the horizontal direction is measured	The minimum length in the horizontal direction is measured based on detected edge	The maximum length in the vertical direction is measured	The minimum length in vertical direction is measured based on detected edge

Table 7.2 Clamp gap setup.

Gap: 2	Gap: 4	Gap: 6

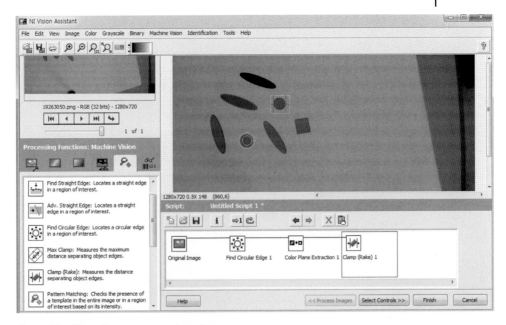

Figure 7.8 Dimension measurement results.

be processed. So, the proper value for gaps needs to be selected considering accuracy and efficiency.

3. Select **OK** and you can confirm the overlaid results using **Find Circular Edge** and **Clamp** to measure circle 1 and circle 2, respectively, as seen in Figure 7.8.

7.1.3
Caliper Function

To measure the distance between circle 1 and circle 2, select the **Caliper** function from **Processing Functions: Machine Vision**. Figure 7.9 shows the **Caliper** setup. You will need to select a measurement item from Figure 7.9 ①. Select a geometric feature of caliper from the available features, as summarized in Table 7.3.

To measure the distance between the two circles using Caliper function, complete the following two steps:

- **Step 1: Finding Center of Circle 2**
  1) Select **Mid Point** from the **Geometric Feature** list, as seen in Figure 7.10 ①. By selecting the Mid-Point ① between the two points, you can obtain the center location of circle 2.
  2) Select the **Point 1** and **Point 2** of circle 2, as seen in Figure 7.10 ②, which corresponds to horizontal maximum and minimum points.

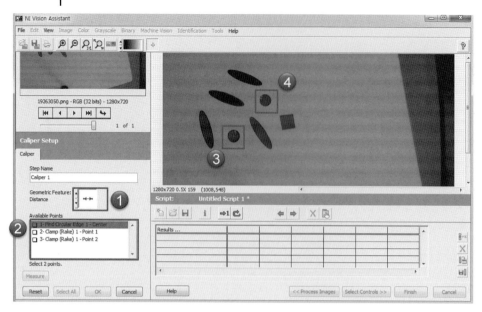

Figure 7.9 Caliper setup.

Table 7.3 Measurement items for caliper.

Distance	Midpoint	Perpendicular projection	Lines intersection	Angle from horizontal
⊶⊷	⊶⊷	⊥	⊷	∠
Angle from vertical	**Angle defined by three points**	**Angle defined by four points**	**Bisecting line**	**Mid line**
∠	∠	∠	⊿	⊥
Center of mass	**Area**	**Line fit**	**Circle fit**	**Ellipse fit**
△	★	⁄	◔	⬡

3) Select **Measure** as seen in Figure 7.10 ③ to obtain the midpoint of **Point 1** and **Point 2**. The midpoint corresponds to the center location of circle 2, as seen in Figure 7.11. As a result, you can get X and Y center position of circle 2, as seen in Figure 7.11.

4) Select **OK** to proceed to next step.

Caliper Setup

Caliper

Step Name

Caliper 1

① Geometric Feature:
Mid Point

Available Points

☐ 1- Find Circular Edge 1 - Center
✓ 2- Clamp (Rake) 1 - Point 1
② ✓ 3- Clamp (Rake) 1 - Point 2

Select 2 points.

③ Measure

Reset   Select All   OK   Cancel

Figure 7.10 Finding center location from **Clamp** function results.

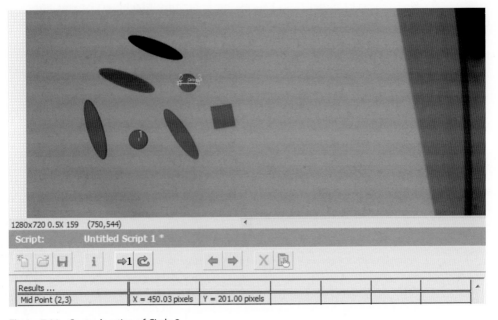

1280x720 0.5X 159 (750,544)

Script: Untitled Script 1 *

Results ...							
Mid Point (2,3)	X = 450.03 pixels	Y = 201.00 pixels					

Figure 7.11 Center location of Circle 2.

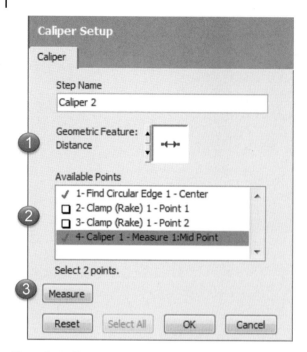

Figure 7.12   Distance measurement of two circles.

- **Step 2: Finding Distance between Circle 1 and Circle 2**
  5. Select **Caliper** from **Processing Functions: Machine Vision»Caliper** to measure the distance between two circles.
  6. Select **Distance** as seen in Figure 7.12 ① from the **Geometric Feature**.
  7. Select **Center** (item No. 1) and **Mid Point** (item No. 4) to measure the distance between the circles. Here, **Mid Point** corresponds to the center of circle 2.
  8. Select **Measure** ③.

As a result of the measurement, you can see the distance between two circle centers, as seen in Figure 7.13.

7.2
VI Creation for Dimension Measurement

7.2.1
Vision Assistant Express VI for Dimension Measurement

After confirming the results from Vision Assistant, create controls and indicators by clicking **Select Controls>>**. Here, two ROI Descriptors (Figure 7.14 ①

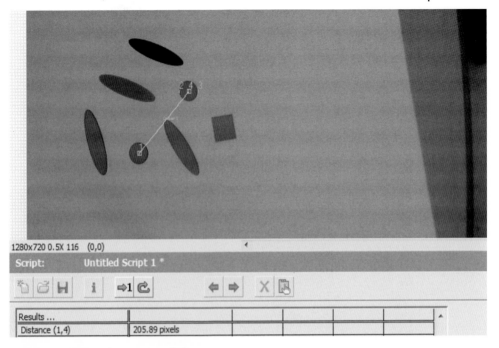

Figure 7.13 Distance between two circles.

and ②) and one caliper results (Figure 7.14 ③) are selected as controls and indicator, respectively, as seen in Figure 7.14. If you then select **Finish**, the Vision Assistant Express VI will have inputs and outputs that can be accessed from the block diagram, as seen in Figure 7.15.

As seen in Figure 7.15, there are two **ROI Descriptors** for the annulus and rectangle ROIs as input terminals of the Vision Assistant created VI. The ROIs will be defined interactively from the Image display on the front panel during execution. The methods for creating the two different ROIs will be discussed in Section 7.2.2.

7.2.2
ROI Array

To effectively deal with more than two different ROIs, we recommend the use of a ROI array. Note that there are two ROIs, which are different in type, location, and size to measure the center of two circles using different functions.

You can create a ROI array by using the following processes shown in Figure 7.16.

1) Place an **Array** control in the front panel (step 1 in Figure 7.16).

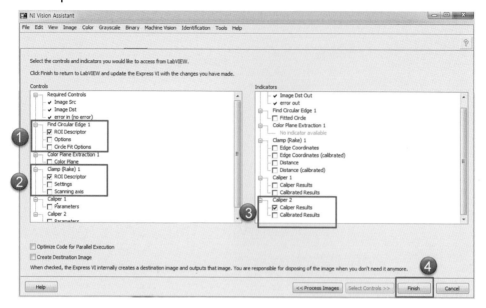

Figure 7.14 Selection of controls and indicators.

Figure 7.15 Vision Assistant VI for measuring distance between two circles.

2) From Control palette, go to **IMAQ Vision Controls** from the **Vision** palette and select **ROI Descriptor** ( ) (step 2 in Figure 7.16).

3) Drag the **ROI Descriptor** and drop it into the **Array** control (step 3 in Figure 7.16).

The ROI array is used to handle more than one ROI descriptors from the main program. The first element in the ROI array is the **Annulus**-type ROI for **Find Circular Edge** function, whereas the second element of the ROI array is a

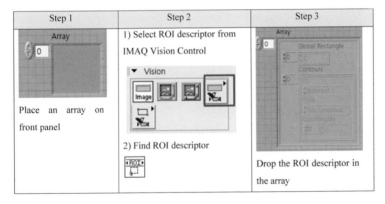

Figure 7.16   ROI Array.

Rectangle type for the **Clamp** function. If wrong types of ROI are connected to controls of Vision Assistant Express in Figure 7.15, there will be errors during the measurement process.

7.2.3
Front Panel of Main VI

Figure 7.17 shows the front panel of main program to measure the distance between two circles. Note that the approach used in this example may not be the preferred method for your application. So, you may want to modify this proposed method according to your applications.

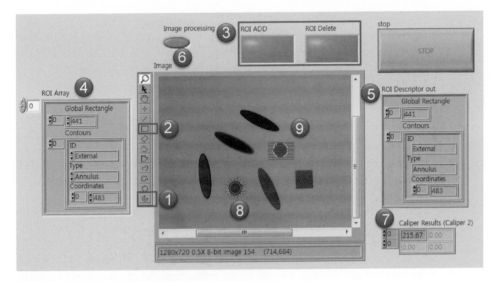

Figure 7.17   Front panel of main program.

The main feature of the program is that two different types of ROI are used to measure the locations of two circles. For this purpose, a ROI array is used, as seen in Figure 7.17 ④. In the main VI, one type of ROI can be added by user selection on image display. To show more than one ROI on the image display, all the ROI elements in the ROI array are grouped, as seen in Figure 7.17 ⑤. The details of dealing with multiple ROIs will be discussed later.

Figure 7.17 ③ shows the Boolean controls to add or delete a ROI from ROI array. By clicking the Boolean control (**ADD**), a user-selected ROI on the image display can be added to the ROI array. To select different types of ROI, the ROI tools can be used. In this example, annular and rectangular types of ROI can be selected from ROI tool, as seen in Figure 7.17 ① and ②. Finally, the **Caliper** function is used to calculate the distance (Figure 7.17 ⑦) between two circles if the Boolean switch (**Image Processing**) in Figure 7.17 ⑥ is true.

To calculate the distance between the two circles, the following steps needs to be taken.

1) Select **Annulus ROI** by using ①.
2) Draw out the ROI on the circle of ⑧ on the image display.
3) Click **ROI ADD** in ③ in order to add annulus-type ROI to ROI array.
4) Select rectangle ROI ②.
5) Draw out the rectangle ROI on the circle of ⑨ on the image display.
6) Click **ROI ADD** to add the rectangle ROI to ROI array.
7) Activate **Image Processing** (Boolean control) in ⑥.
8) The result of the distance measurement is then displayed in ⑦.

7.2.4
Block Diagram of the Main VI

Figure 7.18 shows the block diagram for the circle distance measurement. The Vision Assistant Express VI, described in Section 7.2.3, is used for image analysis. Here, an **Event** structure is used to coordinate the acquisition and analysis of the images, as seen in Figure 7.18.

Figure 7.18 shows the **Timeout** event. If no value is connected at ②, the default value will be −1 and the timeout case will never be processed. In this example, the value is set to 300. As a result, the timeout event will be executed once every 300 ms if there are no other events. In this way, one frame per 300 ms is shown on Image front panel display. In addition, if the Boolean control of **Image Processing** is true, then the image analysis within Vision Assistant Express VI (③) will be executed to measure the distance between the circles. Note that image conversion from color to grayscale is included in the Vision Assistant Express function. So, if the Vision Assistant Express is executed, the color image is automatically changed to grayscale. If you want to keep original image, you will need to allocate additional image memory with the **IMAQ Create** function and connect it to the image destination (**Image Dst**) input of Vision Assistant Express VI in Figure 7.18 ③.

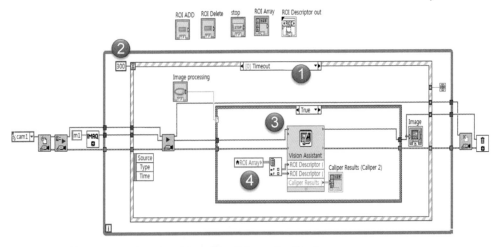

Figure 7.18   Timeout event in main program (Image Processing: True).

If Boolean control of **Image Processing** is false, then only the acquired image will be shown on front panel (**Image** display) without any image analysis, as seen in Figure 7.19.

Figure 7.20 shows the stop event. This event occurs when the value of stop (Boolean) changes, the program will be terminated.

The method to create ROI arrays will now be discussed. Figure 7.21 shows the event structure to create and add an ROI to the ROI array. The **ROI ADD** event shown in Figure 7.21 will be executed when the **ROI ADD** Boolean control on the front panel changes its value when the user clicks on it. In Figure 7.21 ① and ③ show the local variable for the **ROI Array**. Figure 7.21 ② shows the property node of the **Image** to retrieve the current ROI information.

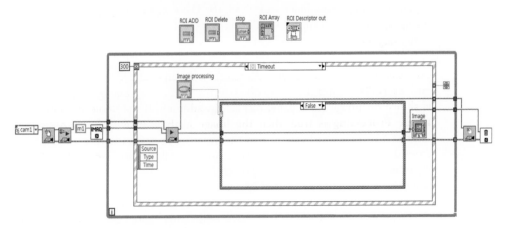

Figure 7.19   **Timeout** event (Image Processing: False).

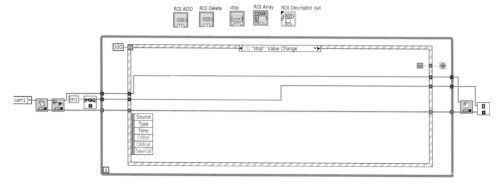

Figure 7.20   Stop event.

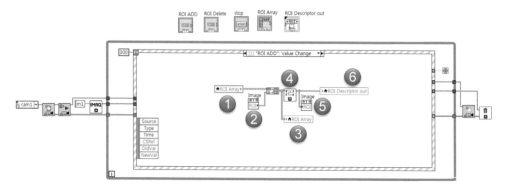

Figure 7.21   ROI ADD event.

As seen in Figure 7.21, the current ROI information of the image can be added to the ROI array by using the **Build Array** function in Figure 7.22. Note that when **Building Array** function is used, the **Concatenation** input option should be selected (right click on the **Building Array** icon to select the **Concatenation** option).

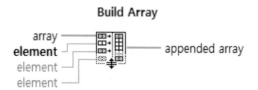

Figure 7.22   Build array.

IMAQ Group ROIs

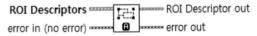

ROI Descriptors ═══════ ▦ ═══════ ROI Descriptor out
error in (no error) ━━━━━ 🅰 ┅┅┅┅ error out

Builds a single ROI descriptor from an of array ROI
descriptors.

Figure 7.23   Group ROIs.

The **ROI Array** needs to be reformed in a way that is compatible with the ROI data contained in the Image display. For this purpose, **IMAQ Group ROIs** function (Figure 7.21 ④) is used. This will result in the multiple ROIs being displayed in the Image display on the front panel. The **IMAQ Group ROIs** function can be found in function palette: **Vision and Motion»Vision Utilities»Region of Interest** (Figure 7.23).

The grouped ROIs can be supplied as an input into the **Image** display by using **Image ROI** property node (with write option), as seen in Figure 7.21 ⑤. In this way, you can see more than one ROI on the image display.

In some cases, the size of the ROI array may need to be reduced. For this purpose, to reduce the size of the ROI array, an **ROI Delete** event can be created, as seen in Figure 7.24. In the ROI delete event, the ROI element with highest index will be deleted from the ROI array.

Figure 7.24 ① and ③ show the local variable of **ROI Array**. By using a **Delete from Array** function ②, an element of ROI array with maximum index is deleted and thereby the size of the array can be reduced by 1. The reduced ROI array can be grouped using **IMAQ ROI Group** function. The grouped ROI can be displayed on the front panel **Image** display with the use of **Image ROI** property node in ④.

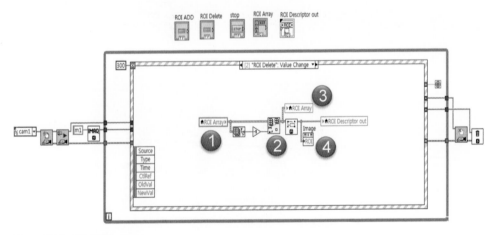

Figure 7.24   ROI Delete event.

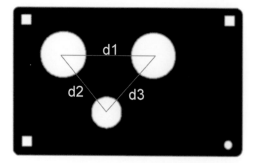

Figure 7.25 Distance among holes.

In this example, the number of elements in ROI array was two since two ROIs are required to measure the distance between circles. However, you can define as many as ROIs according to your applications by using the ROI arrays.

Exercise 7.1

Use the **Caliper** function to calculate the distances (d1, d2, d3) among three holes as seen in Figure 7.25. The image can be found from *C:\Program Files\National Instruments\Vision\Examples\Images\Holes.tif.*

8
Dimension Measurement Using Coordinate System

To measure the dimensions of an imaged object, a ROI is used to define the measurement location as discussed in previous chapters. In most cases, the object under inspection may shift and/or rotate in the viewing field of the video image. If a static ROI does not incorporate the entire object under investigation, the dimension may not be measured. For this case, the ROI location will need to be shifted and rotated according to the objects location. To enable this dynamic ROI location, a reference coordinate system can be used to define the measurement area around the object relative to the reference location of the object. The reference coordinate system is based on a characteristic feature of the object. To locate a reference coordinate system relative to the object, pattern matching or edge detection can be used. The ROI defined with respect to the reference coordinate system is then used to measure the dimension of a part of the object.

The example using a reference coordinate system can be found from the following folder:

C:\Program Files\National Instruments\LabVIEW 2013\Examples\Vision\Vision Assistant Express VI\Battery Clamp Inspection (Express).vi

As seen in Figure 8.1, a reference coordinate can be located irrespective of any shift and/or rotation of the object in an image via pattern matching. From the reference coordinate, the ROI used for measurement can be automatically located on a part of the object that is of interest.

8.1
Measurement Based on a Reference Coordinate System Using Vision Assistant Express

Example: Dimension Measurement Using a Reference Coordinate System

In this example, a measurement of a circle fit and clamp distance shown in Figure 8.1 is discussed in detail to create a VI for dimension measurement based on a reference coordinate system (Figure 8.2). A modification to the NI-provided

Practical Guide to Machine Vision Software: An Introduction with LabVIEW, First Edition.
Kye-Si Kwon and Steven Ready.
© 2015 Wiley-VCH Verlag GmbH & Co. KGaA. Published 2015 by Wiley-VCH Verlag GmbH & Co. KGaA.

example is incorporated to use continuous image acquisition from a camera. The user-defined ROI in Figure 8.1 is used to define image processing area for pattern matching. The object image, which can be found in *C:\Program Files \National Instruments\Vision\Examples\Images\Battery\Image00.jpg*, is printed on paper and imaged by the video camera. It is assumed that the location of the object is unknown and can be placed anywhere in the acquired image by moving and rotating of printed paper. Complete the LabVIEW code to measure clamp distance, the circle center, and diameter by using Vision Assistant Express.

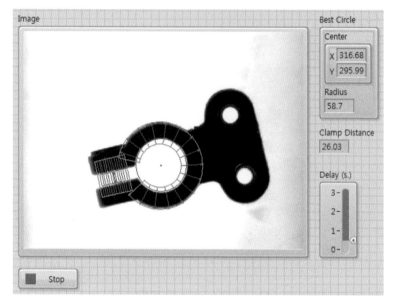

Figure 8.1 Example VI for coordinate system.

Figure 8.2 Example image for dimension measurement.

8.1.1

Pattern Matching

If the location of object in the image is not initially known, a distinct feature of the object needs to be located to define a reference coordinate system. In this example, pattern matching is used to find the location of object and determine the coordinate system.

As a first step, create a VI for continuous image acquisition, as discussed in Chapter 2 (Figure 2.12). Then, one of the acquired images is saved as a file for image processing using Vision Assistant Express. The Vision Assistant Express VI can be dragged down onto the block diagram for image analysis.

The color image should be converted to a grayscale image prior to pattern matching by using **Color plane Extraction** function from **Processing Functions: Color.** Here, the **Luminance Plane** from HSL is selected as discussed previously.

To define a reference coordinate system, a subfeature of the object is used with pattern matching to locate the object. Note that the selected subfeature should have parts that are not symmetric so that the angle of the subfeature can be uniquely determined in the pattern matching process. In this example, the end part of the object is selected as a template image for use in searching for object's location. To define reference coordinate system, complete the following steps.

1) Select **Processing Functions: Machine Vision»Pattern matching**.
2) Select **New Template** from the pattern matching setup.
    Note that object may be rotated. To effectively select rotated object, the **Rotated Rectangle** ROI tool in Figure 8.3 ① is used. In this way, the end part of the rotated object can be selected as the template image for pattern matching, as seen in Figure 8.3 ②.

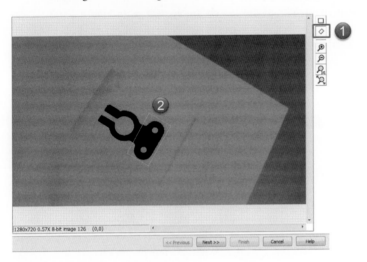

Figure 8.3 Selection of template image.

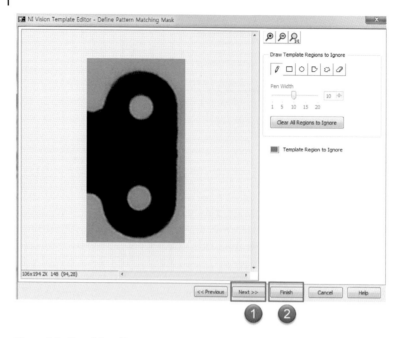

Figure 8.4 Template editor.

3) Select **Next** and then **Finish** (Figure 8.4 ②) if the template image is accept-able and save the template file.
4) Select the **Settings** tab seen in Figure 8.5.
5) Select a ROI (Figure 8.6 ①) to define the search area for the matched pat-tern. Later, two more local ROIs will be defined to measure the dimensions of the object based on the reference coordinate.
6) Check that the results of the search are correct as in Figure 8.6 ③. If the results are not correct, adjust pattern matching settings in ②. For details, refer to Chapter 5. Click on **OK** to proceed to the next step.

8.1.2
Coordinate System

The next step is to define the reference coordinate system based on the matched patterns. This will be accomplished in the following steps:

1) Select **Set Coordinate System** from **Processing Functions: Image** section, as seen in Figure 8.7.
2) Selecting **Horizontal**, **Vertical**, and **Angular Motion** from the **Mode** selections allows the pattern matching function to search for rotated and shifted instances of the pattern in the image, as seen in Figure 8.8. Note that **Pattern Matching 1-Match 1** is reported in the **Origin** and **X-Axis Angle** box. **Pattern Matching 1-Match 1** is the result of the previous

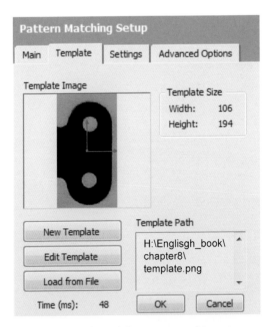

Figure 8.5   Template tab for pattern matching setup.

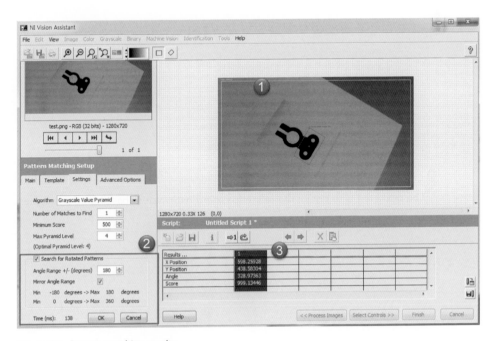

Figure 8.6   Pattern matching results.

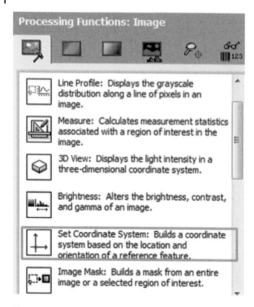

Figure 8.7   Set Coordinate System.

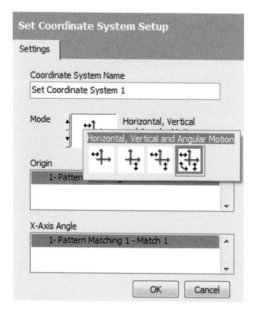

Figure 8.8   Set Coordinate System setup.

pattern matching and is used for defining the origin and reference coordinate system. After finishing the setup, the coordinate system, which has the name of **Set Coordinate System 1**, will be created.

8.1.3
Dimension Measurement Using the Clamp Function

1) The **Clamp** function will be used here to measure distance between the object's edges (Figure 8.9). Here, the **Clamp** functions for dimension measurement can be found from **Processing Function: Machine Vision**. Note that there are other measurement functions that can be used depending on the object shapes to be measured.
2) Select the **Reposition Region of Interest** and **Set Coordinate System 1** from the main tab of **Clamp** setup, as seen in Figure 8.10, in order to use the dynamically defined reference coordinate system from above. In this way, the dimensions of the object will be measured relative to the reference coordinates.

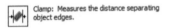
Clamp: Measures the distance separating object edges.

Figure 8.9 Clamp function.

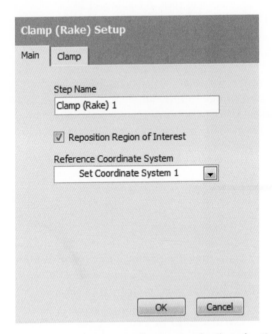

Figure 8.10 Reference coordinate system for Clamp function.

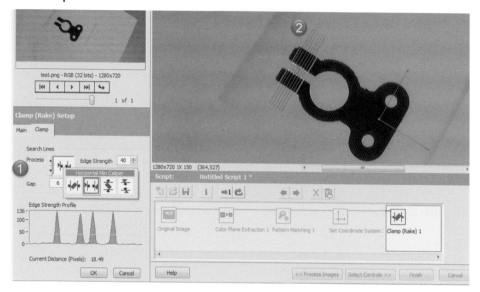

Figure 8.11 Clamp setup.

3) Select the **Clamp** tab from the **Clamp (Rake)** setup. A **Clamp Rake** ROI can be placed on the image. Using the control points on the ROI, rotate, scale, and move this ROI into position as seen in Figure 8.11 ②.

4) Select **Horizontal Min Caliper** from the **Process** selections (Figure 8.11 ①) to measure the gap distance. Since the coordinate system has been redefined dynamically by the previous step (**Set Coordinate System**, Section 8.1.2), the position of the clamp ROI will move with respect to the new reference coordinate system based on the position of the object.

5) Select the **OK** button if all the other setting values are acceptable. Then, you will see that clamp distance can be measured based on the dynamically determined reference coordinate system.

6) Select the **OK** button if the measurement is acceptable.

8.1.4
Measurement of Circle Edge

As a next step, you need to measure the circular edge.

1) Select **Find Circular Edge** setup from **Processing Function: Machine Vision**. Make sure that reference system is correctly selected and the repositioned region of interest is selected as seen in Figure 8.12. Then, select **OK**.

2) Draw out the ROI for **Find Circular Edge** as seen in Figure 8.13 ② and check the settings in Figure 8.13 ① to obtain the best circle results.

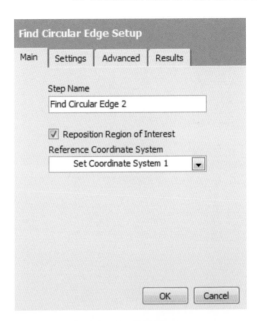

Figure 8.12   Find Circular Edge setup.

3) Select **OK**. You will now see the two measurement results overlaid on the image, as seen in Figure 8.14 ①.

4) Click on **Select Controls≫** (Figure 8.14 ②) to set the controls and indicators we will need in a LabVIEW VI. In this example, the **ROI Descriptor**

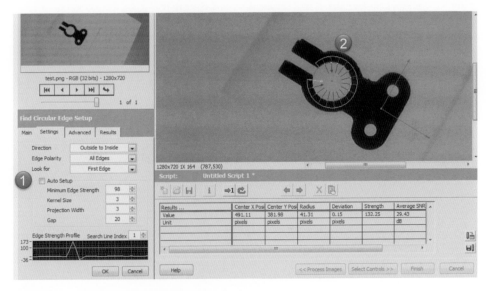

Figure 8.13   Settings for Find Circular Edge setup.

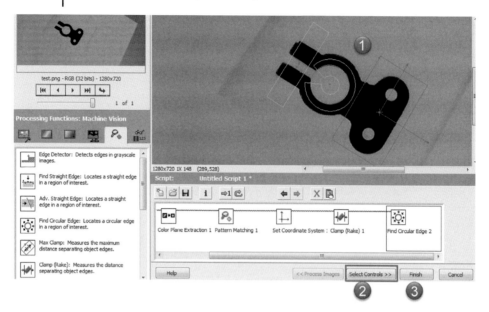

Figure 8.14 Overlaid measurement results.

for pattern matching is selected as a control and **Clamp Distance** and **Fitted Circle** are selected as indicators, as seen in Figure 8.15 ① and ②. After selecting **Finish** ③, a VI having the specified controls and indicators is created (Figure 8.16).

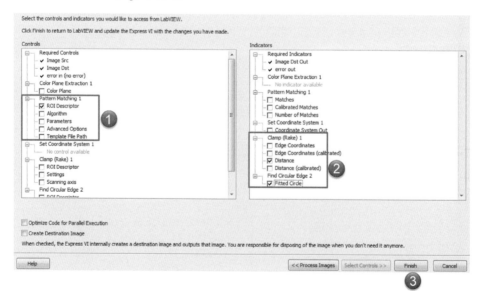

Figure 8.15 Selection of controls and indicators.

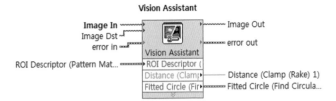

Figure 8.16 Vision Assistant Express VI.

8.2
Conversion of Vision Assistant Express to a Standard VI

We will now modify the resulting function created with Vision Assistant Express. In order to do this, we first need to convert the Vision Assistant Express function to a standard VI by right mouse clicking on the VI icon and selecting **Open Front Panel** from the pop-up window. Then, a standard VI will be created from Vision Assistant.

Figure 8.17 shows a part of the resulting VI that performs pattern matching (Figure 8.17 ①) and defines the reference coordinate (Figure 8.17 ③) based on the matched pattern. Now, by creating an indicator of **Matches** (output of **IMAQ Match Pattern** VI indicated at ②) and connecting it to the terminal of the VI, the match results will be available for the creation of an indicator on the main VI's front panel. Also, the match results will be used to overlay location information on the image.

Figure 8.18 shows the block diagram of the main VI for measuring the clamp gap and inner circle edges. Figure 8.18 ① shows the converted standard VI with file name of **chapter8_sub**.vi. Note that the created output terminal for the pattern matching results is connected to an overlay VI shown in Figure 8.18 ②.

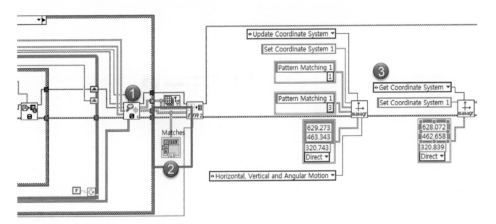

Figure 8.17 LabVIEW code (Coordinate setting via pattern matching).

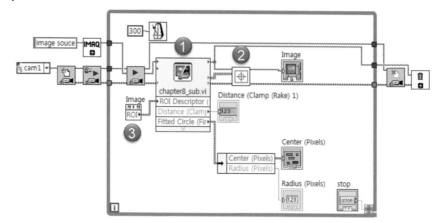

Figure 8.18 Main VI for measurement.

Note that the **Image ROI** property node shown in Figure 8.18 retrieves the ROI information from the **Image** display to define the search area for the pattern matching process. The matched pattern is then used to define the reference coordinate system. For this to be successful, the ROI area should be set large enough to find the part of object that has the reference pattern. If you do not connect this ROI descriptor, the created VI will use the default constant ROI descriptor that was defined in pattern matching setup during the Vision Assistant setup and may not be appropriate for variable imaging situations.

To overlay the pattern matching results on the image display, the previously created **Draw Pattern Matches Position.vi** (Figure 5.14) was modified, as seen in Figure 8.19. The main difference is that the **Clear Overlay** function is not used because it would delete the overlay for **Clamp Distance** and **Find Circle Edge**, which were included from Vision Assistant.

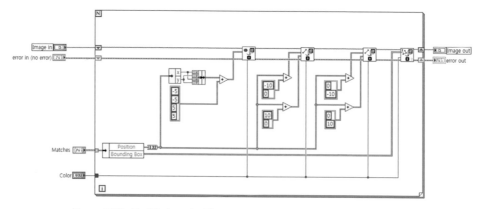

Figure 8.19 Modified overlay VI.

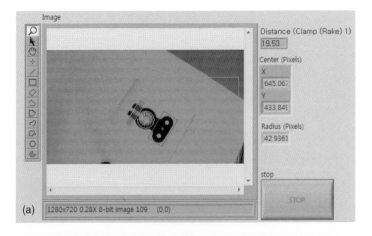

(a)

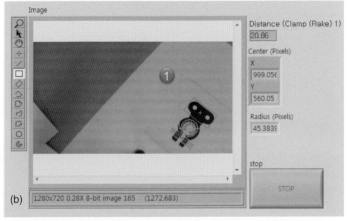

(b)

Figure 8.20 Results of dimension measurement based on coordinate system. (a) Inclusive ROI. (b) Noninclusive ROI.

Figure 8.20 shows the results of dimension measurement based on the reference coordinate system. To validate the VI, the object can be moved and rotated as seen in Figure 8.20a and b. The VI can measure object dimensions irrespective of the object's location and rotation. Therefore, the coordinate system based on pattern matching is useful to measure dimensions of objects when you do not have any prior information on the location of the object in the image.

You may notice that the circular fit results are slightly different according to the location. This is due to the camera axis not being located perpendicular to the object. The perspective errors may be corrected by using the calibrated image, which will be discussed in Chapter 14.

Portions of the object in Figure 8.20b are located outside the ROI. Nevertheless, the clamp gap (**Distance**) and circle radius (**Radius**) were possible since the searched parts of the pattern are still within the ROI.

distance

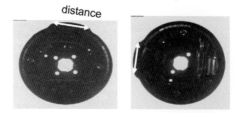

Figure 8.21 Size measurement of the bump part in rotated images.

Exercise 8.1

Use the rotated images from *C:\Program Files\National Instrument\Vision\ Examples\Images\Rotate*. Select one of the images from the folder and make reference coordinate at the bump part (Figure 8.21). By using the reference coordinate, calculate the size of bump part of other images with different rotated angle.

9
Geometric Matching

Pattern matching algorithm described in Chapter 5 uses the pixel intensity information as the primary feature for matching. As an alternative, geometric matching uses boundary edges to characterize the shape of an object and then uses this characterization to search for similar shapes. To use this method, the object and background should be distinguishable by sharply contrasting regions in order to accurately determine the boundary of the object. The boundary shape information of the objects is compared with that of an object in a template image to determine similarity. If the edge of the boundary is not sharp, pattern matching as described in Chapter 5 is recommended. An advantage of geometric matching is that it can find matching objects regardless of shifting, rotating, scaling, and even occlusion (overlapping of objects in the image). Geometric matching can be used in the following applications: gauging, inspection, alignment, and sorting.

Example VI on geometric matching can be found from the following folder:

C:\Program Files\National Instruments\LabVIEW 2013\Examples\Vision\Geometric Matching\Geometric Matching.vi

Figure 9.1 shows example VI provided with LabVIEW. As seen in the **Template** image in Figure 9.1, the object has a distinct boundary to extract the geometric features. By using the appropriate search parameters, the rotation angle, scale, and the location of the matched patterns can be determined. Note that the method detects boundary edges of the object in grayscale images. Therefore, the color images should be converted to grayscale image.

Practical Guide to Machine Vision Software: An Introduction with LabVIEW, First Edition.
Kye-Si Kwon and Steven Ready.
© 2015 Wiley-VCH Verlag GmbH & Co. KGaA. Published 2015 by Wiley-VCH Verlag GmbH & Co. KGaA.

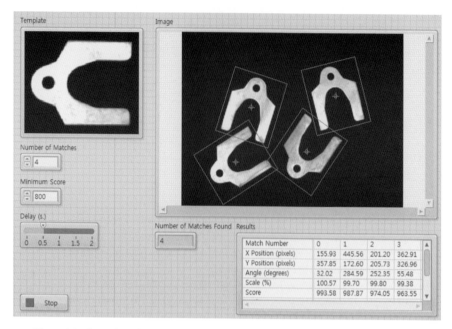

Figure 9.1 Example VI for Geometric Matching.

9.1
Geometric Matching Using Vision Assistant Express

> **Example: Geometric Matching**
>
> Figure 9.2 shows an example image that will be used for geometric pattern matching. Note that this is the same example image used in color pattern matching described in Chapter 6. As seen in Figure 9.2, the objects have distinct boundary edges and thus suitable for geometric matching. There are three different kinds of geometric shapes in Figure 9.2. Among those, find two geometric shapes: circles and ellipses using geometric matching.

The image acquisition VI will be skipped since it has been discussed in previous chapters. The use of Vision Assistant Express for geometric matching will be mainly discussed.

As a first step of Vision Assistant Express, the color image is converted to a grayscale image by using **Color Plane Extraction** function. This image conversion method has been described in Chapter 3.

Since there are two different patterns to search, the geometric pattern matching needs to be repeated: once for locating circles and once for ellipses. Note that if there are many patterns to be located, the use of a **Classification** function

Figure 9.2 Example image for Geometric Matching.

is recommended instead of using the many steps required for geometric pattern searching. Classification functions will be discussed in Chapter 12.

9.1.1
Geometric Matching for Circles

Complete the following steps to find matched geometric patterns for circles.

1) Using Vision Assistant Express, select **Geometric Matching** from **Processing Functions: Machine Vision**.
2) In the **Template** tab within **Geometric Matching Setup**, select **New Template**, as shown in Figure 9.3, to define reference pattern.
3) Using the ROI tool, select one of the circles as the template pattern, as seen in Figure 9.4.
4) Click **Next≫** to proceed to geometric matching. If the setting values are correct, the boundary curve of the template pattern will be indicated by an overlay, as seen in Figure 9.5 ①. If the boundary curve is not quite right, the parameter values in ② can be adjusted until the overlaid boundary line perfectly outlines the object.
5) Click on **Next≫** and you may draw regions to ignore, as seen in Figure 9.6.
6) Select **Next≫** to set up matching parameters for the geometric matching, as seen in Figure 9.7.
7) By modifying the **Match Offset** value, as seen in Figure 9.7 ①, the object's location coordinates based on the **Match Offset** can be adjusted within the object template. You can also allow for rotation and scaling changes of the searched object by using the **Match Range** variables in Figure 9.7 ②.
8) Select **Finish** and save the template image to a designated folder. The **Template Image** will be displayed within the template tab in the **Geometric Matching Setup** window, as seen in Figure 9.8.

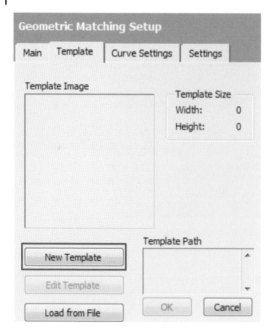

Figure 9.3 Geometric Matching setup.

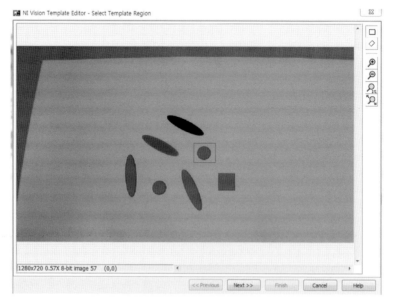

Figure 9.4 Selection of template image.

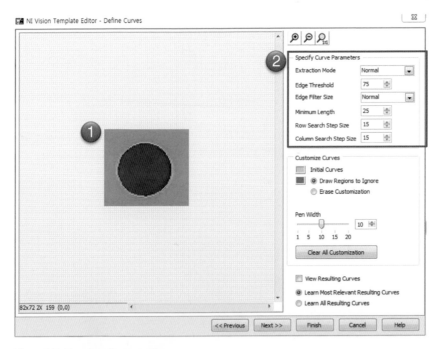

Figure 9.5 Template image setting.

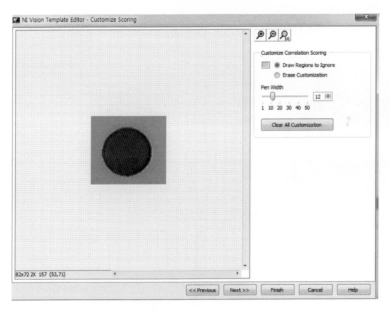

Figure 9.6 Draw regions to ignore.

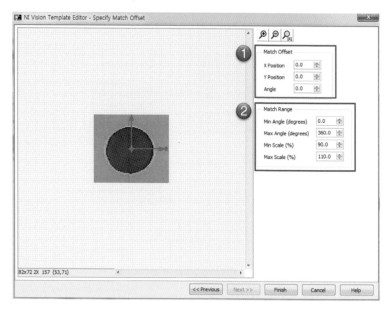

Figure 9.7 Match offset and range.

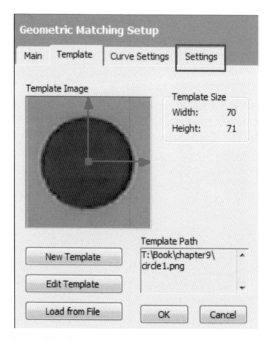

Figure 9.8 Geometric Matching setup for circle.

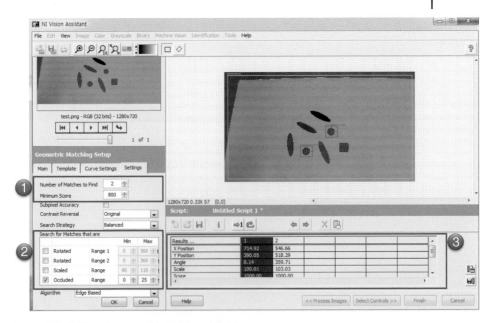

Figure 9.9 Settings for geometric matching (circle).

9) Select the **Settings** tab in Figure 9.8 to set up other parameters. As seen in Figure 9.9 ①, the number of objects to find as well as the minimum score can be selected. The minimum score value ranges from 0 to 1000. Note that the more perfectly matched patterns are located when higher score value is used. In this example, the score value of 800 was used. You can also search for the patterns that are rotated, scaled, and occluded with proper selection of these setting values. For example, in Figure 9.10 ②, if you use the occluded value of 25, then about 25% of an occluded pattern may be matched. Figure 9.10 ③ summarizes the results on the matched patterns using geometric matching. Among the matched results shown are object location, angle, scale, and score.

10) Select **OK** to search for circles based on geometric matching if the setting values are acceptable.

9.1.2
Geometric Matching for Ellipses

After searching for circles, the same steps using **Processing Functions: Machine Vision» Geometric Matching** should be repeated to search for ellipse pattern. Here, the detailed explanation on the similar steps will be skipped for brevity.

1) Select **Geometric Matching** from Vision Assistant Express and set up an ellipse template. When you set up an ellipse reference template, you

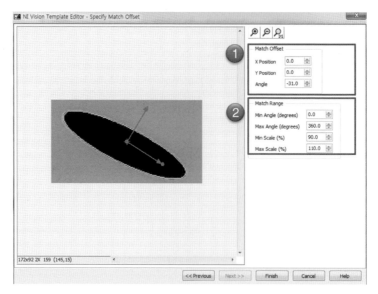

Figure 9.10 Setting for template (ellipse).

can reference the angle of major axis of the ellipse so that the object's angular orientation is reported relative to this axis. In this example, the angle of the ellipse shown at the match offset is set to be −31° (Figure 9.10 ①) for this purpose. Also, the **Match Range** of the angle and scale can be set according to your application requirements, as seen in Figure 9.10 ②.

2) Select **Finish** and save the template image.

3) After saving the template image, select the **Settings** tab to set parameters for geometric matching of the ellipses, as seen in Figure 9.11 ① and ②. Then, from Figure 9.11 ③, you can evaluate the information on the matched ellipses in terms of center locations, angle, scale, and score.

As a result of the two steps of geometric matching, two different geometric patterns can be searched: circles and ellipses.

Figure 9.12 shows the final results of geometric matching using Vision Assistant. As seen in Figure 9.12, matched circles as well as ellipses can be located. Note that since we used two steps of geometric matching, you may use two different ROI tools to define the search areas for each geometric matching. However, in this application, only one ROI tool was used for searching two different patterns. This will be discussed later.

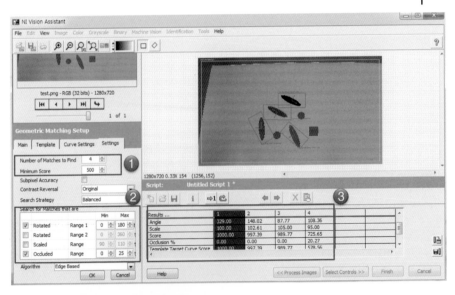

Figure 9.11 Setting parameters (ellipse).

As a final step of Vision Assistant Express, controls and indicators need to be selected, as seen in Figure 9.13, so that they can be accessed from LabVIEW. Since there are two steps for geometric matching, circle and ellipse, two different **ROI descriptors** and two sets of results of **Matches** (Figure 9.13 ① and ②) are selected.

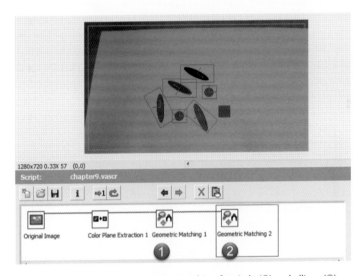

Figure 9.12 Two steps of geometric matching for circle (①) and ellipse (②).

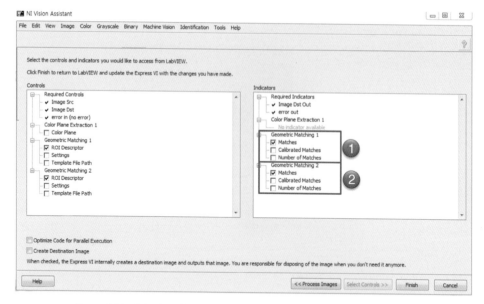

Figure 9.13 Selection of controls and indicators for geometric matching.

9.2
VI Creation for Geometric Matching

Figure 9.14 shows a main VI block diagram for continuous image acquisition with the VI created with Vision Assistant Express VI (Figure 9.14 ②) for geometric matching of both circles and ellipses. The two template images (circle image and elliptic image) saved from Vision Assistant will be used for geometric matching. The file paths for the template images were set as constants within the Vision Assistant setup.

Note that the ROI information is supplied as an input to the SubVI from main VI. For this case, an image ROI property node (Figure 9.14 ①) will be used to define the search area for both circles and ellipses.

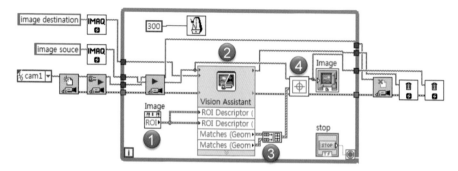

Figure 9.14 Main VI for geometric matching.

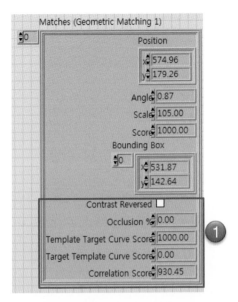

Figure 9.15 Matches (result from geometric matching).

The results from the geometric matching operations are to be shown on the image display by using an overlay function. For this purpose, the overlay SubVI, **Draw Pattern Matches Position.vi** (Figure 9.13 ④), which was discussed in Chapter 5, was used to overlay results of geometric matching. However, the previous SubVI cannot be used directly since the result of **Matches** (Figure 9.15) is a little different from that of pattern matching. We obtained the matched results (positions, angle, scale, and score) as a result of geometric matching. Note that information on the degree of occlusion is additionally provided, as seen in Figure 9.15 ①, compared with the previous pattern matching results. A subset of the results from **Matches** needs to be extracted in order to be compatible with the input to the overlay SubVI.

The variable **Matches** in Figure 9.15 is an array that contains information on the matched objects. The size of this array corresponds to the number of found objects. Two geometric matching results for circles and ellipses can be concatenated into one array, as seen in Figure 9.14 ③. In this way, both results can be overlaid using the single overlay SubVI.

Figure 9.16 shows a result of the front panel for the main VI that uses the Vision Assistant Express-created SubVI for geometric matching described in this section.

9.3
Shape Detection

The geometric matching described in Section 9.2 searches matched pattern based on template images. In this section, the method to find matched geometric

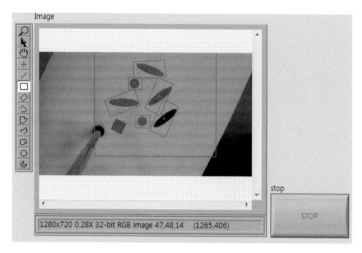

Figure 9.16 Front panel of main VI for geometric matching.

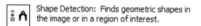

Shape Detection: Finds geometric shapes in
the image or in a region of interest.

Figure 9.17 Shape matching functions.

shapes without a template image will be discussed. For this purpose, the **Shape Detection** function shown in Figure 9.17 can be selected from **Processing Functions: Machine Vision** in Vision Assistant.

When you select the **Shape Detection** function, you can then select a specific **Shape Type** from the menu in Figure 9.18. The available shape types include circles, ellipses, rectangles, and lines. By using shape detection, we can find the objects that match predefined shapes and obtain information on location and size. This method has advantages because matched results can be obtained without the use of any template images.

For example, if objects with an ellipse shape need to be located within an image, **Ellipses** can be selected from the available **Shape Types**, as seen in Figure 9.18. Note that the circle is a special case of ellipse with the equal major and minor radiuses. The ellipse size for shape detection can be set by using the specified range (min and max) to the minor and major radii of the ellipse.

As a result of shape detection, **Major Radius**, **Minor Radius**, **Angle**, and **Center** location information can be obtained, as seen in Figure 9.18.

If you finish with the shape detection setup, the controls and indicators of Vision Assistant can be selected, as seen in Figure 9.19.

The result indicator for the ellipse is shown in Figure 9.20. Note that the result items are quite different from that of geometric matching. As a result, it is difficult to use the overlay SubVI that has been used for geometric or pattern matching.

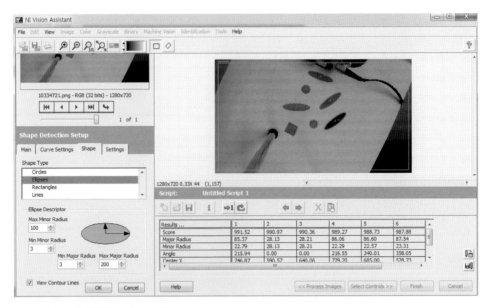

Figure 9.18 Shape detection results.

The results include **Position**, **Orientation** (angle), and **Major** (or **Minor**) **Radius**. By comparing the major and minor radius, we can determine whether the searched ellipse is close to circular in shape. For example, the results of major (85.4) and minor radius (22.8) in Figure 9.19 indicate that the ellipse is not a circle.

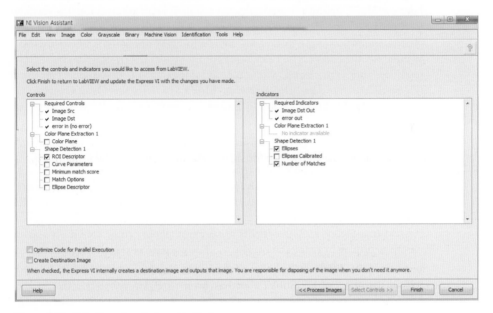

Figure 9.19 Selection of controls and indicators.

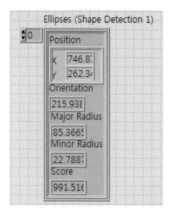

Figure 9.20 Results of shape detection for ellipse.

You may want to use the overlay SubVI that is provided by LabVIEW to show the results effectively. You can find overlay examples from *C:\Program Files\National Instrument\LabVIEW 2013\Examples\Vision\Overlay Utilities*. In this example, we will use the overlay SubVI named **Overlay Points with User-Specified Size** to indicate the matched objects with circle overlays. However, the current results from shape detection are in a data format that is not compatible with this overlay VI and so the data format will need to be modified. For example, you may want to use the major radius of the found ellipse for the circle radius. On the other hand, the point diameter in Figure 9.21a ② cannot use multiple size results (major/minor radius) according to the size of objects. To overlay circles according to the size of the found objects, the major radius data from the results array of Figure 9.21b ② are used as input for the SubVI. The calculation for the size of the overlay can be slightly modified and **For Loop** with the autoindexing of the radius is used (Figure 9.21b ③). Also, the **Drawing Mode** input to the **Oval Overlay** VI (Figure 9.21a ③) should be set to **Frame**, as seen in Figure 9.21b ④ in order not to fill the overlay outline.

Figure 9.22 shows the block diagram of the main VI to search and overlay of the found ellipses. To use the **Major Radius** and **Position** information for overlay purpose, the information is extracted from the result cluster as seen in Figure 9.22 ①. Then, the modified **Overlay** SubVI in Figure 9.22 ②, of which block diagram was shown in Figure 9.21b, is used to show the searched results effectively.

As seen in Figure 9.23, the results of searched ellipse can be effectively shown on image display by using the overlay VI. The purpose of this overlay example is to show readers how to use and modify the overlay VI examples provided by LabVIEW. You may choose different VIs to show the results effectively or you may build your own VI.

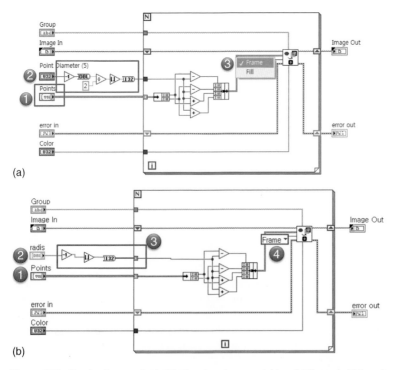

(a)

(b)

Figure 9.21   Overlay for searched objects using shape matching. (a) Example VI "overlay points with user-specified image. (b) Modified overlay SubVI used in Figure 9.22 ②.

Shape detection is a simple and effective method, but has limitations due to the fact that you can search for only a few predetermined geometric shapes. If other shapes need to be searched, the geometric matching with reference template images should be considered.

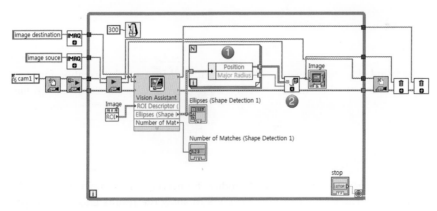

Figure 9.22   Main VI for shape matching.

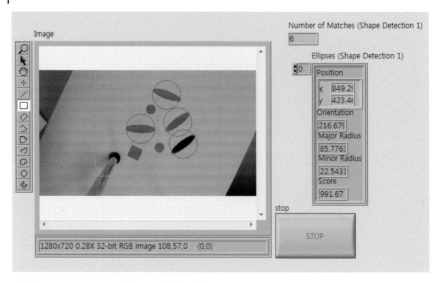

Figure 9.23 Shape matching results for ellipse.

Exercise 9.1

Find an image file (**Parts00.png**) from *C:\Program Files\National Instruments\ Vision\Examples\Images\Parts* (Figure 9.24). Use geometric pattern matching to find motor from the other images (Parts01.png, Parts02.png, etc.).

Figure 9.24 Example image for geometric matching.

10
Binary Shape Matching

In this chapter, shape matching based on binary images will be discussed. The use of binary images for shape matching has advantages because morphology functions can be used prior to shape matching to modify the binary image resulting for better results.

Binary shape matching is different from geometric matching and pattern matching, which are based on edge curve extraction and pixel intensity variation in an image, respectively. Each method has advantages and disadvantages, which should be considered before selecting a particular algorithm. Binary shape matching is an efficient and effective method to determine the center of mass of matched objects from its shape. However, this method cannot find occluded objects since two objects in a binary image whose features overlap are not indistinguishable from a single object with different shape.

To use shape matching in a binary image, a color or grayscale image needs to be converted to a binary image. Prior to conversion, the objects to identify in the image should have good contrast with respect to the background so that the boundaries of each object can be accurately represented when converted to a binary image.

By using shape matching, sorting and inspection of objects are possible. The shape of the objects can be classified (sorted) and defects can be determined by comparison with a reference image (inspection).

An example of finding objects using binary shape matching is discussed in this chapter. Every object has its own shape features and so it is possible to find each object by using the binary shape matching.

Example for Binary Shape Matching

Go to folder: *C:\Program Files\National Instruments\Vision\Examples\Images\Parts*. There are five image files including **Parts00.png**, which is shown below. Read the image files from the folder and use the binary shape matching to find the motors and worm gears from among the several different parts (Figures 10.1 and 10.2).

Note: The template images, **motor01.png** and **wormgear00.png**, can be found from the folder *C:\Program Files\National Instruments\Vision\Examples\Images\ Classification*.

Practical Guide to Machine Vision Software: An Introduction with LabVIEW, First Edition.
Kye-Si Kwon and Steven Ready.
© 2015 Wiley-VCH Verlag GmbH & Co. KGaA. Published 2015 by Wiley-VCH Verlag GmbH & Co. KGaA.

Figure 10.1   Example image for binary shape matching (Parts00.png).

(a)   (b)

Figure 10.2   Template images for binary shape matching. (a) Motor (motor01.png). (b) Worm gear (wormgear00.png)

10.1
Accessing Previously Saved Images with Vision Acquisition Express

Vision Acquisition Express can be used to read images from a folder.

1) For this purpose, the Vision Acquisition Express function in Figure 10.3 can be dragged onto a block diagram to setup image acquisition.
2) From the pop-up window, you can select **Folder of Images** to read images as seen in Figure 10.4. Then, select **Next≫**
3) There are only five images to read in the folder. So, the **Finite Acquisition with inline processing** is selected as seen in Figure 10.5. Then, select **Next≫**.

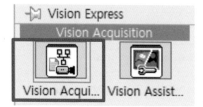

Figure 10.3   Vision Express.

Figure 10.4 Acquisition source selection.

Figure 10.5 Finite acquisition with inline processing.

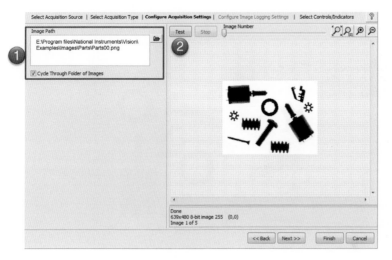

Figure 10.6 Configure Acquisition settings.

4) With the **Image Path** (Figure 10.6 ①) and **Cycle Through Folder of Image** selected, clicking on **Test** (Figure 10.6 ②) will sequentially show the images as seen in Figure 10.6. Then, select **Next≫**.
5) Select the **Controls and Indicators** as seen in Figure 10.7. Then, select **Finish** to create the VI for image acquisition.

Figure 10.8a and b shows the block diagram and front panel of the created VI. When you run the VI, you will see the five consecutive images in the front panel image display.

Figure 10.7   Selection of controls and indicators.

(a)

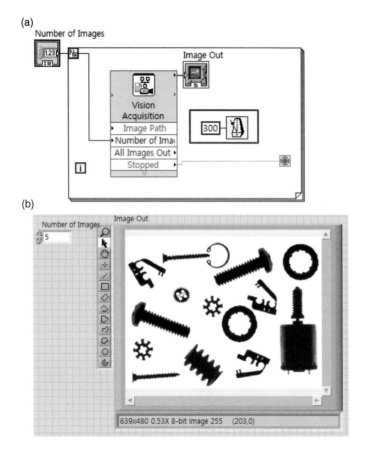

Figure 10.8   VI to read finite images from folder. (a) Block diagram. (b) Front panel.

10.2
Binary Shape Matching Using Vision Assistant

After the acquisition of images is set up in Vision Assistant, complete the following steps to search objects based on binary shape. In this example, an intended target template image is provided by a separate image file. To use the template image file for binary shape matching, you will need to convert the image into binary and save it for use as a template file.

10.2.1
Binary Template Images

1) As a first step, a binary template image is required for binary shape matching. Select **Open Image** (Figure 10.9 ①) to read in the template image
   of a motor (Figure 10.9 ②), which can be found from *C:\Program Files\
   National Instrument\Vision\Examples\Images\Classification\motor01.
   png.*
2) Select **Threshold** from **Processing Functions: Grayscale** to change the
   image to binary for the template image. Note that the motor image is
   darker than the background. Therefore, **Dark Objects** is selected
   (Figure 10.10 ①). By choosing a proper threshold value, you can obtain an
   accurate binary representation of the motor, as seen in Figure 10.10 ③.

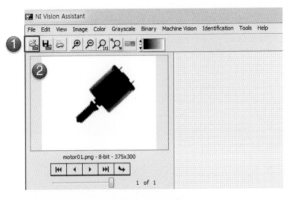

Figure 10.9 Read in template image of motor.

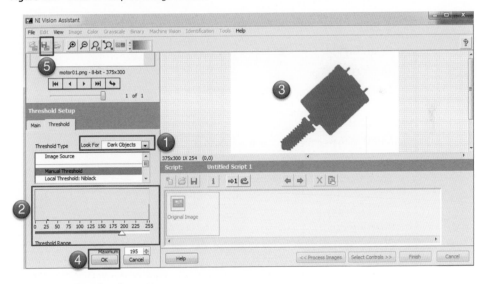

Figure 10.10 Template for motor.

3) Select **OK**. As a next step, morphology functions may be used prior to saving the template image to remove unwanted pixels. In this example however, morphology functions may not be required since the motor image should be well distinguished from the background and easily rendered as a binary image object.

4) Save the template image file by selecting **Save Image** (Figure 10.10 ⑤). There is check box to select **Expand Dynamic of Binary Image**. If it is selected, the grayscale representation of the image (0 and 255 pixel values) is saved. The gray image has only two values of 255 for the object (motor) and 0 for the boundary. If it is not selected, the image will have two values of 0 and 1. The option of **Expand Dynamic of Binary Image** should be considered since some other imaging software expects binary images to be represented with 0 for background and 255 for object. In this example, save the file with the name of **bolt_binary.bmp** with the expanded format.

5) The same process is repeated for the wormgear00.png to create and save the binary image as **Wormgear_binary.bmp**. After saving all the files, proceed to image processing using Vision Assistant.

10.2.2
Binary Shape Matching

With the task of creating and saving template images completed, the Vision Assistant Express can be restarted by selecting **New Script,** as seen in Figure 10.11.

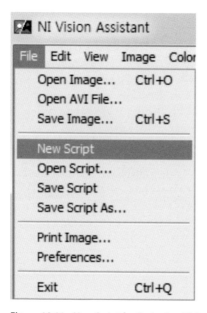

Figure 10.11 New Script for Restarting Vision Assistant.

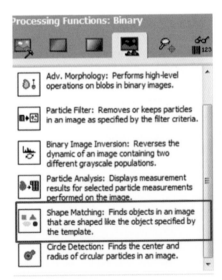

Figure 10.12 Binary shape matching.

In this way, the previously created script for binary template image creation is not included in the new script for binary shape matching.

1) Open the image of **part00.png** from *C:\Program Files\National Instruments\Vision\Examples\Images\Parts*.
2) Prior to using binary shape matching, convert the gray image to binary using **Threshold** from **Processing Functions: Grayscale**. Here, details of using threshold will be skipped.
3) Select **Shape Matching** from **Processing Functions: Binary** (Figure 10.12).
4) Select **Load from File** (Figure 10.13 ①) to use the binary template image for the motor, which was saved prior to binary shape matching. Choose an appropriate minimum score and select the check box for **Scale Invariance** in Figure 10.13 ②. Then select **OK** after confirming the matched results, as seen in Figure 10.13 ③.
5) The same step can be repeated for shape matching of worm gear, as seen in Figure 10.14.
6) Select **OK**. The script in Figure 10.15 is then displayed showing the two steps of binary shape matching (for the motor and for the worm gear).
7) Proceed by clicking on **Select Control≫** in Figure 10.15 ③.
8) Select **Number of Matches** and **Shape Reports** for indicators (Figure 10.16) that will be used in LabVIEW.

The **Shape Report** will be in the form of an array of clusters as seen in Figure 10.17. The size of the array equals to the number of matches. The results include information related to location (**Global Rectangle**, **Centroid**), size (**Object Size**), and **Score**, as seen in Figure 10.17.

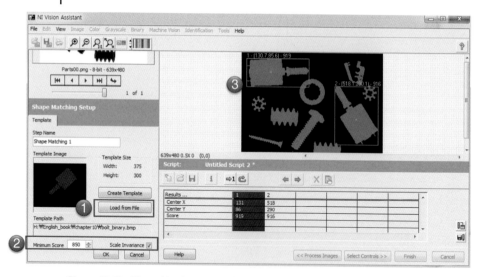

Figure 10.13 Shape Matching Setup for motor.

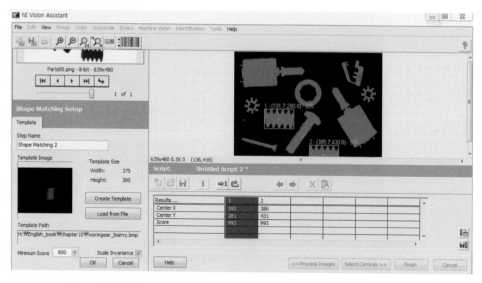

Figure 10.14 Shape Matching Setup for worm gear.

10.3
Overlay VI Creation for Shape Matching

We will now discuss the overlay SubVI for binary shape matching. To overlay the matched result, the **Global Rectangle** (Figure 10.18 ①) information from the **Shape Report** is used as input to the **IMAQ Overlay Rectangle** VI

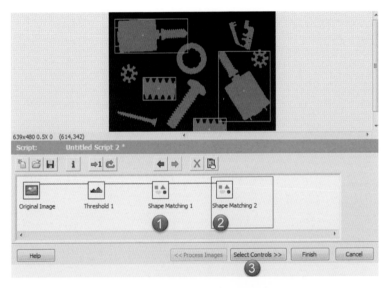

Figure 10.15 Results from two steps of binary Shape Matching.

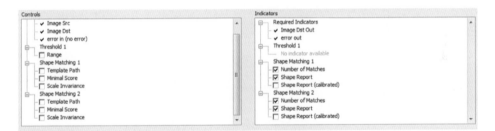

Figure 10.16 Selection of controls and indicators for Shape Matching.

(Figure 10.18 ②), as seen in the figure. When this overlay function is used, you may encounter errors in cases where there are no matched results. To avoid such errors, the size of the array needs to be checked. If there exist no matched results, the overlay function should be skipped, as seen in Figure 10.19.

10.4
VI for Binary Shape Matching

Figure 10.20 shows the block diagram for locating the two objects: motors and worm gears. Vision Express wizards are used for both image acquisition (Figure 10.20 ②) and image analysis (Figure 10.20 ③). The results from shape matching are delivered to the **Shape Report** and **Number of Matches** indicators.

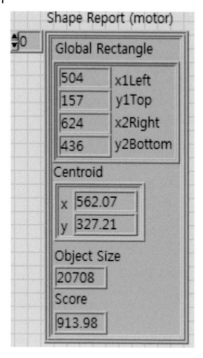

Figure 10.17 Shape Report.

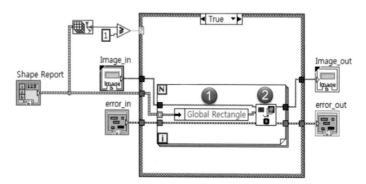

Figure 10.18 Overlay VI for global rectangle.

Due to the requirement that binary shape matching operates on binary images, all target images need to be converted to binary. In order to preserve the original image, additional image memory needs to be allocated (Figure 10.20 ①) and connected to the image destination input of Vision Assistant shown in Figure 10.20 ③.

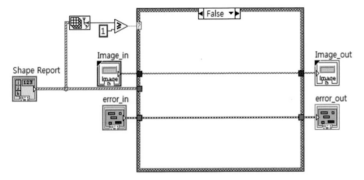

Figure 10.19 False condition for skipping overlay if no search results.

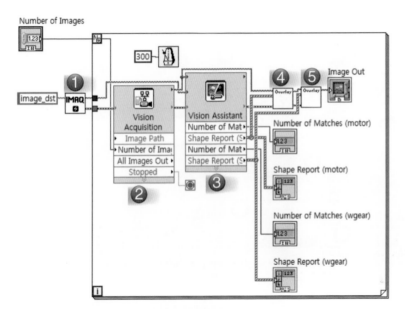

Figure 10.20 Block diagram for shape matching.

Figure 10.21 shows a screen captured of the main VI front panel after it is executed. As seen in Figure 10.21, motors and worm gears are successfully located based on shape matching from the binary image. The matched shape results are displayed as an array of clusters.

To overlay results to indicate the found objects in the image display, we used a SubVI as shown in Figure 10.20 ④ and ⑤. The block diagram for the overlay SubVI was shown in Figures 10.18 and 10.19.

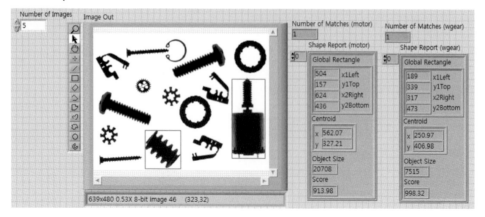

Figure 10.21 Front panel for shape matching.

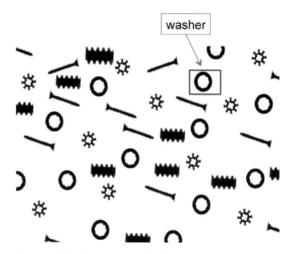

Figure 10.22 Exercise image for binary shape matching (**Particle 01.png**).

Exercise 10.1

Find **Particle 01.png** from *C:\Program Files\National Instruments\Vision\Examples\Images*. Use the binary shape matching to find all the washers and provide a function to indicate the locations with an overlay (Figure 10.22).

11
OCR (Optical Character Recognition)

OCR (Optical Character Recognition) is machine vision software that translates images of characters into text. To identify characters in an image, the LabVIEW software needs to be trained to identify each character. A data set of trained characters is created and saved as a character set file in advance. The set of trained characters are compared with character objects in an image for recognition.

The example of OCR provided in LabVIEW can be found from the following folders:

C:\Program Files\National Instruments\LabVIEW 2013\examples\Vision\OCR

Figure 11.1 shows the screen-captured image of the example **OCR.vi**. In this example, characters in the image are recognized and converted into a character string.

Some industrial applications of OCR for machine vision include inspecting labels, sorting, tracking packages, and verifying parts during manufacturing process.

11.1
OCR Using Vision Assistant

Example: OCR

Train the character sets in Figure 11.2 and identify numeric characters in Figure 11.3 via OCR functions. Note that the size and font of the characters may be different from those of the trained characters.

11.1.1
Character Training Using Vision Assistant

The **OCR** function using Vision Assistant offers an excellent procedure to train the software to recognize the imaged characters. For this purpose, complete the following steps:

Practical Guide to Machine Vision Software: An Introduction with LabVIEW, First Edition.
Kye-Si Kwon and Steven Ready.
© 2015 Wiley-VCH Verlag GmbH & Co. KGaA. Published 2015 by Wiley-VCH Verlag GmbH & Co. KGaA.

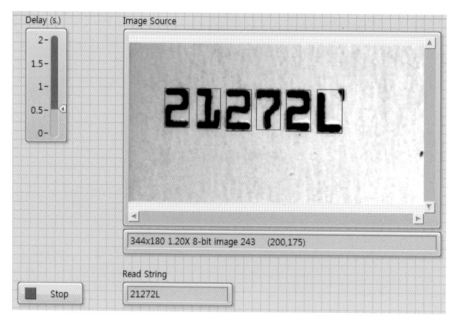

Figure 11.1 Example VI for OCR.

1 2 3 4 5 6 7 8 9 0
1 2 3 4 5 6 7 8 9 0
+ - * /

Figure 11.2 Characters to be trained.

1) Launch Vision Assistant and select **Open Image** to train characters in the image. The image from Figure 11.2 will be used to train the numeric characters as seen in Figure 11.4.
2) Select the **OCR/OCV** function icon (Figure 11.5) from **Processing Functions: Identification» OCR/OCV**. You will then see the menu for the **OCR/OCV Setup**, as shown in Figure 11.6.
3) Select **New Character Set File** from the menu in Figure 11.6. A pop-up window will appear, as seen in Figure 11.7, to train characters.

21+77   **21+77**

978 - 74221   200/123

Figure 11.3 Characters to be identified.

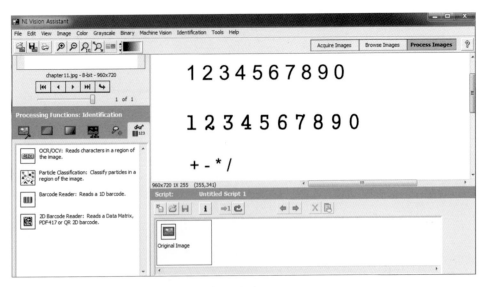

Figure 11.4   Open image file of characters to be trained.

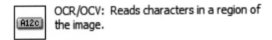

OCR/OCV: Reads characters in a region of the image.

Figure 11.5   OCR/OCV function.

4) Drag out a rectangle to create a ROI area around the characters to train in the image as seen in Figure 11.7 ①. The OCR function automatically separates each character from image background. As a result, there will be small rectangles that will indicate the location of the found image for each character. The character sets can be selected in groups or individually. Then, **Train All Characters** (②) is selected to begin the training process.

5) Key in the corresponding character string in the proper sequence so that the software can equate the imaged characters with the correct text, as seen in Figure 11.7 ③.

6) Select **Train**, as seen in Figure 11.7 ④, to train the characters in the ROI. It can be the case that the text characters to be recognized are of different fonts. Training the software with all the character fonts to be recognized will produce a more accurate and reliable result. In this example, two different fonts of numeric characters and the math symbols are trained.

7) Select the **Edit Character Set File** tab in Figure 11.7 ⑤. You will then see the trained characters as shown in Figure 11.8.

8) You may rename or delete the trained character sets from the **Edit Character Set File** Tab.

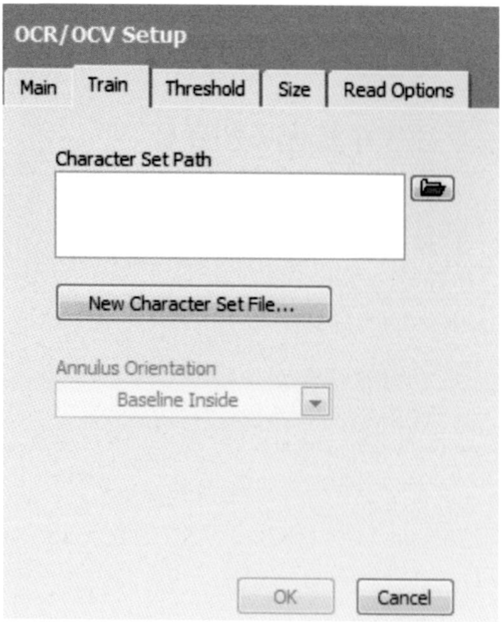

Figure 11.6 OCR Setup.

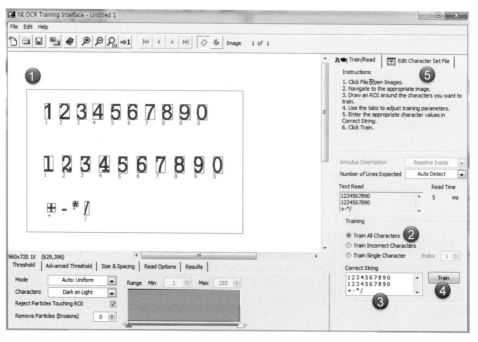

Figure 11.7 OCR Training interface.

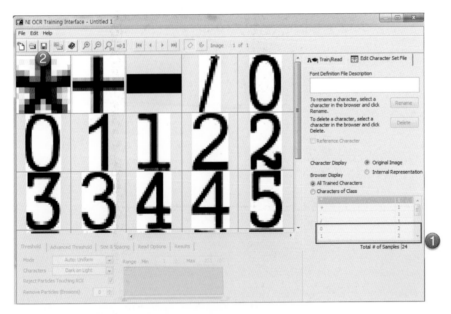

Figure 11.8 Edit character set file.

9) Save the character set file by selecting the **File Save** icon in Figure 11.8 ②
   as the final step for training of a character set. As a suggestion, you might
   save it as a file named **char.abc**.

11.1.2
Character Identification Using Vision Assistant

In this section, a USB camera is used for image acquisition. To identify characters from acquired images, OCR will be discussed and used to build a VI. This
process will use the previously saved character set file. To gain understanding of
real-time text identification using OCR, a set of characters is printed out on
paper and then a camera is used to take images of the printed paper. Note that
the size of the character and image quality of the acquired image can be significantly different from the image that was used for training.

1) Launch NI Vision Assistant and select **New Script** from **File** menu.
2) Select **Acquire Images** in Figure 11.9 ①.
3) Select **Acquire Image (1394, GigE, or USB)** if you are using USB camera.
4) Select the **Acquire Continuous Images** icon to continuously acquire
   images (Figure 11.9 ②).
5) Select the **Store Acquired Image in Browser** icon (Figure 11.9 ③) to save
   the acquired image for image processing using Vision Assistant. Then,

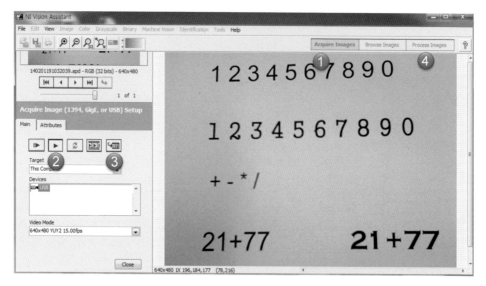

Figure 11.9 Acquisition of image characters.

select the **Image Process** icon button in Figure 11.9 ④ to start image processing.

6) Select **OCR/OCV** from **Processing Functions: Identification**, as seen previously in Figure 11.4.

7) Select **Train** Tab from **OCR/OCV Setup**.

8) Select **Character Set Path** to load the Characters Set File (Figure 11.10 ①), which was saved during the training process (Figure 11.8).

9) Use the mouse to drag out a ROI rectangle around the characters as seen in Figure 11.10 ②.

10) The recognized characters are then indicated by rectangular outlines. The images of the trained characters are also overlaid on the recognized characters. The characters at the bottom of the rectangles correspond to the recognized text. The identified results from the OCR process are shown in Figure 11.10 ③. Note that the condition of the acquired image using digital camera is significantly different from that of the image used for training character. Nonetheless, the characters from the camera are identified as seen in Figure 11.10.

You can check whether the characters with different fonts are identified correctly by placing ROI around other examples of imaged characters, as seen in Figure 11.11. As we can see in this figure, some characters may not be identified due to differences in font. Here, the unrecognized character is marked with a question mark, "?."

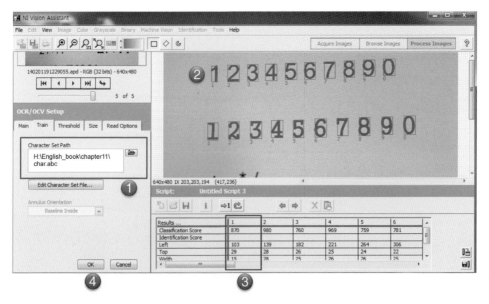

Figure 11.10   OCR/OCV setup.

By lowering the **Acceptance Level** score value in the **Read Options** tab as seen in Figure 11.12, previously unrecognized characters may be identified as similarly trained characters.

For example, if the **Acceptance Level** is reduced from 700 to 300, as seen in Figure 11.12, every character except 74 can be identified. The two numeric characters of 7 and 4 were overlapped in the horizontal directions and cannot

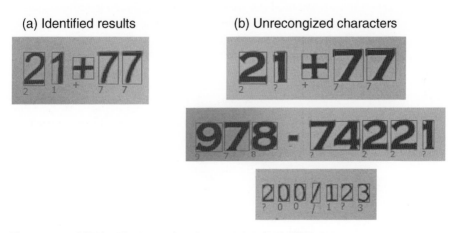

Figure 11.11   OCR identification results using acceptance level of 700.

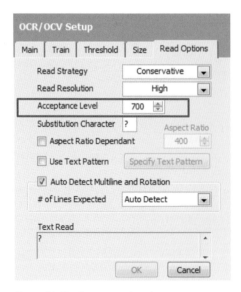

Figure 11.12 Acceptance Level.

be separated by using rectangle ROI. The two characters might be considered as a single character, as seen in Figure 11.13a. Note that there is a trade-off in selecting an **Acceptance Level**. If a high value is used for the acceptance level, an identified character is likely to match a trained character perfectly. However, there may be other missed characters. On the other hand, more characters can be identified by lowering **Acceptance Level**, although some characters may not be identified correctly due to the low tolerance. For example, 1 (one) is identified as 7 (seven) in Figure 11.13b. To improve identification results, more character sets with different fonts should be trained during the OCR setup training process.

11) If the identified results are acceptable, select **OK** (Figure 11.10 ④).

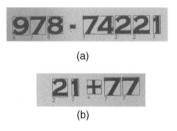

(a)

(b)

Figure 11.13 OCR identification failures. (a) Improper spacing. (b) Incorrect identification due to low acceptance level.

11.2
VI for OCR

11.2.1
VI Creation for OCR Using Vision Assistant

In this section, an OCR VI, which performs real-time character identification, will be discussed. We will use the OCR function to identify characters from an imaged printed paper. A USB camera is used to acquire images of the printed characters. To identify the characters from the acquired image, a VI created using Vision Assistant will be modified as a SubVI.

You need to first select **Tools»Create LabVIEW VI** (located in the NI Vision Assistant tool bar menu) upon finishing the OCR setup in Vision Assistant (Section 11.1). From the **LabVIEW Create Wizard – Step 3 of 4,** select **Image Control** (Figure 11.14) to use this VI as a SubVI, which will receive acquired image from main VI.

By selecting **Next** in the **LabVIEW VI Creation Wizard – Step 4 of 4**, you can select **Controls** and **Indicators**, as seen in Figure 11.15.

Here, **Image Src** (source) and **Image Dst Out** (destination) are automatically selected for controls and indicators in Figure 11.15 so that an acquired image can be received from main VI and the processed image can then be returned.

11.2.2
SubVI for OCR

To read characters within an image, the LabVIEW VI created from Vision Assistant is modified to a SubVI having inputs and outputs as seen in Figure 11.16.

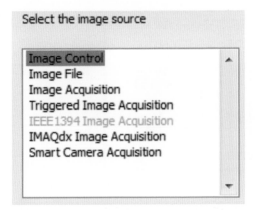

Figure 11.14   Selection of the image source.

Select the controls and indicators to create on the front panel of the VI.

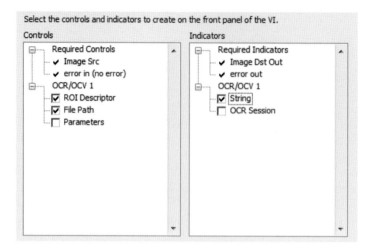

Figure 11.15   Selection of controls and indicators.

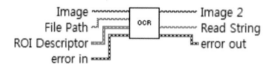

Figure 11.16   OCR SubVI.

Figure 11.17 shows the block diagram of a SubVI for performing the OCR, which has been slightly modified from the VI created with Vision Assistant. As seen in Figure 11.17, controls of **ROI Descriptor** and the acquired **Image** are used as inputs of the SubVI to receive information from the main VI. As a result

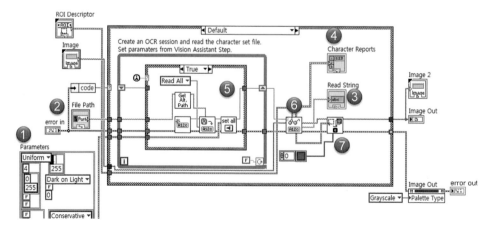

Figure 11.17   OCR SubVI block diagram.

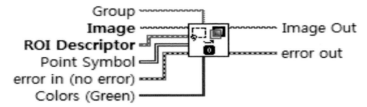

IMAQ Overlay ROI

Overlays a region of interest (ROI) on an image.

Figure 11.18 Overlay function.

of OCR processing, the character string (**Read String**) is obtained and used as an output of the SubVI.

To use the OCR function, a character set file having trained character information is required. For this purpose, the character sets file (file name: char.abc) saved previously in this chapter is used. Figure 11.17 ② shows the control for the path of the character set file. The previously selected **Parameters** values for OCR character identification can be found in Figure 11.17 ①. After reading in the character set file (Figure 11.17 ⑤), the characters in the image are identified by using the **OCR Read Text** function (Figure 11.17 ⑥). The resulting recognized text corresponding to each identified character is in the **Read String** indicator shown in Figure 11.17 ③. To draw an overlay on each identified character, the overlay function in Figure 11.17 ⑦ is used. Note that **IMAQ Overlay ROI** shown in Figure 11.18 is used since ROI descriptor bounding the characters from the **OCR Read Text** function is compatible with this overlay function.

Figure 11.19 shows the first result in the **Character Reports** indicator in Figure 11.17 ④. The **Character Reports** provides useful information for debugging purpose. The **Character Reports** has the form of a cluster array with the size of the array equal to the number of characters identified. Each array element of **Character Reports** contains information such as character value, score, character location, and character size.

11.2.3
Main VI

Figure 11.20 shows the block diagram of a main VI for real-time OCR analysis. The SubVI for OCR described in Figure 11.16 has been used to perform the OCR analysis.

Figures 11.21 and 11.22 show the character identification results when the main VI is executed. To identify characters in the image display, a ROI is placed around the character set to be identified. As seen in Figure 11.21, character identification is possible even though character fonts, as well as the font size, are different from the character set file. Also, you may rotate the paper to check if

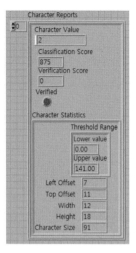

Figure 11.19 Character Reports.

OCR function can read characters properly. In this example, character identification was possible in cases where the paper is slightly rotated.

However, if the image is not clear and/or the characters do not have proper spacing, character identification may fail as seen in Figure 11.22. Also, the characters in the image need to have a minimum size, which is a measure of the total number of pixels in a character. It is recommended in NI Vision Concept manual that the character size be more than 25 pixels to successfully identify characters using the OCR function.

Note that identified character sets include numbers. If a numeric calculation is needed from the numerals identified, they will need to be converted from text to numeric values before mathematics functions are used.

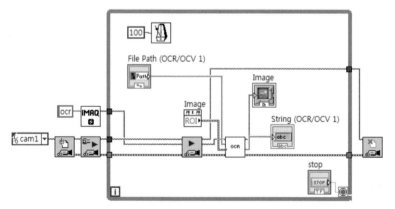

Figure 11.20 Main VI for real-time OCR analysis.

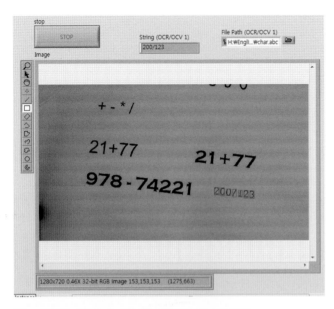

Figure 11.21 Character identification results (success).

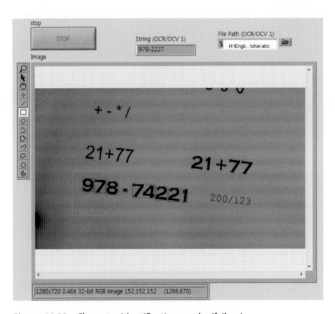

Figure 11.22 Character identification results (failure).

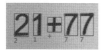

Figure 11.23 OCR identification and the numeric calculation.

Exercise 11.1

Create an application that can read number and symbol characters of an equation, complete the calculation, and return the results. For example, the results of Figure 11.23 would be 98.

Exercise 11.2

Find image files from **C:\Program files\National Instruments\Vision\Examples\Images\Lcd**. Build an application that reads the characters from the images, as seen in Figure 11.24.

Figure 11.24 LCD image.

12
Binary Particle Classification

By using classification functions, objects with various shapes can be recognized, characterized, and sorted. Binary particle classification identifies an unknown object in a binary image by comparing a set of its significant features with a set of features that conceptually represent classes of known samples. For this purpose, the software needs to be trained using individual object images with significant unique features to create classes. The classes will be compared with unknown image samples during the classification process. The **Binary Particle Classification** method is different from geometric matching and pattern matching in that it is based on particle analysis of binary images. While **Binary Particle Classification** is discussed here, keep in mind that geometric matching is based on extraction of information on the boundary curve of objects and pattern matching is based on pixel intensity of image. The merits and demerits for each of the image analysis methods should be considered before selecting the best algorithm for sorting or inspecting of objects.

Binary particle classification is a fast method when the objects need to be sorted. However, this method will not find occluded objects because the method is based on binary images and two or more occluded objects are considered as one object of a different shape. Note that any acquired grayscale image of the objects will need to have good contrast with respect to background and that the boundaries of the object should be accurately represented as a result of the binary image conversion.

By using classification, sorting and inspection of objects are possible. An object can be classified (sorted) according to the shape and defects of the imaged object can be determined by the comparison with referenced features (inspection).

An example demonstrating classification can be found in folder

C:\Program Files\National Instruments\LabVIEW 2013\Examples\Vision\Classification.

Figure 12.1 shows the front panel of the example VI for classification (**Particle Classification.vi**). The objects are classified according to the known features.

Practical Guide to Machine Vision Software: An Introduction with LabVIEW, First Edition.
Kye-Si Kwon and Steven Ready.
© 2015 Wiley-VCH Verlag GmbH & Co. KGaA. Published 2015 by Wiley-VCH Verlag GmbH & Co. KGaA.

Overview: Demonstrates how to use the **IMAQ Classify** function with a binary classifier file to dynamically find the bounding box of the particles and classify them.
Requirements: Vision Development Software.
Instructions: Run the VI.
Image

Figure 12.1 Example VI for binary classification.

12.1
Vision Acquisition Express to Load Image Files

In this chapter, example images are used to practice classification function. The images can be found in

> *C:\Program Files\National Instruments\Vision\Examples\Images\Parts.*

Complete the following steps using Vision Assistant for classifying objects.

Begin by using Vision Acquisition Express to load images from the image folder. Drag the Vision Acquisition Express icon from the functions palette on to the block diagram and perform the following steps:

1) Select **Folder of Images** as an option of **Select Acquisition Source** (step 1 of 5).
2) Select **Finite Acquisition with inline processing** (step 2 of 5) to load the five files from the folder, as seen in Figure 12.2.

Finite Acquisition with inline processing
This acquisition is used for acquiring a fixed number images once. When an image is acquired, it will be available for image processing. This is useful if you want to display or process your images before the acquisition is done.

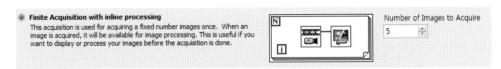

Number of Images to Acquire

5

Figure 12.2 Finite Acquisition with inline processing.

3) Select **Image Path**, navigate to the folder identified above, and select **Cycle Though Folder of Images.** Then, by clicking on **Test**, the five images will be loaded and displayed one after the other, as seen in Figure 12.3 (step 3 of 5). Use the **Image Number** slider at the top to cycle through each of the five images.
4) Skip the next step of **Configure Image Logging Settings** (step 4 of 5).
5) Select any desired **Controls** and **Indicators** (step 5 of 5) before selecting **Finish.** When running the created VI, you will see one of the loaded images on the image display in the front panel of the VI, as seen in Figure 12.4.

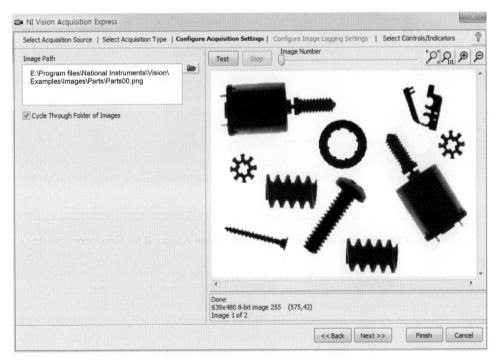

Figure 12.3 Select Image Path.

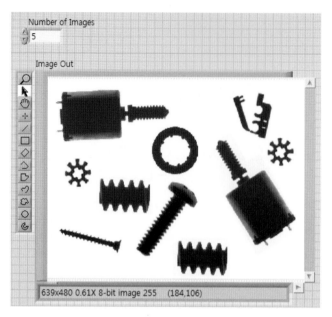

Figure 12.4 VI for loading images from folder.

12.2
Vision Assistant Express for Classification

Drag the Vision Assistant Express icon from the functions palette onto the block diagram. Then, follow the steps below to complete classification using Vision Assistant:

1) Load the image file of **Parts01.png** from Vision Assistant Express (Figure 12.5 ①).
2) Select **Particle Classification** from **Processing Functions: Identification**, as seen in Figure 12.5 ②.

12.2.1
Train for Particle Classification

1) In **Particle Classification Setup** under the **Train** tab, select **New . . .**, as seen in Figure 12.6 ①. Then, you will see the pop-up window of **NI Particle Classification Training Interface**, as seen in Figure 12.7.
2) Select Zoom out in Figure 12.7 ① in order to view the whole image in the NI Particle Classification Training Interface.
3) Draw a region of interest (ROI) around the sample you want to add as a class. For example, a bolt is selected, as seen in Figure 12.7 ②.

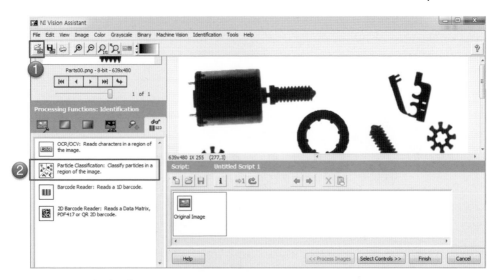

Figure 12.5 Particle classification.

4) Select the threshold method used to convert the grayscale ROI image to binary image. In this example, **Clustering (Auto-Thresholding)** is selected (Figure 12.7 ③).
5) Select **Dark Objects** from **Look For** as seen in Figure 12.7 ④ since objects are darker than the background.

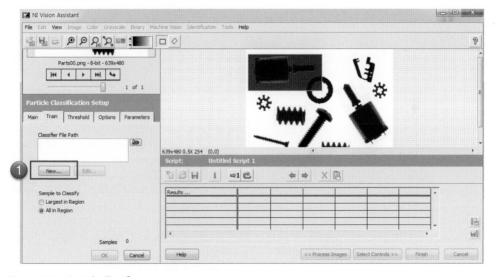

Figure 12.6 Particle Classification setup.

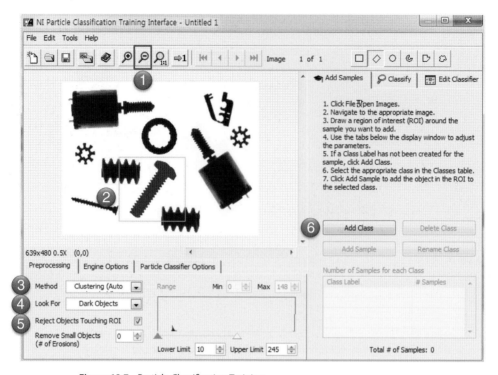

Figure 12.7 Particle Classification Training.

6) Select **Reject Objects Touching ROI** as seen in Figure 12.7 ⑤. In this way, if an object intersects the ROI boundary, the object is excluded from the training process and image analysis. In the case of the ROI shown in Figure 12.7 ②, only the bolt is selected. Other parts touching the ROI are excluded from training.

7) Select **Add Class**, as seen in Figure 12.7 ⑥. You will then be required to enter a name for the new class label. For example, you can type **bolt** in the **Class Label** pop-up menu in Figure 12.8.

Figure 12.8 New class label.

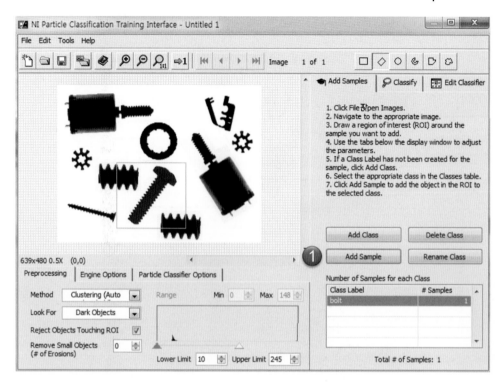

Figure 12.9 Add sample.

8) Select **Add Sample** as seen at ① in Figure 12.9. Thus, the bolt image object will be added to the class **bolt**. You can add more samples to the class. In this way, you can have better training results for the class.

9) Repeat **Add Class** and **Add Sample** to train all the significant features. Then, you can see # **Samples** for each class, as shown in Figure 12.10 ①. In this example, four classes are used: **bolt, motor, screw,** and **washer**. Note that two samples are added for motor and there are objects in the image with shapes that are not included among the trained classes.

10) Select the **Classify** tab in Figure 12.10 ② after finishing the adding of classes and samples process.

11) Now, select **Train Classifier** in Figure 12.11 ②.

12) You can select any objects from the image to verify classification results. For example, a motor is selected as seen in Figure 12.11 ①. You then see the classification results as in Figure 12.11 ③. The class label is motor. Here, the classification score is 1000, which means perfectly matched with trained class. The **Distances** information (Figure 12.11 ④) in this context indicates how closely each class resembles currently selected class. The **Distance** of 0 indicates a perfect match.

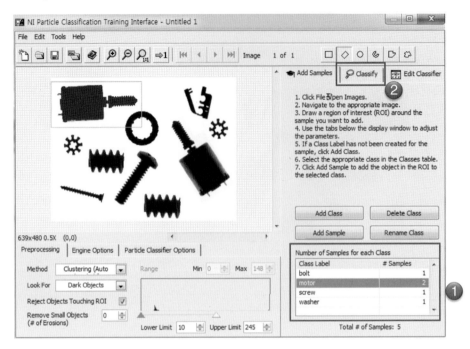

Figure 12.10 Particle classification training results.

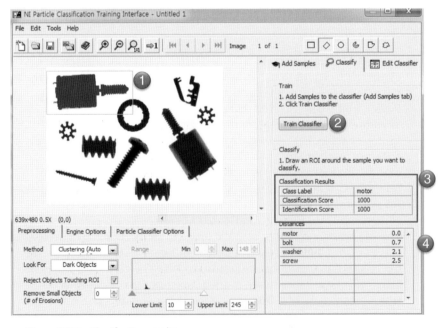

Figure 12.11 Classification results.

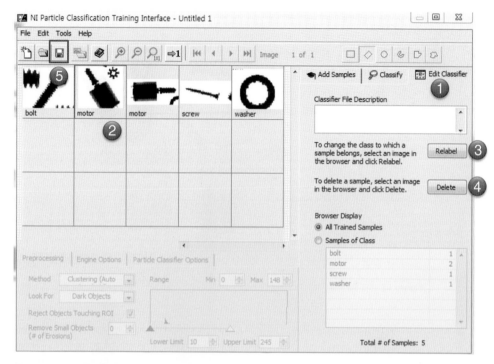

Figure 12.12 Edit classifier.

13) Select **Edit Classifier** in Figure 12.12 ① to change the class label or delete the samples. For example, if you want to edit the class of a sample, select the sample as seen in Figure 12.12 ②. Then, you can change the class label of the sample (③) or delete the sample (④).

14) Save the classifiers (Figure 12.12 ⑤). The file will be saved with the file-name extension .clf. You now can exit **Particle Classification Training Interface** by closing the window.

12.2.2
VI Creation

1) The classification results need to be confirmed from the particle classification setup. By dragging out a rectangular ROI in the processing window in Figure 12.13 ①, you can get the classified results of all objects within the ROI, as seen in Figure 12.13 ②. If you select one of these results as in Figure 12.13 ④, it will indicate the corresponding object with a rectangle around the object in the processing window, as shown in Figure 12.13 ③. Also, you can evaluate the accuracy of the classification from classification score of the selection. If the score is close to 1000, the classified result is likely to be accurate. Note that the classification score in Figure 12.13 ④ is

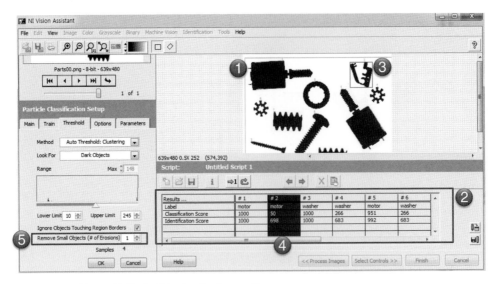

Figure 12.13 Particle classification results.

50. In this case, even though it was classified as motor, the score indicates that the classified result might not be correct. The classified object's classification score below a set threshold value may indicate that the object should be ignored.

2) You have the option of using **Remove Small Objects** in Figure 12.13 ⑤ in order to preprocess the image to eliminate small particles that may be left over from the binary conversion process.

3) If the results are acceptable, select **OK**.

4) Complete the Vision Assistant Express by determining the controls via **Select Controls>>** at the bottom of the window.

5) Select **Finish** to create a VI.

6) Connect inputs and outputs of the created VI, as seen in Figure 12.14a. Then by executing the VI you will obtain the classification results as seen in Figure 12.14b.

12.3
VI Modification

To fully use the results of the identified objects, such as the location and identification scores, the Express VI will need to be converted to a standard SubVI. To do this, right click the mouse on Vision Assistant Express icon and select **Open Front Panel** from pop-up window. By doing this, you can modify the converted VI according to your needs and save it to a project directory. Figure 12.15 shows a portion of converted VI's block diagram.

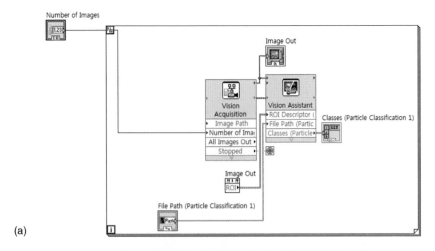

(a)

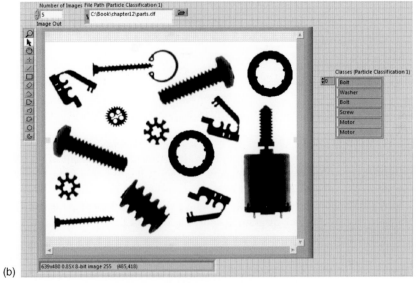

(b)

Figure 12.14 Created VI for classification. (a) Block diagram. (b) Front panel.

Please focus on the function icon, **IVA Classification Classify All Objects.vi**, located in Figure 12.15 ①. This VI function has inputs and outputs as seen in Figure 12.16.

To classify each object, a binary image template is used to find the particles (objects). During the particle identification process based on the template, each found particle will be assigned its own ROI, which identifies the location of each of the classified objects within the image.

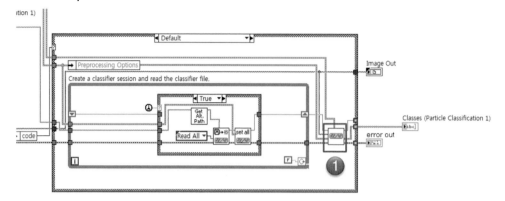

Figure 12.15 Part of VI for classification converted from Vision Assistant Express.

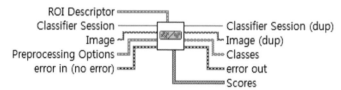

Figure 12.16 Inputs and outputs of **IVA Classification Classify All Objects** (Figure 12.15 ①).

However, the RIO descriptors are not initially provided as a result of the **IVA Classification Classify All Objects.vi**. So, we will need to create the ROI descriptors as seen in Figure 12.17 ①.

You can access the VI by double clicking the function icon (Figure 12.15 ①) and then display its block diagram as shown in Figure 12.17. The VI can then be modified according to your requirements.

The **ROI Descriptors** are in the form of an array of clusters, which holds information on the locations of all the classified particles. As a final step, modify the VI for use as a SubVI by adding the **ROI Descriptors** indicator for output (①), in addition to the already supplied **Classes** (②) and **Scores** (③) outputs.

Now, the results of the classification analysis, **ROI Descriptors, Classes,** and **Scores** are supplied in the form of arrays. The size of the output arrays of the **ROI Descriptors, Classes**, and **Scores** is the same as the number of particles found and the indexes of these arrays are associated with a specific particle with that index.

The classes are one-dimensional string arrays containing **Class Labels**, which identify the classified objects with the particle templates. In observing the results of the scores, you can evaluate how well the algorithm classified the objects. The scores have two values: a **Classification Score** and an **Identification Score**. The classification score indicates how much better the indicated class represents

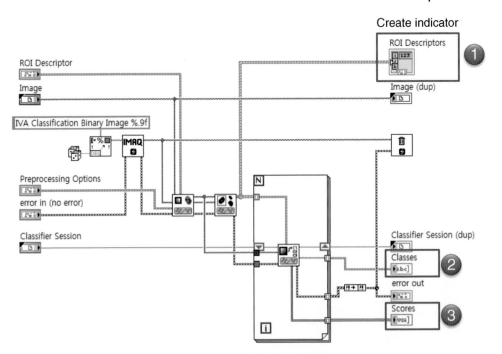

Figure 12.17 Modified block diagram of **IVA Classification Classify All Objects** (Figure 12.15 ①).

the input sample than other available classes. The **Identification Score** indicates how closely the object matches to a specifically matched class.

Then, the results of the modified **IVA Classification Classify All Objects.vi** (Figure 12.17) can be used in a **classification_sub.vi**. As seen in Figure 12.18,

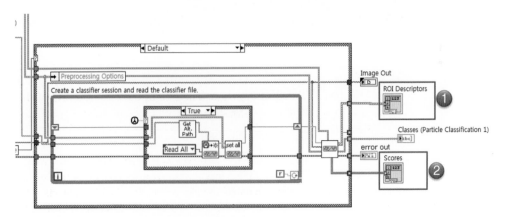

Figure 12.18 Block diagram of modified classification_SubVI from VI shown in Figure 12.15.

Vision Assistant
[classification_sub.vi]

Image In · Image Out
Image Dst · · · · · · · · · · · · · · · · · · · ROI Descriptors
error in · Scores ①
classification_su
b.vi · · · · · · · · · · error out

ROI Descriptor (Particle Cl... · · · · · · ROI Descriptor (
File Path (Particle Classif... · · · · · · File Path (Partic
Classes (Particle · · · · · · · · · · Classes (Particle Classific...

Figure 12.19 Inputs and outputs of classification_sub.vi.

you can add two more indicators (**ROI Descriptors and Scores**) that were obtained from modified **IVA Classification Classify All Objects.vi** in Figure 12.18.

The two indicators (**ROI Descriptors** and **Scores**) are added as output terminals of the SubVI so that additional outputs of this **classification_sub.vi**, as seen in Figure 12.19 ①, can be accessed by a main VI.

12.4
Overlay for Classification

The output results of the classification SubVIs can be used to overlay the results. In this way, the classification results may be effectively evaluated by the user of the program. In this section, we will show you an example of overlay VI that uses the classification results as seen in Figure 12.20.

The block diagram of the SubVI for overlaying is shown in Figure 12.21. In this SubVI, the **ROI Descriptors**, **Classes**, and **Scores** are used as inputs from

classification_overlay.vi

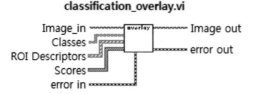

Image_in · · · · · · · · · · [overlay] · · · · · · · · · · Image out
Classes · error out
ROI Descriptors · · · · · ·
Scores · · · · · · · · · ·
error in · · · · · · · · · · · ·

Figure 12.20 Overlay for Classification results.

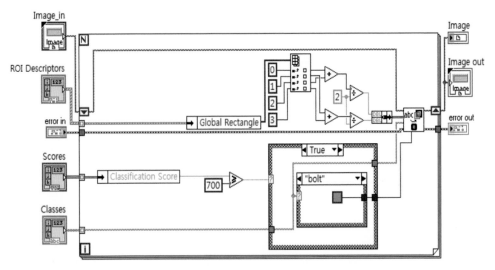

Figure 12.21 Block diagram for overlay (with classification score higher than 700).

the main VI. These array variables all have the same number of elements, which is related to the number of classified objects.

As seen in Figure 12.21, auto-indexing is used with a FOR loop to overlay all the classified objects. For this overlay function, **IMAQ Overlay Text** in Figure 12.22 is used to label the class on the location of classified objects in the output image.

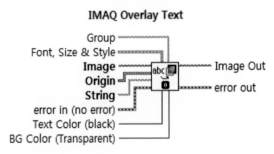

Figure 12.22 IMAQ Overlay Text.

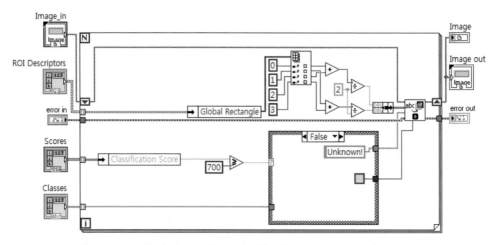

Figure 12.23 Block diagram for overlay (classification score lower than 700).

To use the **IMAQ Overlay Text** function, both the locations (**Origin**) and texts to show (**String**) are required. In this example, the location information in the ROI array is used to place the text labels. The text string labels are obtained from the identified object's class. The class is a character string that identifies the class. Note that the object's class may not be reliable if unknown or unclassifiable objects in the image exist. In this example, a classification score of 700 is used so that objects identified with a value below 700 will be classified as an unknown object, as seen in Figure 12.23. For each of the classification labels, a unique color can be selected for the overlaid text within the case structure.

12.5
Main VI for Classification

Figure 12.24 shows the main VI's block diagram for obtaining the classification results. Vision Assistant Express was used to both load the image (①) and classify objects in the image (②). Then, the results of the classification were overlaid on the image (③). Each process was discussed in previous sections.

As discussed earlier, the classification result may not be absolutely accurate. By using the score values, objects with low score can be indicated as unknown to increase the reliability of the classification results as seen in the front panel of the VI in Figure 12.25.

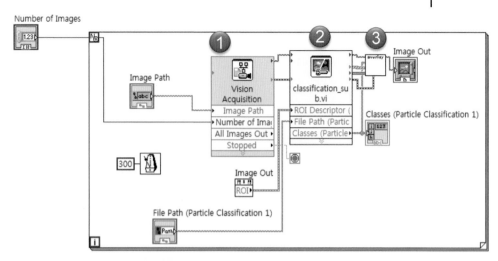

Figure 12.24 Block diagram of main VI.

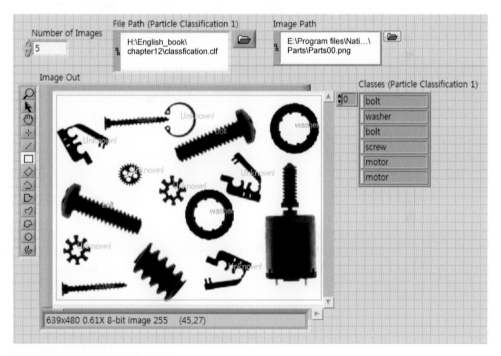

Figure 12.25 Front panel of main VI.

Exercise 12.1

Using the image file, **Parts01.png** (Figure 12.26) from *C:\Program Files\ National Instruments\Vision\Examples\Images,* create a program utilizing binary classification to classify each object and overlay the identified class names on the objects.

Figure 12.26 Image for classification exercise.

13
Contour Analysis

Contour analysis is often used to detect defects in objects by analyzing the object's contours. Boundary curves of objects are connected to produce contours. For this purpose, the objects in the image should have clear boundary edges to accurately distinguish its location from the image background. Since boundary curves are a set of edge points, the color image should be converted to 8 bit grayscale or binary image for the edge detection.

Figure 13.1 shows the basic process for contour analysis to find defects in objects.

To analyze the contour of objects, curvature profile is often used. The curvature profile is effective in detecting defects in places where the contour changes abruptly. However, some objects may have abrupt contour changes even though there are no defects. In such cases, defect detection using the curvature may be impossible.

On the other hand, you may use a reference template image to detect defects in an object by the comparison of contours. Alternatively, if the contour has a standard geometric general shape, such as line, circle ellipse, polynomial, and B-spline, the contour of the object may be numerically fitted to find abnormal parts in an object.

The example for detecting defects of an object can be found from the following folder:

C:\Program Files\National Instruments\LabVIEW2013\Examples\Vision\Contour Analysis

Figure 13.2 shows the front panel for the example VI, **Contour Defect Inspection.vi**.

As seen in Figure 13.2, certain types of defects can be effectively located by using contour analysis. The method shown in Figure 13.2 uses fitted circle for comparison. The difference (distance) in the contours compared with the fitted circular shape is used to find defects in this object.

In some cases, curvature profiles can be used alone and do not require comparison with a fitted shape, reference template, or reference contour. Applying

Practical Guide to Machine Vision Software: An Introduction with LabVIEW, First Edition.
Kye-Si Kwon and Steven Ready.
© 2015 Wiley-VCH Verlag GmbH & Co. KGaA. Published 2015 by Wiley-VCH Verlag GmbH & Co. KGaA.

Figure 13.1 Defect detection process using contour analysis.

the method of curvature profiles may be easier to use in some applications. Figure 13.3 (**contour analysis.vi**) shows the example of using curvature profile to detect abnormalities in a simple pattern.

13.1
Contour Analysis

> **Example: Defect Detection Using Contour Analysis**
>
> Figure 13.4 shows two ellipses. Note that the one ellipse has a defect. Use contour function to determine the size and location of the defect. These shapes are printed on paper and we will use USB camera to acquire the image. Use contour analysis to detect possible defects in the ellipse.

13.1.1
Image Acquisition Using a USB Camera

1) Drag the Vision Acquisition Express icon from the function palette to the block diagram.

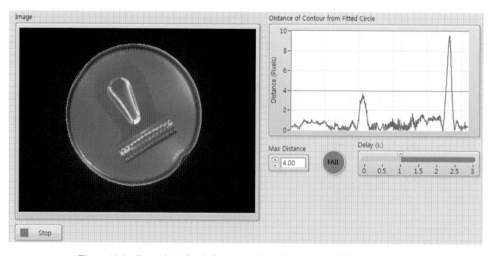

Figure 13.2 Example VI for defect detection using contour difference (reference: circle).

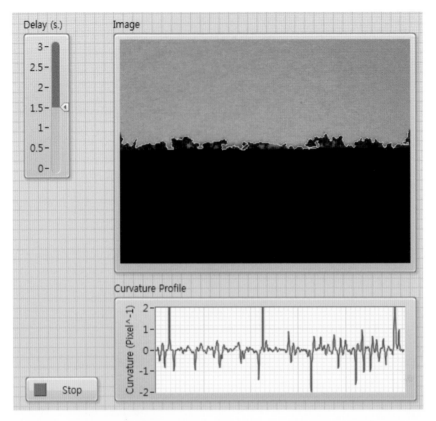

Figure 13.3 Example VI for defect detection using curvature profile (**Contour Analysis.vi**).

2) Complete the creation of a continuous acquisition with inline processing as seen in Figure 13.5. The details can be referenced from previous chapters.

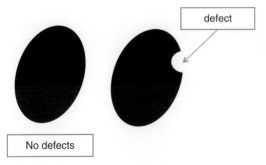

Figure 13.4 Defect detection using contour.

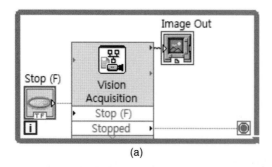

(a)

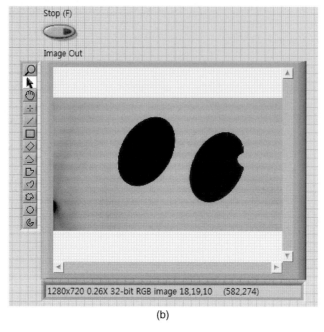

(b)

Figure 13.5 Continuous image acquisition. (a) Block diagram. (b) Front panel.

3) Right click the mouse on the front panel image display in Figure 13.5b and save the acquired image for image processing using Vision Assistant.

13.1.2
Contour Analysis Using Vision Assistant

1) Drag the Vision Assistant Express icon from the functions palette to a block diagram.
2) Select **Open Image** to open the previously saved image file for contour analysis.

Contour Analysis: Analyzes the contour of objects for defects.

Figure 13.6 Contour analysis.

3) Convert the color image to grayscale or binary for detecting edges since contour of an object (boundary edge curve) is extracted from a grayscale or binary image. For this process, select **Luminance** plane from HSL from **Color Plane Extraction** function.
4) Select the **Contour Analysis** function icon from **Processing Functions: Machine Vision** in Vision Assistant, as seen in Figure 13.6.
5) Appropriate parameter values need to be selected for the contour analysis setup. Figure 13.7 shows the example of the **Extract Contours** tab under

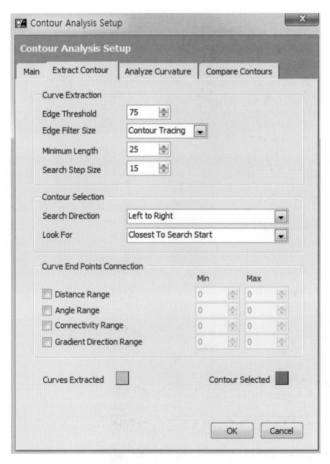

Figure 13.7 Contour analysis setup.

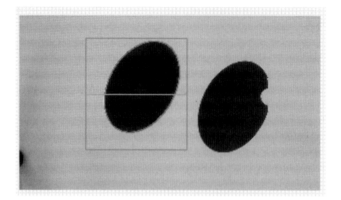

Figure 13.8 Reference image for contour analysis.

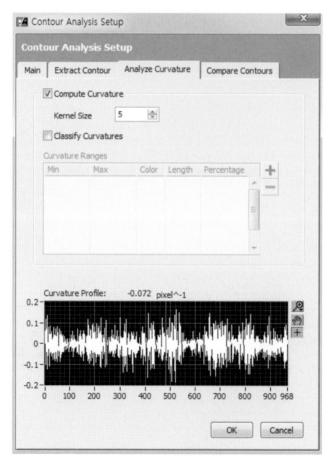

Figure 13.9 Curvature analysis of contours with no defects.

the **Contour Analysis Setup** to extract contours of the objects. The setup values should be adjusted by observing the perimeter contour line overlay on the objects in the displayed image. If the setup values are correct, the overlaid line lies exactly along the contour of the objects within ROI, as seen in Figure 13.8.

13.1.3
Defect Detection Using Curvature

Select the **Analyze Curvature** tab to verify from the **Curvature Profile** that the contour extraction is successful. Since there are no defects, the graph in Figure 13.9 shows no significant variation throughout the curvature of the object's boundary.

For the case of the notched ellipse, Figure 13.10b shows how the curvature profile reveals defects, as seen in Figure 13.10a. Note that you can change Kernel size such that the curvature profile can adequately detect possible defects. You can see the sudden large value change in curvature profile as seen in Figure 13.10b ①. In this way, you can identify the location of the defect as well as determine its severity. Note that the value of curvature profile is not related to

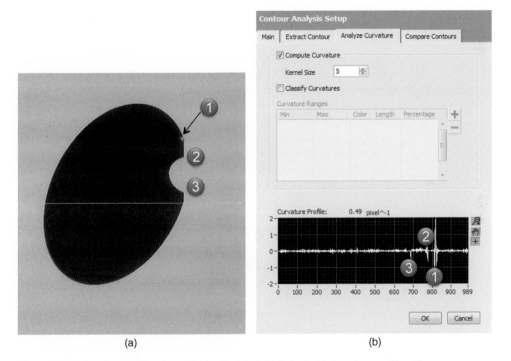

(a)   (b)

Figure 13.10 Curvature profile of an object with defect. (a) Defects. (b) Curvature profile with defects.

amount of defects, but to the rate of change of the contour. For example, the defect in Figure 13.10a ① is smaller in size than that of the defects along ② and ③. However, the curvature graph shows a significant value in defect at ①. The detection of the defect based on curvature is effective in identifying defects due to irregularity of the contour (smoothness).

13.1.4
Defect Detection by Comparing Contours

In some cases, objects may intentionally have irregularities to their shape, which do not indicate a defect in the object. In the presence of an irregular shape, which is normal for the object, large values of curvature profile may be observed. Thus, defect detection using the curvature profile method may not be appropriate. In these cases, the comparison of contours using a reference template image is perhaps better choice for the detection of defects.

The two different approaches may be used to compare contours: the use of fitted data with a reference contour as seen in Figure 13.11 ① and the use of reference template image as seen in Figure 13.11 ②. In this section, the method using the reference template will be discussed. This method uses the contour of an object and a reference template to detect defects by comparing the two contours. To use the reference template method, we need to create a template file. Complete the following steps to detect defects based on template image.

1) Select **New** (Figure 13.11 ③) to create template file. A pop-up window will appear to create a new contour template as seen in Figure 13.12.
2) Identify the reference template image area by using a ROI, as seen in Figure 13.12 ①.
3) Select **OK** and save the template contour to a file in the form of a **.png** image. As a suggestion, save the contour in a file named **reference.png**. After saving the reference contour, you can drag out a ROI around the target object to detect defects by means of distance (**Distance**) between the contour and the reference contour. Figure 13.13b shows the distance graph of the defective object. From Figure 13.13a and b, the point ① shows the largest difference and is easy to detect based on the compare contour method. However, even though the curvature is very large, the defect area at ② in Figure 13.13 may not be noticed using this detection method since the contour distance is relatively small.

The defects can be detected by comparing the distance against a threshold tolerance. If the distance is larger than the threshold at a location, the location can be identified as a defective part. An overlay on the image can be used to show the detection results effectively. The details of this will be discussed later.

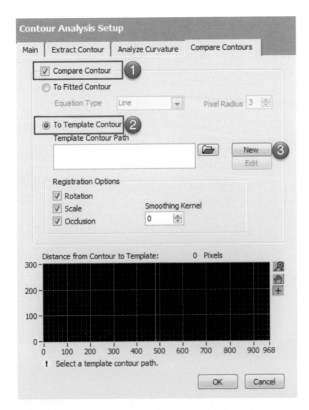

Figure 13.11 Contour analysis setup.

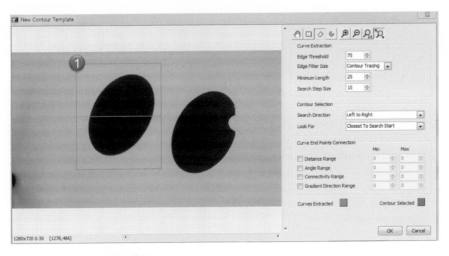

Figure 13.12 Contour template.

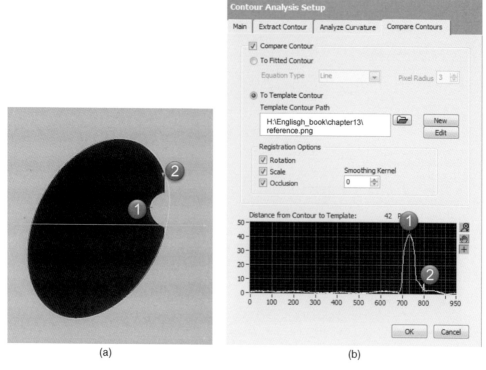

(a)　　　　　　　　　　　　(b)

Figure 13.13 Defects detection using template contour. (a) Defects. (b) Contour analysis setup.

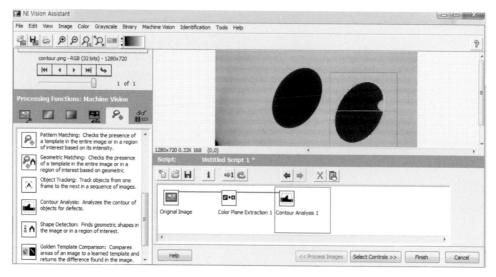

Figure 13.14 Vision Assistant Express for contour analysis.

Figure 13.15 Selection of controls and indicators.

13.1.5
VI Creation

When the contour analysis setup is complete, the results of the analysis are indicated as an overlay on image, as seen in Figure 13.14.

As a final step, click on **Select Controls≫** to choose the **Controls** and **Indicators**, as seen in Figure 13.15.

As seen in Figure 13.15, you can access two different results of contour analysis in the forms of **Curvature Profile** and **Distance**. In this way, you can choose contour results according to your requirement of defect detection.

13.2
VIs for Contour Analysis

13.2.1
Main VI

After finishing the selection of controls and indicators, a Vision Assistant Express VI can be created, as seen in Figure 13.16 ①. To build up the main VI, you may want to connect the inputs and outputs of the Vision Assistant Express VI as seen in Figure 13.16.

In this example, two different methods (with and without reference contour) are compared to detect defects using contour analysis. The two methods include the use of curvature profile and distance between contours.

The template image, which was saved previously using Vision Assistant, is used for contour comparison based on distance.

The acquired image (**Image_In**) is used as the input of the SubVI and the ROI (Figure 13.16 ②) is used to define the image area of the object for defect detection so that the object in the ROI is compared with the template image. Note that the **Contour Analysis** method based on distance is related to the direct comparison of the target object with the template object. Therefore, the template and target objects should be matched properly since the target object may be

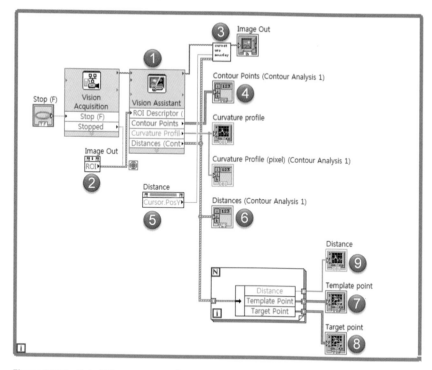

Figure 13.16 Main VI for contour analysis.

rotated as well as translated in the ROI region. Therefore, the matching process should be included in the contour analysis to acquire the intended results.

As an alternative method, curvature profile of the object can be used to detect defects without a reference contour.

The results of **Contour Comparison** between target and template contour points are in the form of cluster array, as seen in Figure 13.17. In the cluster, you can find the template contour (**Template Point**) and matched contour locations (**Target Point**) in their X and Y locations. Also, the distance between two contours can be obtained.

For better understanding of extracted contours of objects, the **Template Points** and **Target Points** can be plotted on a graph, as seen in Figure 13.18.

Based on the contour of the template and target points, curvature and distance can be obtained as seen in Figure 13.19a and b, respectively.

As seen in Figure 13.19, a horizontal line cursor can be added to the graph and used to graphically modify the threshold value from within the graph. In this way, the setting and modifying of threshold value can be made easy and straight-forward. To add the line cursor, right click the mouse on waveform. Then, in the pop-up window, you can add cursors from **Cursors** tab of **Graph Properties** menu, as seen in Figure 13.20.

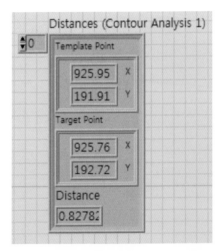

Figure 13.17 Contour analysis result (**Distances**).

You can now move the cursor on the graph and the value at the cursor can be used in the block diagram. To access this value, right click the mouse on the graph indicator in block diagram (Figure 13.16 ⑨). You will then see the pop-up window to select **Create»Property Node»Cursor»Cursor Position» Cursor Y**. From the created property node, you can obtain the cursor value from the graph, as seen in Figure 13.16 ⑤. The value can then be used as the threshold value for identifying defects.

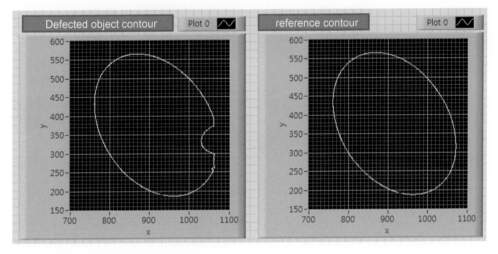

Figure 13.18 Template and target points.

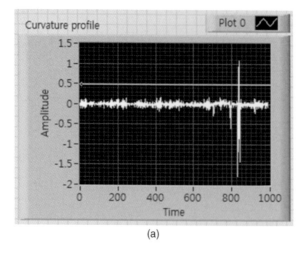

(a)

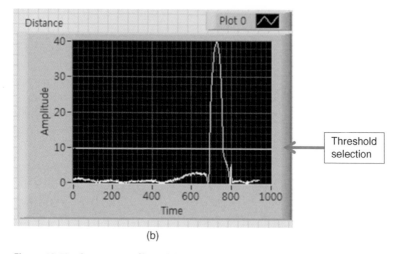

(b)

Figure 13.19 Curvature profile and distance. (a) Curvature profile. (b) Distance.

13.2.2
Overlay for Defects

An overlay of the template contours and target contours for comparison are automatically generated from Vision Assistant Express. However, you may want to add a highlight overlay to indicate the defect area. To detect possible defects, a threshold value is used to identify severe defects by comparing the value with the curvature variation or the distance. If the distance value is higher than the threshold, the location can be classified as defective part. The defective parts can be effectively shown on the image display by using overlay SubVI. Figure 13.21 shows the inputs and outputs of the SubVI.

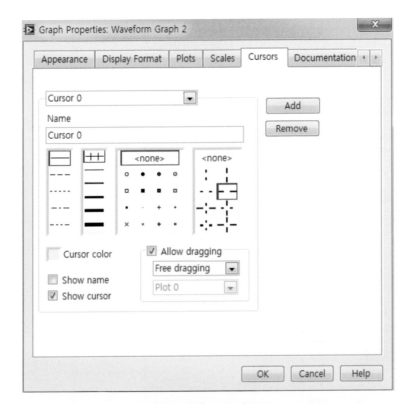

Figure 13.20   Cursor creation from waveform graph.

Figure 13.22 shows the block diagram for the SubVI to overlay multiple lines on defected parts. To overlay highlights on defective parts, the locations for the distance or curvature profile greater than the threshold value will be added to an array receiving the defect location information.

For defect detection, we will discuss the method of using the distance values. As seen in Figure 13.22a, if the distance is larger than the threshold value, the size of array of detects location will be increased accordingly (②) and the array will be plotted using overlay multiline function. On the other hand, if the distance is lower than threshold value, the locations will not be used for overlay, as seen in Figure 13.22b.

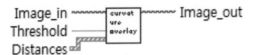

Figure 13.21   Inputs and outputs of overlay SubVI for defects.

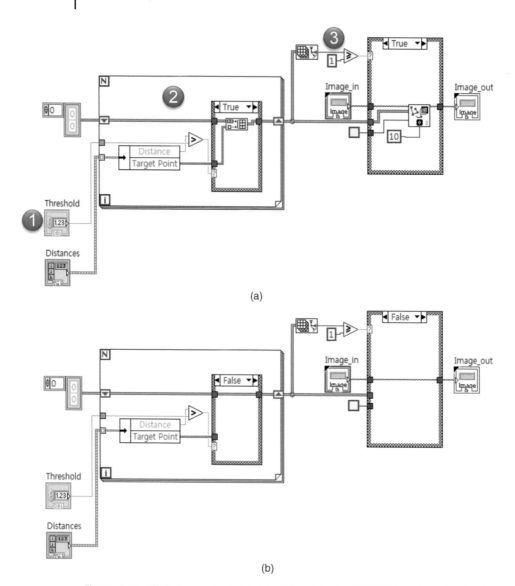

Figure 13.22: (a)

(b)

Figure 13.22 Block diagram for defect detection and overlay. (a) Distances above threshold value. (b) Distances below the threshold value.

To overlay on defect locations, the overlay function of **IMAQ Overlay Multiple Line 2** in Figure 13.23 is used, which can be found from **Vision and Motion»Vision Utility»Overlay**. As seen in Figure 13.22, line segments (Line End Points) specified with X and Y location data are used as input to the **IMAQ Overlay Multiple Lines 2** function.

IMAQ Overlay Multiple Lines 2

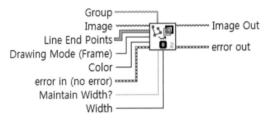

Overlays multiple lines, as either a polyline or a
polygon, on an image.

Figure 13.23 Overlay Multiple Line function.

Figure 13.24 shows the overlay results that use the threshold value from the
Distance graph. As seen in Figure 13.24, the defect location can be identified
and effectively indicated on image display by using the overlay SubVI.

Note that defect detection may not always be successful because of image distortions due to perspective errors. When object under inspection is not located
on the same position where template image is taken, the results are likely to be
affected by perspective errors depending on camera alignment. The perspective
issue in image will be discussed in Section 13.2.3 and Chapter 14.

13.2.3
Perspective Errors in Images

As seen in Figure 13.25, the shape of an object and its contour is affected by the
alignment of the camera. So, if the camera is not exactly perpendicular to the

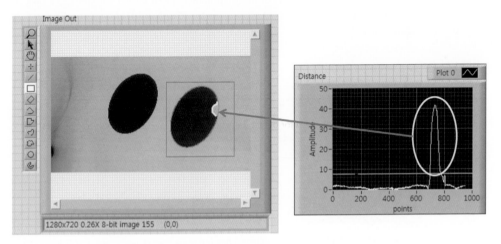

Figure 13.24 Identified defects based on the threshold value.

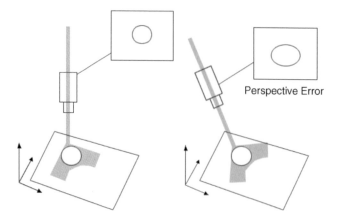

Figure 13.25 Distorted image due to perspective error (size, shape).

object, perspective errors will occur. The distortions include size as well as the shape. Due to the distortions, it may be difficult to determine the defects from the contours analysis.

Therefore, it is advisable to position your camera perpendicular to objects under inspection. In the case that the camera position may not be controlled, the distortion can be corrected using software. The calibration method for correcting distortions using the software will be discussed in Chapter 14.

Exercise 13.1

Find images in *C:\Program Files\National Instruments\Vision\Examples \Images\Cans*.

Use Vision Assistant Express to build your own VI to detect the defective part of the cans (Figure 13.26). You may refer to the **Contour Defect Inspection.vi** in Figure 13.2.

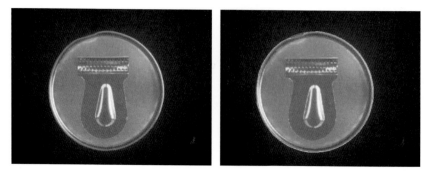

Figure 13.26 Example images for defect detection.

14
Image Calibration and Correction

If the camera axis is not perpendicular to the object, perspective errors will occur. Due to perspective errors, the acquired image might be distorted and the distortion will vary according to the distance and angle between the objects and camera lens. To reduce perspective errors, the alignment of the camera's axis with respect to objects is important. In addition, you may observe nonlinear distortions caused by optical errors (lens distortion) in camera lens. These distortions can be corrected by using NI Vision calibration tools. During the correction process, you can also acquire conversion information for converting from pixels to the real-world dimensions. This will allow you to measure the size and location of objects in physical measurement units using vision analysis.

In this chapter, image calibration and correction methods using **NI Vision Calibration** tools are discussed to increase the accuracy of image processing results. By using the calibration tools, an image is calibrated to obtain conversion information in real-world units as well as corrections for image distortion. Then, the image along with the calibration information is saved to a file. The file with the imbedded calibration information is used to correct newly acquired images. This results in a distortion corrected image and measurements are made in physical measurement units.

14.1
Method for Creating an Image Correction File

To generate an image calibration file, a grid pattern of dots with 5 mm spacing in the X and Y directions is printed on a paper as seen in Figure 14.1a. Then, an image of the printed grid pattern is taken by a camera, as seen in Figure 14.1b. Since the camera's axis is not set perpendicular to the target object, pattern distortion is observed, as seen in Figure 14.1b. The distortion is to be corrected to increase the accuracy of image analysis results.

Practical Guide to Machine Vision Software: An Introduction with LabVIEW, First Edition.
Kye-Si Kwon and Steven Ready.
© 2015 Wiley-VCH Verlag GmbH & Co. KGaA. Published 2015 by Wiley-VCH Verlag GmbH & Co. KGaA.

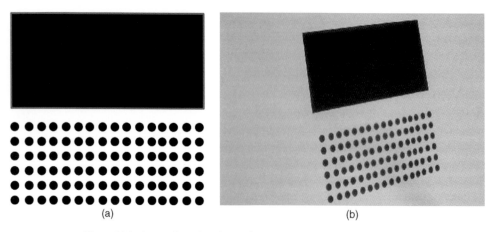

(a)   (b)

Figure 14.1 Image distortion due to the camera misalignment (perspective error). (a) Original image. (b) Image acquired using camera.

14.1.1
Image Acquisition

Prior to image correction, the Vision Assistant Express is used to acquire continuous images as seen in Figure 14.2. Here, the camera's axis is intentionally set to be off perpendicular to the target objects in order to understand the effects of image corrections.

From the acquired image shown in Figure 14.2b, right click on image display and save the acquired image as **image_cal.png** so that it can be used for image calibration and correction using Vision Assistant.

14.1.2
New Calibration File

To correct image distortion, create a calibration file by completing following steps.

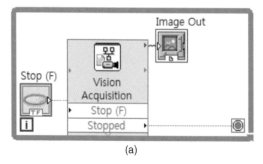

(a)

Figure 14.2 Continuous image acquisition. (a) Block diagram. (b) Front panel (image display with perspective errors).

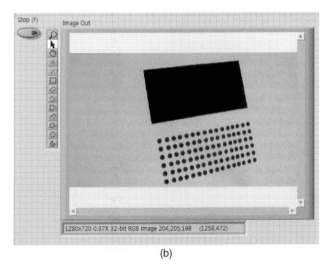

(b)

Figure 14.2 (*Continued*).

1) Drag the Vision Assistant Express icon onto a block diagram.
2) Open the saved image (**image_cal.png**) from Vision Assistant Express.
3) Convert the color image to a grayscale image. The calibration procedure is based on binary images and it is much easier if the calibration process is started with a grayscale image. To convert the color image to grayscale, select the Luminance plane from the HSL color image representation using the **ExtractColorPlanes** function.
4) Select **Image Calibration** function (Figure 14.3) from **Processing Functions: Image** in Vision Assistant.
5) From the **Image Calibration Setup**, select **New Calibration . . .**, as seen in Figure 14.4 ①, to set up a new calibration file. Perform the several steps needed to set up the calibration file.

Step 1: Select Calibration Type
Select a calibration type. In this example, select **Distortion Model (Grid)** as seen in Figure 14.5. The calibration types are compared in Table 14.1. Note that the grid type (**Distortion Model**) can correct distortion caused by both perspective errors and lens distortion.

 Image Calibration: Calibrates an image to perform measurements in real-world units.

Figure 14.3 Image calibration.

Figure 14.4 Image calibration setup.

Table 14.1 Image Calibration type for flat objects.

Simple calibration (point distance calibration)	Calibration using user-defined points	Grid calibration (Distortion Model, Camera Model)
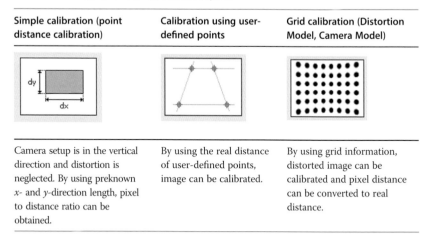		
Camera setup is in the vertical direction and distortion is neglected. By using preknown *x*- and *y*-direction length, pixel to distance ratio can be obtained.	By using the real distance of user-defined points, image can be calibrated.	By using grid information, distorted image can be calibrated and pixel distance can be converted to real distance.

Step 2: Select Image Source

You may add or delete images to calibrate grid images. For example, you may use acquired images from the camera to add image files for calibration. In this example, we used the default saved image as seen in Figure 14.6. Select **Next>>** to proceed to the next step.

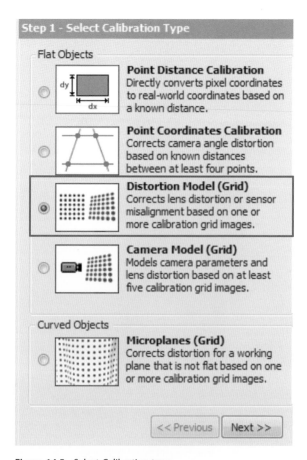

Figure 14.5 Select Calibration type.

Step 3: Extract Grid Features

Select proper threshold parameters to extract grid features as seen in Figure 14.7. First, select a ROI area on the grid in the image, as seen in Figure 14.7 ①. Select **Dark Objects** ② in the **Look For** drop down box since the grid of dots is darker than the image background. Since this method is based on binary images, we need to select a threshold method to convert the grayscale image to binary. By observing the converted image (blue: grid, white: background), the threshold value can be adjusted so that the binary converted image accurately overlays on the imaged grid of dots. In this example, the **Local Threshold: BG Correction** method was selected. By using the binary converted grid pattern, the distortion to the grid pattern is easily identified. Select **Next>>** in Figure 14.7 ③ to proceed to the next step.

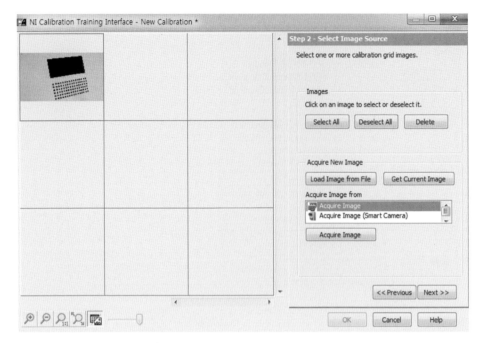

Figure 14.6   Select Image Source.

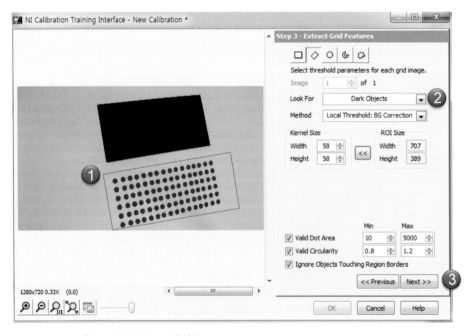

Figure 14.7   Extract Grid Features.

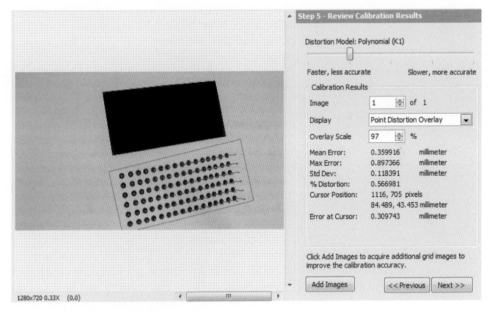

Figure 14.8 Specify Grid Spacing.

Step 4: Specify Grid Parameters
The grid spacing, which is used for calibration and correction, can be specified as seen in Figure 14.8. In this example, the grid spacing was 5 mm.

Step 5: Review Calibration Results
By selecting **Next>>**, you can review the calibration results as seen in Figure 14.9.

Step 6: Specify Calibration Axis
Now we are asked to set up a calibration axis as seen in Figure 14.10. The calibration axis on the image display can be adjusted by using the mouse or by

Figure 14.9 Review calibration results.

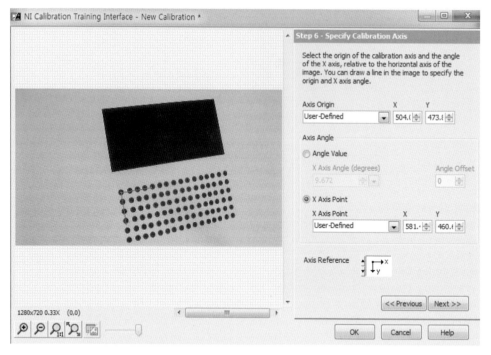

Figure 14.10 Calibration axis setup.

changing numerical values of the angle in the X-axis. In this example, angle of the X-axis is aligned along the grid X direction so that corrected grid X direction will be aligned along horizontal direction of the image.

Step 7: Summary

Figure 14.11 shows the summary of the calibration information from the steps 1–6. Finally, select **OK** if the calibration results are sufficient. You will now be able to save the calibration file, which contains the trained calibration information. In this example, image file named **cal.png** is saved.

14.2
Image Correction

14.2.1
Image Correction Using Vision Assistant Express

After saving the calibration image, the information in this image file can be used to correct other images acquired with the same camera setup that produces the observed image distortion. In this section, the method to correct images based on the calibration image is discussed.

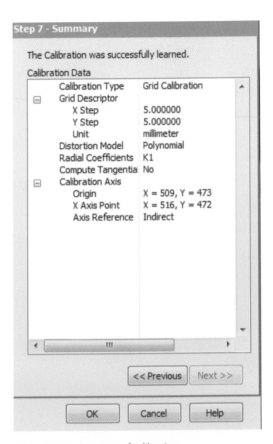

Step 7 - Summary

The Calibration was successfully learned.

Calibration Data

	Calibration Type	Grid Calibration
⊟	Grid Descriptor	
	X Step	5.000000
	Y Step	5.000000
	Unit	millimeter
	Distortion Model	Polynomial
	Radial Coefficients	K1
	Compute Tangentia	No
⊟	Calibration Axis	
	Origin	X = 509, Y = 473
	X Axis Point	X = 516, Y = 472
	Axis Reference	Indirect

<< Previous   Next >>

OK   Cancel   Help

Figure 14.11 Summary of calibration.

1) Start with the Vision Assistant again by selecting new script.
2) Select the **Image Calibration** function from **Processing Functions: Image**.
3) Select **Calibration File Path** to load and use the saved file containing the calibration information.

   If you check the checkbox in **Preview Corrected Image** as seen in Figure 14.12, you can preview the corrected image as seen in Table 14.2. Note that the size of the corrected image may differ from the image before correction. The corrected X direction is aligned with horizontal direction of the image. There will be black regions surrounding the original image background, which has been added to show the correction of the entire original image in the rectangular window.
4) Select **OK** in the Image Calibration Setup.
5) Select **Image Correction** function (Figure 14.13) from **Processing Functions: Image**.

Image Calibration Setup

Main | Calibration Data

Step Name

Image Calibration 1

Calibration File Path

C:\Book\Chapter 14\Cal.png

[New Calibration...] [Edit Calibration...]

☐ Preview Corrected Image

Interpolation Type   Replace Value

Zero Order   ▾   0   ⬍

[OK] [Cancel]

Figure 14.12 Image Calibration setup.

Table 14.2 Image correction comparison.

Before correction (1280 × 720)	After correction (1564 × 846)
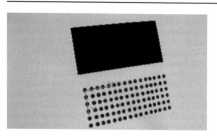	
There is image distortion according to camera alignment and position.	The image corrected for distortion.
	In calibrated image, image values with zero (black image) appear near the boundary.
	X direction of grid pattern is aligned with respect to horizontal direction due to the calibration angle setup.

Image Correction: Transforms a distorted image acquired in a calibrated setup into a corrected image.

Figure 14.13 Image Correction.

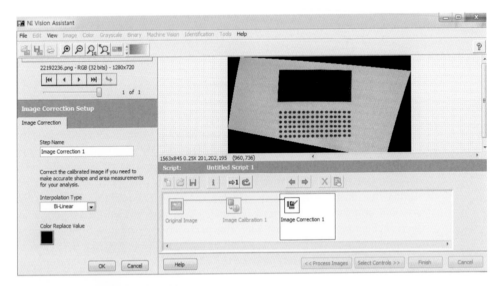

Figure 14.14 Image Correction setup.

You will now be able to view the corrected image as seen in Figure 14.14. By using image correction, the grid spacing will be more uniform compared with the uncorrected image. However, note that other objects might be influenced by the correction. For example, the nearby rectangular object as well as the shape of paper has been affected.

6) Select **OK** to finish image correction based on the image calibration file.
7) As a final step of Vision Assistant Express, click on **Select Controls>>** so that you select controls and indicators, as seen in Figure 14.15. Then, select **Finish** to create a Vision Assistant Express VI to perform image correction.

14.2.2
VI Creation for Image Correction

The corrected images can be obtained by continuously taking images using a USB camera. Figure 14.16 shows VIs created from Vision Assistant Express for the real-time correction of acquired images.

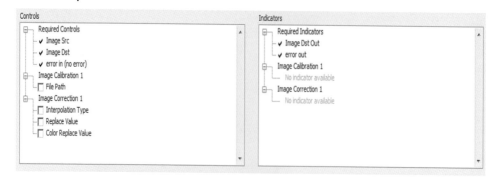

Figure 14.15 Selection of controls and indicators.

Figure 14.16 ① shows the **Image Create** function, which is used to allocate memory for the corrected image (**Image Out** ⑤). By connecting the created image to the **Image Dst** (Image destination) in Figure 14.16 ④, we can keep a version of the original image (Figure 14.16 ③), which will be unaffected during the image correction. If you run the LabVIEW code in Figure 14.16, you can compare the acquired original image with the corrected image as seen in Figure 14.17. In this way, the perspective error due to the camera alignment can be effectively corrected in real time. Note that the best correction can be obtained in the area of the image where the grid calibration has been performed.

As a next step, the corrected image can be used for various machine vision purposes such as measurement of size, image location of an object, or inspection of the possible defects.

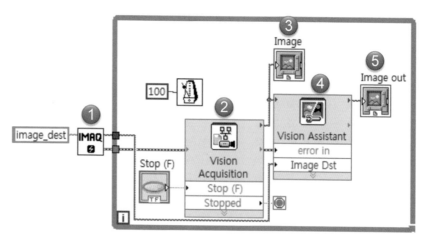

Figure 14.16 VI for real-time image correction.

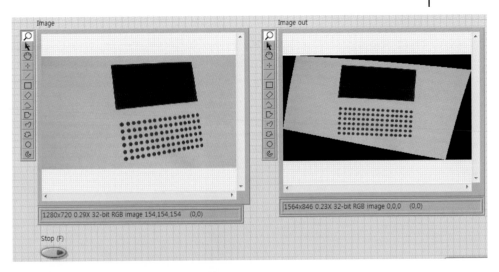

Figure 14.17 Real-time image correction results.

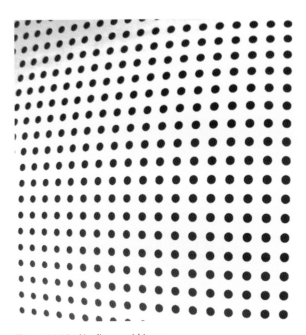

Figure 14.18 Nonlinear grid image.

Exercise 14.1

Find **Nonlinear grid.png** from *C:\Program Files\National Instruments \Vision\Examples\Images*. Assume that the grid is equally spaced with distance of 1 mm. Use Image Calibration and Image Correction functions to correct the image (Figure 14.18).

15
Saving and Reading Images

15.1
Saving Image

You can save images using **IMAQ Write File** as seen in Figure 15.1, which is found from the function palette in **Vision and Motion»Vision Utilities»Files**.

As seen in Figure 15.2, various kinds of image formats such as **BMP, JPEG, PNG,** and **TIFF** can be selected to save image file using the **IMAQ Write File** function.

The available types of images are summarized in Table 15.1.

When using **IMAQ Write File**, you can specify the **Compression Ratio** or **Image Quality**, as seen in Figure 15.3 (**IMAQ Write** file for JPEG) and Figure 15.4 (**IMAQ Write** file for JPEG2000).

For example, the default value for **Image Quality** is 750 in case of saving a JPG file. The value for **Image Quality** ranges from 1 to 1000 depending on the image quality required. Note that even if the quality value of 1000 is used for saving jpg file, there might be some amount of image data loss due to compression. In case of JPEG2000, **Compression Ratio** is used to define image quality. If the compression ratio is 50, the size of the file can be reduced 50 times smaller.

Example: Saving Image

Build LabVIEW code that can save image from USB camera twice a second.

Figure 15.5 shows a block diagram of a VI, which can save acquired images twice a second to a designated folder.

Figure 15.5 ① shows the SubVI to create a folder and specify a path to save the acquired image. At Figure 15.5 ③, a programmatically created file name for an image is added to the specified folder path. The file names for the images will be **imagxx.bmp,** where xx indicates numeric characters in sequential order from the **While Loop** increment. Note that we have added the file extension **bmp** since image file type to be saved is in Microsoft bitmap format. As specified in the block diagram, the wait function at ② is used to save the acquired image twice a second (every 500 ms).

Practical Guide to Machine Vision Software: An Introduction with LabVIEW, First Edition.
Kye-Si Kwon and Steven Ready.
© 2015 Wiley-VCH Verlag GmbH & Co. KGaA. Published 2015 by Wiley-VCH Verlag GmbH & Co. KGaA.

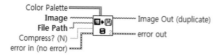

Figure 15.1 IMAQ Write File.

Figure 15.2 Image selection.

Table 15.1 Image type.

BMP (BitMaP image)	JPEG (Joint Photographic Coding Experts Group)	PNG (Portable Network Graphics)	TIFF (Tagged Image File Format)
Image from camera is bitmap image, which has the image values on each pixel location. The bitmap image is not compressed	JPEG is one of the image compressing methods. The color image can be effectively compressed by using JPEG. Here, the quality and the size of the image can be adjusted	PNG has been widely used in the Web to realize bitmap image	The data information of image was saved in the form of Tag in front of the image. From this, image type can be recognized

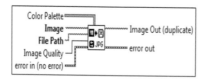

Figure 15.3 IMAQ Write File (JPG save).

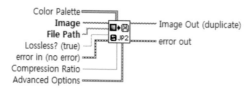

Figure 15.4 IMAQ Write File (JPG2000 save).

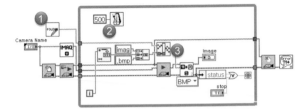

Figure 15.5 IMAQ image save (BMP) of acquired image.

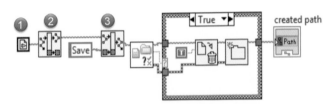

Figure 15.6 Block diagram of SubVI to create a folder.

SubVI for Creating a Folder

In this section, the SubVI (Figure 15.5 ①) for creating folder will be discussed. You may skip this section if you are familiar with creating folders. Figure 15.6 shows the block diagram of the SubVI used in Figure 15.5 ①. As seen in Figure 15.6, the output of the SubVI is the path information of **created path**.

To save the acquired images, the folder name of **Save** is created as a subfolder of the current VI's path. For this purpose, **Current VI's Path** (Figure 15.7) is used, which can be found in **Programming»File I/O»File constants** function palette.

The **Strip Path** function in Figure 15.8 separates the directory path from file name. In this way, only path information for the folder, where current VI exists, is obtained.

Current VI's Path

 path

Returns the path to the file of the current VI. If the VI never has been saved, this function returns <Not A Path>.

Figure 15.7 Current VI's path (Figure 15.6 ①).

Strip Path

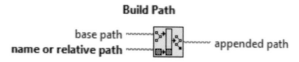

path ～～～ stripped path
name

Figure 15.8 Strip path (Figure 15.6 ③).

Build Path

base path ～～～
name or relative path ～～～ appended path

Figure 15.9 Subfolder generation from current folder (Figure 15.6 ②).

Check if File or Folder Exists.vi

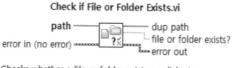

path ～～～ dup path
error in (no error) ～～～ file or folder exists?
error out

Checks whether a file or folder exists on disk at a
specified path. This VI works with standard files and
folders as well as files in LLB files.

Figure 15.10 Check if a file or Folder Exists.vi (Programming»File I.O»Advanced File Functions).

The subfolder name **Save** is added to the path using the **Build Path** function seen in Figure 15.9. The final result is a file path to a folder where image files will be saved.

The path information for the folder is connected to **Check if File or Folder Exists.vi** function in Figure 15.10 to see if the folder already exists.

The Boolean output of **File or Folder Exists?** is used to check the existence of the folder. In case the folder already exists, the folder including all the files contained in the folder is deleted by using **Delete** function (**Programming»File I.O»Advanced File Functions**). Then a folder with the same name is created using the **Open/Create/Replace File.vi** (**Programming»FileI.O» Advanced File Functions**), as seen in Figure 15.11.

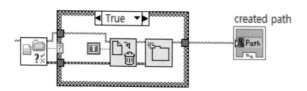

created path

Figure 15.11 Delete the existing folder and create a new folder.

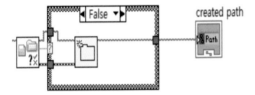

Figure 15.12 Folder creation.

If there is no folder by that name, a new folder is created, as seen in Figure 15.12.

The **created path** for the folder is used as the output of the SubVI in Figure 15.5 ①.

15.2
Image Read from File

15.2.1
IMAQ Readfile

In Chapter 2, the Vision Acquisition Express was used to read images from files. In this section, methods to read image files using **IMAQ Readfile** are discussed. The method using **IMAQ Readfile** has advantages because it is more effective method in building your own VI to meet your requirements.

The use of **IMAQ Readfile** to read image file is simple. As a first step, **IMAQ Create** function should be used to allocate memory space for the image to be read in. Then, the **IMAQ Readfile** function is used to read an image file. Figure 15.13 shows the typical block diagram of VI to read an image file.

IMAQ Readfile function (Figure 15.14) can be found in **Vision and Motion ≫ Vision Utilities ≫ Files**.

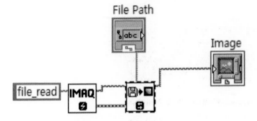

Figure 15.13 Block diagram for image read.

IMAQ ReadFile

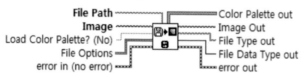

File Path ～～～～～～～～～～ Color Palette out
Image ～～～～～～～～～～ Image Out
Load Color Palette? (No) ～～ File Type out
File Options ━━━ File Data Type out
error in (no error) ━━━ error out

Reads an image file. The file format can be a standard format (BMP, TIFF, JPEG, JPEG2000, PNG, and AIPD) or a nonstandard format known to the user.

<u>Detailed help</u>

Figure 15.14 Image Read function.

15.2.2

Example of Reading Image from Image Files

Example: Image Read
Build a VI to read image files that were saved using the VI in Figure 15.5. Then, show the images on image display in sequential order.

Figure 15.15 shows an example of a block diagram to read image files in sequential order and show the images in the **Image** display on the front panel. By using the VI shown in Figure 15.15, the sequential images will be displayed with the same time interval as the images were acquired and saved. As a result, the images appear on the display window as if the images were being acquired in real time.

To read image files from the image folder, the folder is scanned of its contents to obtain the number of saved image files in the folder. Then, the number of files is used for the number of iterations in the FOR loop. The **Recursive File List** function in Figure 15.16 ① is used to analyze the contents of the folder.

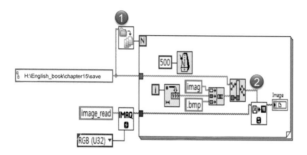

Figure 15.15 Block diagram for VI to read image files.

Recursive File List.vi

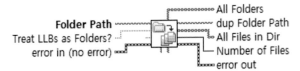

Lists the contents of a folder or LLB. In order for this VI to work correctly, the LLB must have a .llb file extension.

Figure 15.16 Recursive File List.vi.

Recursive File List.vi can be found in **Programming»File I/O»Advanced File Functions**. The file names of imagexx.bmp (xx = 1,2, . . .), which were file names previously saved using block diagram in Figure 15.5, are created in sequential order by using the index of FOR loop (Figure 15.5). In this VI, the saved image files in Figure 15.5 can be read in using the **Image Read** function in Figure 15.15 ②.

Exercise 15.1: Image save

From the continuous acquired images, you can drag out a ROI and save the image portion as defined via the ROI. As a result, the size of image to be saved will be reduced accordingly (Figure 15.17).

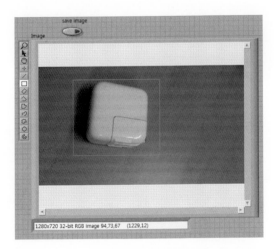

Figure 15.17 Saving a part of an image defined by a ROI.

NI_Vision_Development_Module.lvlib:IMAQ Extract Tetragon

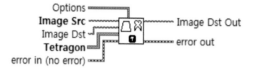

Figure 15.18   IMAQ Extract Tetragon.

Note:

You can use **IMAQ Extract Tetragon function** (**Vision»Vision Utilities» Image Manipulation**) to reduce the size of the image by using ROI information (Figure 15.18).

16
AVI File Write and Read

The AVI (Audio Video Interleaved) file format contains audio and video information within a single file. The audio part will not be discussed here. We will mainly be focusing on video and image aspects of AVI files. Specifically, methods to create AVI file from image files and read image frames from AVI file will be discussed in detail.

16.1
AVI File Creation Using Image Files

In Chapter 15, images acquired using LabVIEW were saved in sequential order. In this section, these sequential images are used to make an AVI file. Figure 16.1 shows the block diagram for making an AVI file using the saved images.

As seen in Figure 16.1, two paths are used: one folder path from which to read image files and another to save the image sequence as an AVI file. From Figure 16.1 ②, the **Recursive File List.vi** retrieves the number of files found in a folder and is used to specify the number of files read in using a **FOR** loop. All these images in the folder are then read using the **Image Read** function ④ in sequential order via an indexed **FOR** loop. Each image from the folder of previously stored image files is used to make the AVI file. For this purpose, the following three functions are required to create AVI file.

IMAQ AVI Create
The basic parameters to initialize and create an AVI file are set by using the **IMAQ AVI2 Create** function (**Vision and Motion»Vision Utilities» Files»AVI**).

As seen in Figure 16.2, the **IMAQ AVI2 Create** function requires the name of the codec (**Codec**) used to write the frames to the AVI file. Codecs are used to compress the image sequence into the AVI file. You may need to call **IMAQ AVI2 Get Codec Names** function to get the lists of codecs that are available on your computer for creating the AVI files (Figure 16.3).

In this example, **Microsoft Video 1 (index 0)** codec is used from the list of codec names identified by the **IMAQ AVI2 Get Codec Names** function.

Practical Guide to Machine Vision Software: An Introduction with LabVIEW, First Edition.
Kye-Si Kwon and Steven Ready.
© 2015 Wiley-VCH Verlag GmbH & Co. KGaA. Published 2015 by Wiley-VCH Verlag GmbH & Co. KGaA.

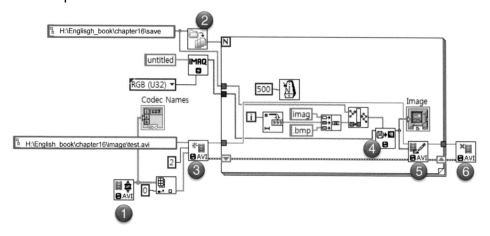

Figure 16.1 Block diagram for making an AVI file using existing image files.

IMAQ AVI2 Create

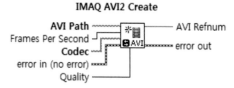

Figure 16.2 AVI Create (Figure 16.1 ③).

Figure 16.3 IMAQ AVI2 Get Codec Names (Figure 16.1 ①).

In this example, the frame rate (**Frames per Second**) input to the **Create AVI** function was set to 2 as seen in Figure 16.1 ③ since images were acquired and saved two times per second from the exercise in the previous chapter. If you use 20 for the frame rate instead of 2, playback speed of AVI would appear to be 10 times faster than the speed at which the images were acquired.

IMAQ AVI Write Frame

A set of images can be sequentially saved in an AVI file by using **IMAQ AVI Write Frame** function (Figure 16.4), as seen in Figure 16.1 ⑤. Note that each image will become one of the frames in AVI file.

IMAQ AVI2 Write Frame

Figure 16.4 IMAQ AVI2 Write Frame.

IMAQ AVI2 Close

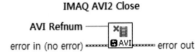

Figure 16.5 IMAQ AVI2 Close.

IMAQ AVI Close

As final step, **IMAQ AVI2 Close** (Figure 16.5) function closes AVI file as seen in Figure 16.1 ⑥.

16.2
AVI File Creation Based on Real-Time Image Acquisition

In this section, a set of images acquired using the **Grab** function will be saved in the form of an AVI file. Figure 16.6 shows an example VI, which makes an AVI file by using the acquired images. Each acquired image from the **Grab** function (③) is provided as an input of **IMAQ AVI Write Frame** (④).

For most applications, the **AVI Frame Rate** should be equal to the rate at which the images are acquired. In the following example, 10 fps were used for the frame rate value as seen in Figure 16.6 ②, which corresponds to an image acquisition period of 100 ms (⑤). Note that codec name obtained from the **IMAQ AVI2 Get Codec Name** function (Figure 16.6 ①) is used.

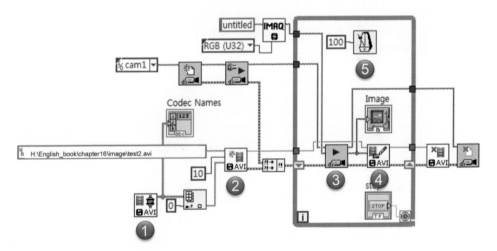

Figure 16.6 Example VI for making AVI file using image acquisition.

Figure 16.7 AVI Read Procedure.

IMAQ AVI2 Get Info

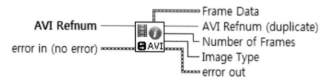

Obtains information about the AVI file associated with AVI Refnum.

Figure 16.8 IMAQ AVI Get Info.

16.3
Read Frame from AVI Files

An Image from an AVI file can be read by specifying the frame number in **AVI Read Frame** function. As an example, you may want to extract the last 10 image frames from the saved AVI file and then save each frame to an image file with a separate file name. For this purpose, the following procedural sequence will be used as seen in Figure 16.7.

As a first step, the **IMAQ AVI Open** function is used to open an existing AVI file. Then, the AVI file information is obtained with **IMAQ AVI Get Info** in Figure 16.8. The obtained AVI information includes **Image Type** (RGB, gray image, etc.), the **Number of Frames** (the number of frames in the AVI file), and the **Frame Data**.

Figure 16.9 shows the **Frame Data** information that was obtained by using **IMAQ AVI Get Info**. The Frame Data information consists of image size (width and height), **Frames per second**, and **Codec** information.

To read the image of a specified frame in an AVI file, **IMAQ AVI Read Frame** (Figure 16.10) is used. With a frame number specified, the image associated with the frame number is returned (**Image Out**). Note that the frames are numbered starting from 0 to the **Number of Frames**-1.

- **Read a series of frames from an AVI file**.

Figure 16.11 shows a block diagram that reads the last 10 frames in the AVI file, displays the images on the front panel image display, and writes the images to separate numbered image files in a sequential order. By using the number of

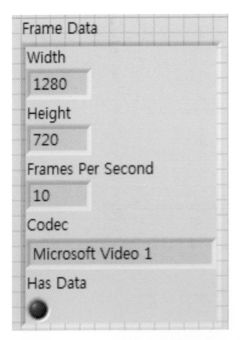

Figure 16.9 **Frame Data** information.

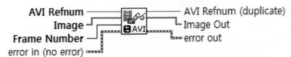

Reads an image from the AVI file specified by **AVI Refnum**.

Figure 16.10 IMAQ AVI Read Frame.

frames information from the **AVI Get Info** function (Figure 16.11 ①), the frame numbers for the last 10 frames can be programmatically determined, as seen in Figure 16.11 Then, the last 10 image frames from the AVI file are retrieved using **IMAQ AVI2 Read Frame** (Figure 16.11 ④) and saved using **IMAQ Write** (Figure 16.11 ⑤).

Exercise 16.1

Using the front panel shown in Figure 16.12 as a template, build your own program capable of reading a specific frame image (Figure 16.12 ②) from an AVI file and display the selected image (Figure 16.12 ①). Also, build a VI, which can

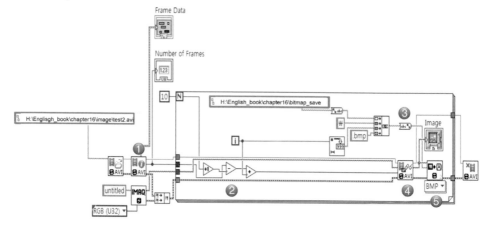

Figure 16.11   Reading image frame from AVI file and saving it as separate image file.

Figure 16.12   Front panel of VI to create a new AVI file from the existing AVI file.

create a new AVI file consisting of a set of selected frames from an existing AVI file by specifying the selected frames with a start frame (③) and end frame number (④). For example, you can use event structure so that a new AVI file can be created when selecting **New AVI File**, as seen in Figure 16.12 ⑤.

17
Tracking

The tracking algorithm has the ability to identify an object in video images and follow the object in subsequent sequential video frames. This is in order to track the object's trajectory, measure the speed, and/or to investigate the object's interaction with other objects.

Other algorithms such as pattern matching could be used for tracking objects, but they will tend to fail to track the object in the presence of other objects that are too similar. The tracking algorithm used in LabVIEW is based on a mean shift method, which is effective in tracking target objects acquired in sequential images even in the presence of similar other objects.

The current location is searched based on the histogram of the object in the previous image frame and uses the mean shift of the result to find the peak of a confidence map (probability density function) near the object's old position. For this to work correctly, the initial location of the target object needs to be correctly determined. As the video images progress sequentially in time, the target object is searched while ignoring many other similar shaped objects.

You can find the NI-supplied tracking example VI in the following folder: *C:\Program Files\National Instruments\LabVIEW 2013\Examples\Vision \Tracking*, as seen in Figure 17.1. By running example VI, you will see a target object (a car with rectangle overlay) being tracked throughout the video.

17.1
Tracking with the Use of Vision Assistant

In this section, a simple example will be used to help readers implement tracking algorithms using Vision Assistant. In this example image, there are several similar shapes. It is important to identify and locate target objects while ignoring similar shaped objects. To demonstrate the effectiveness of tracking, target objects will be shown to be tracked as their locations move from one frame to the next in the video. In this example, four target objects are printed and two of them are used for tracking purposes. Complete the following steps to implement tracking algorithm using Vision Assistant.

Practical Guide to Machine Vision Software: An Introduction with LabVIEW, First Edition.
Kye-Si Kwon and Steven Ready.
© 2015 Wiley-VCH Verlag GmbH & Co. KGaA. Published 2015 by Wiley-VCH Verlag GmbH & Co. KGaA.

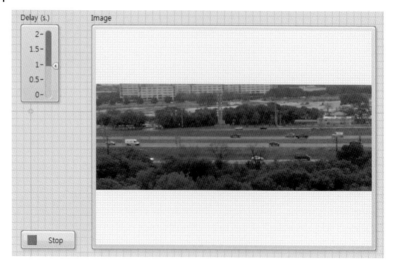

Figure 17.1 Example VI for tracking.

1) Use Vision Acquisition Express to acquire continuous images of the objects you want to track, as seen in Figure 17.2.
2) Save one of the images to a file for use in Vision Assistant Express.
3) Drag the Vision Assistant Express icon from the functions palette on to a block diagram and open the saved image from Vision Assistant.
4) Now, select the **Object Tracking** function from **Processing Functions: Machine Vision** tab as seen in Figure 17.3. You will see the **Object Tracking Setup** as shown in Figure 17.4.

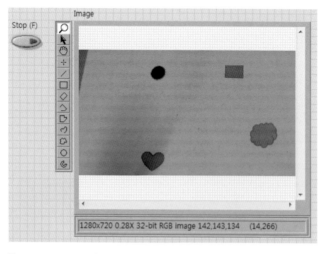

Figure 17.2 Example image for tracking objects.

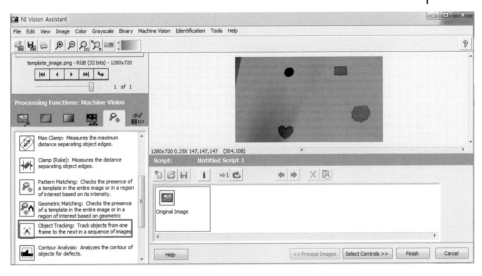

Figure 17.3 Vision Assistant Express for object tracking.

5) Select **New Object Tracking File . . .** ① to create a new tracking file. Now you will see the tracking training interface shown in Figure 17.5.

6) Draw a ROI around the object (Figure 17.5 ①) you want to track and adjust **Histogram Bins** to maximize the contrast of the object against the background shown in the **ROI Back-projected Image** window. Select **Add** (②) to establish the object as the object to track. A representation of the object will appear in the list of chosen objects (Figure 17.5 ③). You

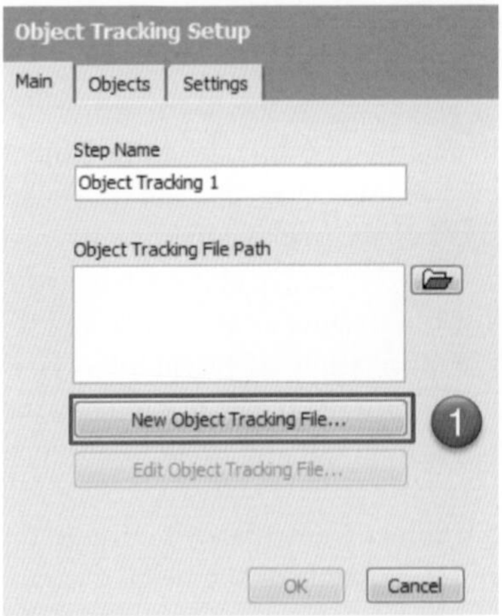

Figure 17.4 Object tracking setup.

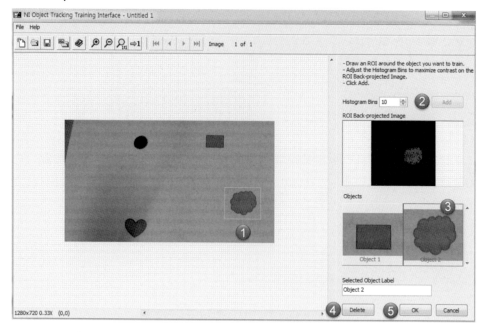

Figure 17.5 Object tracking interface.

can add more objects as well as delete them (④). In this example, we have two objects selected for tracking.

7) Upon selecting **OK**, you will be able to save the trained objects as a **NI Object Tracking File.** The filename will be given an extension of **.nitf**. In this example, the tracking file is saved as **tracking.nitf**.

8) Upon saving the file, the file path will be shown in the **Main** tab of the **Object Tracking Setup**, as shown in Figure 17.6 ①. The **Edit Object Tracking File . . .** button (②) will now become active and will be available if we later want to change some aspect of the tracking file.

9) Figure 17.6 shows the results of tracking the target objects when the tracking file is applied. You can confirm the results as seen in ③ and ④. It should be noted that the initial identification of target objects is important. If the target objects fail to be identified in the first image, the tracking is not likely to be successful throughout the sequential video frames.

10) After selecting **OK**, you can click on the **Select Controls>>** button to set up controls and indicators so that they are available to the block diagram of the LabVIEW VI, as seen in Figure 17.7.

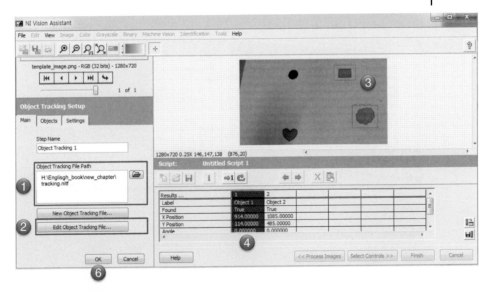

Figure 17.6 Object tracking results.

Figure 17.7 Selection of controls and indicators.

17.2
VI Creation for Tracking Objects

Figure 17.8 shows the block diagram for tracking objects. On the front panel shown in Figure 17.9, the tracked results are automatically overlaid on the image display, so an additional VI for overlaying results is not required. The output of Vision Assistant Express is the cluster array, named **Objects (Pixel)**, which has information on the tracked objects such as score, angle, and location values.

With the use of the tracking method, the location of objects can be identified when the objects move, as seen in Figure 17.9a. However, an initial location of the objects is important to establish tracking because subsequent searches of sequential images are based on previous images. Figure 17.9b shows an example of when the initial location of target objects failed to be identified.

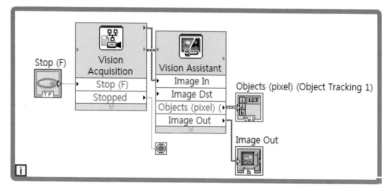

Figure 17.8 Block diagram of tracking.

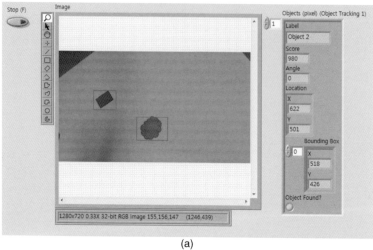

(a)

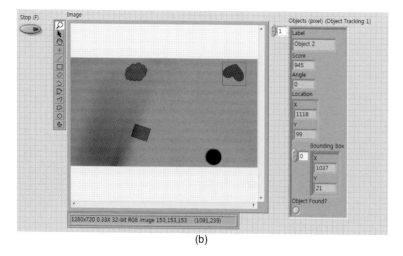

(b)

Figure 17.9 Tracking results when objects are moving.

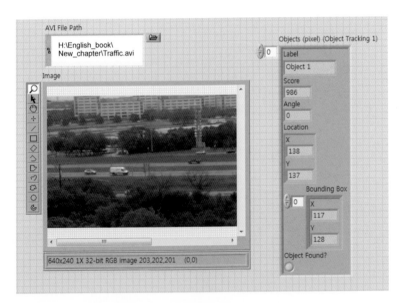

Figure 17.10 Exercise for tracking via Vision Assistant Express.

Exercise 17.1

Find the AVI file named **Traffic.avi** from *C:\Program Files\National Instruments\Vision\Examples\Images\AVIs*. Build your own program using Vision Assistant Express to track a target object as seen in Figure 17.10. You may refer to the example VI in Figure 17.1, which was built via the conventional VI method and compare the results.

18
LabVIEW Machine Vision Applications*

Some of the main applications of machine vision include automatic inspection and gauging (measurement). There are many examples where inspection by the human eye can be replaced and, in most cases, enhanced with the use of machine vision. For many applications, machine vision is the only way to accomplish the task due to advantages of high precision, high speed, and capability of operating in harsh environments. In industry, machine vision is often synchronized with other systems such as motion systems and data acquisition. By using vision algorithms, the movement of a specific object can be measured with respect to time. Also, the motion of the objects can be analyzed. The defects of a product can be inspected and dimensions of an object can be measured rapidly in real time. Information obtained from machine vision can be used for real-time automated motion control, quality assurance, measurement feedback, and process control. Machine vision applications are now essential to many different industries such as manufacturing, semiconductor, surveillance, automobile, and medical applications.

In this chapter, a few examples of machine vision applications will be discussed.

18.1
Semiconductor Manufacturing

In the field of semiconductor industry, machine vision has been used for inspection, positioning, and alignment of substrates. For example, photolithography of VLSI circuits requires critical alignment of an optical mask to prepatterned wafer substrates, as depicted in Figure 18.1. To align a wafer, machine vision is used to determine the position and orientation of the wafer or pattern on the wafer by locating fiducials (i.e., alignment marks). The fiducials are used as known reference positions on the object. Pattern matching or color pattern matching can be used to locate the fiducials for alignment so that a motion-

*All images containing (LabVIEW, IMAQ and LabVIEW Vision applications in chapter 18) are provided by or originate from the hardware and software of National Instruments Corporation and its affiliates. National Instruments reserves all rights including trademarks in such images.

Practical Guide to Machine Vision Software: An Introduction with LabVIEW, First Edition.
Kye-Si Kwon and Steven Ready.
© 2015 Wiley-VCH Verlag GmbH & Co. KGaA. Published 2015 by Wiley-VCH Verlag GmbH & Co. KGaA.

- Wafer Alignment

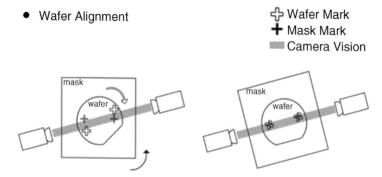

Figure 18.1   Semiconductor wafer alignment.

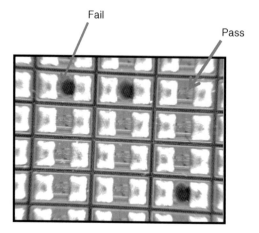

Figure 18.2   Inspection of defects.

controlled stage can move the wafer into an aligned position with an optical mask. It is common to have fiducials for each layer to determine the error, or runout from each added masking layer to track accuracy of aligners.

Machine vision can also be used as inspection tools for measuring the dimension of patterns and shapes after a manufacturing process. Expected features can be inspected for defects as seen in Figure 18.2.

18.2
Automobile Industry

In the auto industry, machine vision measurement has been used to increase assembly accuracy, performance, and reliability. In many cases, machine vision has been incorporated with different kinds of sensor signals acquired by digital acquisition systems.

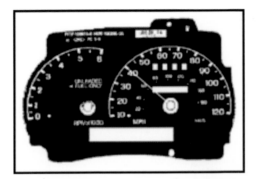

Figure 18.3 Speedometer calibration.

Figure 18.4 Fuse box inspection.

For example, car speedometers can be automatically calibrated via vision measurement, as seen in Figure 18.3. A fuse box in Figure 18.4 is inspected to check for any missing or wrong fuses. Impact analysis such as airbag deployment and safety tests can be performed using vision algorithms, as seen in Figures 18.5 and 18.6.

Figure 18.5 Airbag Test.

Figure 18.6 Collision analysis.

18.3
Medical and Bio Applications

In the medical, pharmaceutical, and bio areas, vision systems can be useful tools for analysis and automation. For example, the human eye movement can be measured and analyzed, as seen in Figure 18.7.

In bio industry, the number of cells as well as the size can be analyzed, as seen in Figure 18.8. Also, the movement can be analyzed in real time.

In the pharmaceutical industry, medicine packages can be inspected. For example, machine vision can inspect whether a medicine is in the right place or can detect incorrect or missing pills in a blister pack, as seen in Figure 18.9.

As another example, the color extraction can be used to classify the drugs and the number of specific medicines can be counted, as seen in Figure 18.10.

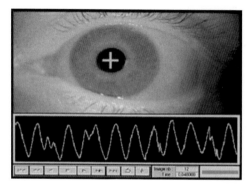

Figure 18.7 Eye tracking.

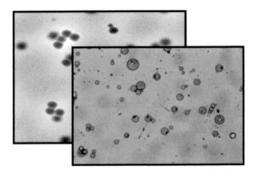

Figure 18.8 Bio applications.

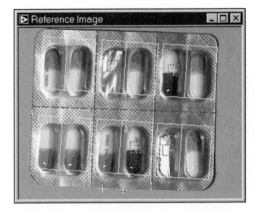

Figure 18.9 Package inspection.

Figure 18.10 Drug classification.

18.4
Inspection

Defects can be detected during the manufacturing process. For example, color pattern matching can be used to inspect complicated printed circuit boards with dense part placement in order to detect assembly mistakes such as missing or incorrect parts and incorrect part orientation, as seen in Figure 18.11.

Machine vision can measure the dimensions at a specific part of an object. Various objects can be classified according to the shape.

Package and label inspection can be possible by machine vision. For example, serial number can be inspected using OCR algorithm, as seen in Figure 18.12.

The infrared light can be used to obtain thermal images of objects (Figure 18.13) instead of the light from visual part of the spectrum. This can be used to detect a heat-generating fault condition in a machine. Still or time-sequenced video thermal images can be used to analyze heat transfer to verify thermal performance of a design.

Figure 18.11   Inspection of PCB manufacturing.

Figure 18.12   Serial number inspection based on OCR.

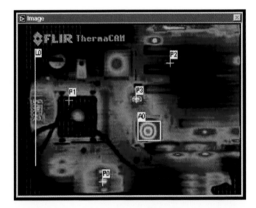

Figure 18.13 Heat analysis from thermal imaging camera.

18.5
Industrial Printing

Machine vision has been used in large-scale printing of graphics and functional materials for the purpose of overprinting alignment (Figure 18.14) and process control. Modern higher end document and graphics printers often have embedded vision systems to monitor four or more color separation and general feature placement as well as color matching control. The real-time monitoring

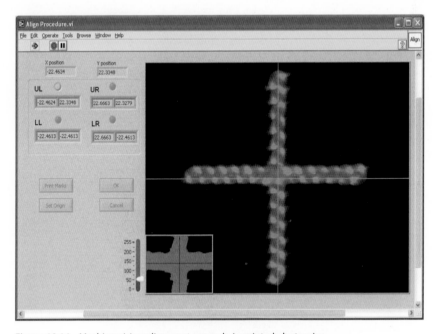

Figure 18.14 Machine vision alignment example in printed electronics.

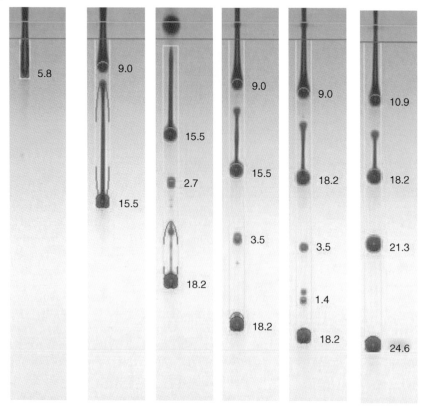

Figure 18.15 Time-elapsed evolution of inkjet droplets using a strobe light to monitor drop volume and production of satellite droplets in real time.

supplies feedback on print runout and color gamut during a print run to ensure uniform quality as aspects of the printing machine change from run to run or even within a print job.

One application that machine vision has had a significant role is in tuning and process control of industrial inkjet printers. The ejection of ink droplets from a multiejector printhead is often characterized using machine vision with the use of freeze frame video by strobe illumination (Figure 18.15). Automated data collection in real time can provide information on droplet size, velocity, angle, and satellite production. These data can be used to monitor multiejector uniformity and performance consistency.

19
Student Projects

Several selected student projects are presented. These tasks are used as final year end test projects for undergraduate students in Soonchunhyang University, South Korea. To be able to use the machine vision concepts learned from this book, we encourage readers to choose at least one team-based student project. The project may be selected from this chapter or self-selected by students. For better evaluations of the suggested projects, screen captures of the student reports are included here. LabVIEW block diagrams are not included in this section. There can be a lot of different approaches to implement the projects and creative programing is always recommended!

Project 1: Noncontact Motion Measurement and Its Analysis

As seen in Figure 19.1, an object is in pendulum motion. The motion is to be measured and analyzed in real time via image analysis. The trajectory of the object is plotted on graph. Also, the overlay on the object in the image display can be used for motion measurement verification. As an example, the period of pendulum motion (T) can be calculated from the measured motion. From the period T, calculate the gravity constant g to confirm that g is about 9.81 m/s at the sea level. Note that the pendulum motion is one of the examples for non-contact motion measurement. You can extend this concept to other noncontact motion measurement applications.

   (*Hint:* Color pattern matching, pattern matching, tracking method)

Project 2: Intelligent Surveillance Camera

Develop a low-cost and multifunction surveillance camera system by using a low-cost USB camera (Figure 19.2). In the case of conventional CCTV (closed circuit television), all the images are being recorded. To investigate and find any unusual occurrences, all the images need to be searched, which may take a significant time. So, unusual occurrences (e.g., people coming in through a door) need to be detected in real time. Then, an image or AVI file of the occurrence is saved. In this way, the use of disk memory for file saving can be minimized. Also,

---

Practical Guide to Machine Vision Software: An Introduction with LabVIEW, First Edition.
Kye-Si Kwon and Steven Ready.
© 2015 Wiley-VCH Verlag GmbH & Co. KGaA. Published 2015 by Wiley-VCH Verlag GmbH & Co. KGaA.

the searching time for events can be reduced significantly. After saving the image files (or AVI), the monitored results (image or AVI files) can be sent to security personnel via e-mail. At the same time, a text message can be sent to the securities via a mobile phone.

Program concept: An image is acquired via USB camera. A template image is saved as a reference image for (color) pattern matching. If the acquired images are different from the reference template image, the acquired images are saved for a specific time period or until they match with the template image. (The image can differ from the template image when the door is open and somebody comes in through the door.)

(*Hint:* (Color) Pattern matching, Image save, AVI write)

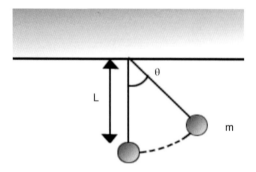

Figure 19.1 Pendulum motion measurement.

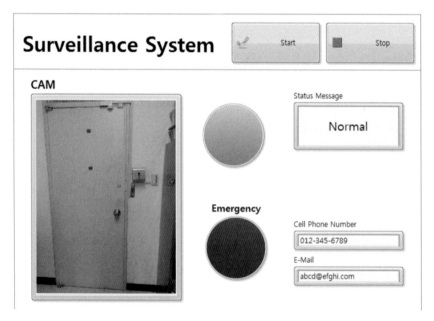

Figure 19.2 Intelligent surveillance system.

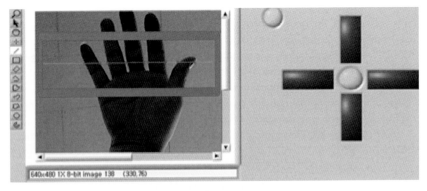

Figure 19.3 Edge detection techniques for finding the number of fingers.

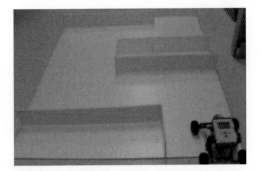

Figure 19.4 Driving a remote control car with figure motion only.

Project 3: Driving a LEGO NXT Car (LEGO Mindstorms) with Finger Motion

Edge detection techniques can find the number of fingers along the ROI line (see Figure 19.3). Use fingers along a ROI line to control remote control device. For example, a remote control car (via Bluetooth) made by Lego NXT can be used. Two different line ROIs may be used to count the number of fingers. If there is no finger in both line ROIs, the remote control car does not move. If there are fingers in the ROI in the left (or right), the remote car makes left (or right) turn. If there are fingers in both ROIs, you can make the remote control car go straight ahead (see Figure 19.4).

 (*Hint:* Multiple ROI, edge detection methods)

Project 4: Piano Keyboard Using Machine Vision

Multiple ROIs can be used as a noncontacting switch or selecting a specific function without actually touching a switch or device. As an example, develop a virtual piano keyboard using multiple ROIs, which will divide the image into many selectable areas. Figure 19.5 shows five different selectable keys. Note that you may make more selections just by making more ROIs. In order to make multiple ROIs, **GetImageSize** is used to obtain the total pixel size of the image. Then, the image is divided by the number of ROIs to define any selectable areas. If you select any ROIs by using finger motion, the existence of fingers in ROIs can be detected by using the particle analysis (Figure 19.6). When the fingers are detected, generate sounds that correspond to the keyboard action.

(*Hint:* Multiple ROI, binary image, particle analysis)

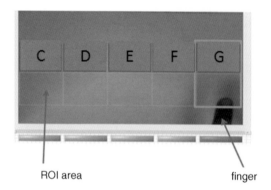

ROI area   finger

Figure 19.5 Piano keyboards using machine vision.

Figure 19.6 Binary image conversion (Particle analysis).

Index

Practical Guide to Machine Vision Software: An Introduction with LabVIEW, First Edition.
Kye-Si Kwon and Steven Ready.
© 2015 Wiley-VCH Verlag GmbH & Co. KGaA. Published 2015 by Wiley-VCH Verlag GmbH & Co. KGaA.